Jack Layton:
Art in Action

Contents

Jack Layton: Arts in Action

Penn Kemp

Jack Layton: Art in Action is a collection of anecdotes, interviews and thoughts about Jack Layton and his involvement with the arts, offered as a way of reflecting his life in politics. Over the last year, I have gathered stories of encounters with Jack in the many arts and cultures that intrigued him. I include pieces on how Jack has continued to influence our lives and our activism; how his spirit has stayed with people since his death in August, 2011. Throughout his long municipal and federal political life, Jack welcomed and encouraged everyone to become an activist to effect change. He certainly inspired me: like so many others, I still feel his motivating spirit strongly. I'd like here to celebrate his legacy and to carry on, with him as example. "What would Jack do?" is my current mantra, as it is for many.

Included in the book are sections on Jack's interest in diverse cultures and his influence on folks of all stripes. Although many of the contributions are from Ontario, Jack touched communities across Canada, especially Québecois, First Nations, and, of course, through his beloved wife and fellow MP, Olivia Chow, Chinese. Activists, artists, politicians, and folks across Canada sent in reflections, anecdotes, poems and photos.

What has moved me most deeply in this process is that while some of the contributors have been high-profile in their field, most of the stories are from the 'ordinary Canadians' whom Jack reached, sometimes just with a word or small kindness, or through media coverage. The anecdotes in the book help us understand who Jack Layton was, where he came from, and the transformational journey that took him and the New Democratic Party so far. Jack was a strong supporter of our many Canadian cultures that offer us diversity and perspective. From a young age, he was an unflagging proponent of social justice and human rights. He was an early champion of environmental protection and the war against homelessness and poverty.

This project lets us reclaim, restore and rejuvenate the Canada we love by focussing on how Jack lived: positively and proactively. My main aim in *Jack Layton: Art in Action* is to encourage folks not to abandon politics but to keep practically optimistic just as Jack would. As I work on the book, Jack continues to have a powerful influence in encouraging me to explore different approaches and avenues for the book and to persevere with Love, Hope, and Optimism!

Olivia Chow endorsed this work by heartily encouraging folks to send stories of Jack's relationship with, and his support of, the arts. "This project is a great opportunity to share our stories about how Jack and the NDP celebrated our Canadian cultures and what we must do together to continue this great relationship. You know he loved to make music and we loved to dance!" When I put out the call for *Jack Layton: Art in Action*, it was primarily artists who first responded. Most of these stories were told to me, but some, especially the poetry, arrived fully formed.

Our publisher is the well-respected publisher, Quattro Books/Fourfront Editions. Appropriately, Quattro Books is a publisher "that wishes to reflect the unique cultural character and dynamism of Canada now: what it has been and what it is in the process of becoming." We've chosen May 2, the anniversary of the New Democratic Party becoming the Official Opposition, to launch the book.

Who is Jack Layton?

We know he was born and raised in Québec, the eldest son of a prominent political family. His blind great-grandfather, Philip Layton, founded the Montréal Association for the Blind in 1908 and later campaigned for disability pensions. His great-great-uncle, William Steeves, was a founding father of Confederation. His grandfather was a Québec provincial cabinet minister. Robert Layton, Jack's father, was first a Liberal and then a Progressive Conservative in Brian Mulroney's Cabinet.

Until 1970, Jack himself was a Liberal. Then, dismayed by Trudeau's War Measures Act in Québec, he joined the New Democratic Party. He admired Tommy Douglas' principled position against the Act. His professor and mentor at McGill, Charles Taylor, advised him to go to graduate school in Toronto, so Jack told me. After his Ph.D. from York, Jack taught political science at Ryerson University. From 1982 to 1991, he served as city councillor in Toronto. The 1990s were not kind to Layton. In 1991, he lost the race to be mayor of Toronto. In two federal elections (1993 and 1997), he ran unsuccessfully for the NDP.

But in 2001, he became head of the Federation of Canadian Municipalities. In 2003, he was elected leader of the federal NDP, supported by former party leader Ed Broadbent. In 2004, Jack served as MP for Toronto-Danforth, a position he maintained until his death. His wife, Olivia Chow, was a fellow Toronto city councillor and then an NDP Member of Parliament, as she still is. The number of federal NDP seats in the House of Commons increased in the last several elections. The May 2, 2011 federal election gave the NDP a majority in Québec. With 103 members in Parliament, Jack became the Leader of the Official Opposition in Ottawa on the rising tide of the Orange Crush. After a tireless campaign, both politically and personally, Jack died of cancer on August 22, 2011 at the age of 61.

Why a book about Jack Layton?

It is intriguing to note how many contributors continued to refer to Jack in the present tense. He lives on in us; his legacy will not die with the man. He himself would always prefer to discuss future plans rather than rehash the past. As an extravert, his art expressed itself in action. But I'm convinced by that old saw that we need to understand the past so as not to risk repeating it. I believe that unless we change ourselves, we will repeat the pattern of confrontation. To whom can we look as model, as local hero? Jack is an exemplary citizen, a mentor. There is a little bit of Jack in every activist.

Jack and Me.

I first met Jack when I lived on Toronto Island throughout the seventies, fighting City Hall to "Save Island Homes." Jack campaigned for and with the Islanders until a settlement was reached. We were connected through mutual friends. My daughter took a course from him at the University of Toronto. My son, on stilts, informed him of a dead body spotted on the street during the 1996 Toronto Caribana. In 1997, upon meeting my husband, Gavin Stairs, I became part of his extended family: Gavin's brother Joe is married to Jack's sister, Nancy Layton. Jack warmly welcomed me with his customary inclusivity. I called him my outlaw; he called me sister. We had many a conversation about activism in both arts and politics: he convinced me that poetry and politics could be more compatible than combatable. I never saw any discrepancy between his public persona and his private self, though he was funnier off the record. I've just collated all his emails to Gavin and me; they include some fascinating discussions on the role of the arts. They're bitter-sweetly sad to read now, given all we have lost in Jack ... but we continue in hope.

Jack and the Arts.

Jack was a master of numerous art forms, in the widest sense. The whole country was his canvas. His was an art of delight in facing the world. Here are some of the art forms he adeptly juggled.

The Art of Action.

Let us recall Jack's call to action. Just think: culture produces wine, yogurt and Art, in the Heart of Community. Spring forward, write on, act out! As poet William Blake wrote, "If the sun and moon began to doubt, They'd immediately go out." Jack was a practical idealist. His brand of optimism included a realistic appraisal that then reached further into what was possible. From perception, he moved swiftly into action. His politics was personal down to the marrow.

The Art of Politics.

Jack Layton lived his politics and politics was his art form. He embodied integrity. It takes courage and confidence to cross the transformational threshold from private to public life. Jack and Olivia slipped between with such grace and evident joy in each other and in their proposals. They carried themselves lightly but they wielded the power of influence, persuasion and action.

How should we respond to perceived iniquity? I am dismayed by the harm that the Harper government has inflicted upon Canada. The damage to our rights as citizens; to our environment; to social justice; to our commitments on the world stage; to our sense of identity; to our reputation, is close to irreparable. What has happened to democracy in this country? To our sense of ourselves as peace-keepers, as models to the world? The nearly daily list of affronts to democracy is so deeply shocking that each new betrayal no longer has the same effect on public awareness. Shock has become the new normal and *The Shock Doctrine* a reality. At this juncture, we cannot afford to settle back into our more or less comfortable lives.

Indignation can stew in its own juices; the recital of wrongs does not necessarily lead to action. Some of us counter the daily news by writing politics and political activism off as lost causes. It seems easier to turn a blind eye and retreat to personal concerns. Who has the energy to respond with the anger necessary to challenge Mr. Harper? How do we confront the dogged, but extremely focussed, commitment of the Conservative government? Following Jack's example, I've chosen an affirmative approach by collecting these anecdotes, as well as harping on Harper. The Jack book is my defense against despair.

The Art of Actual Listening.

Jack's ability to listen with full attention is the quality that permeates nearly every anecdote. Of all the themes that weave this book together, the quality of Jack's listening is paramount. Where did that gift come from? When I asked Olivia what she had taught Jack, she hesitated. It wasn't a question she had anticipated. "I taught him," she answered slowly, "to listen more." Aha! Such a spaciousness opened up in hearing her response.

Jack paid attention. He cared and he remembered. His memory was always strong, reports his mother. Wayne Marston, NDP MP for Hamilton East-Stoney Creek, writes: "One of the most important attributes of Jack Layton was his ability to pass through crowds, talking to a large number of people and leaving each of them with the feeling he had actually listened to them. When Jack looked you in the eye, the connection left you with that feeling. But what people didn't get to see was him sitting with our caucus, relating what people had told him. You see, Jack really was listening. That was what made him the person Canadians accepted as a good friend or a Bon Jack."

The Art of Encouraging, Enthusing and Enlisting Others.

Jack has been behind this project all along, in spirit and in memory, encouraging me to contact folks who might have an anecdote up their sleeve, just as he encouraged likely NDP candidates to run for office, and all of us to engage in civic action. After every interview, I seem to hear the sound of one Jack clapping. He was proud of our accomplishments but he did not hesitate to ask for more from us. Jack's was not a one man show: his caucus was collegial; his approach to everyone congenial. He was the politician folks would most enjoy having a beer with.

In his piece called "Jack and the Ben Talk," journalist Ben Benedict writes: "I remember meeting Jack Layton on several occasions. He was always quick with a smile and an extended hand. His passion for life made a passion for politics easy. Each time we met there would be a brief discussion about the arts and diversity that always ended in a brief yet direct statement: 'You should be a candidate for our party.' His enthusiasm was infectious. It did make me consider running, and with his legacy that seed continues to germinate in my head. In knowing Jack, we all realized that his leadership was about serving our nation by doing what is right and good, a principle that remains close to my own heart."

The Art of Balance.

Jack lived well, balancing work and play with exercise, fun and the long hours necessitated by strenuous campaigns. It was interesting to watch Jack grow over the years. As Toronto councillor, he would hammer aggressively on his desk to deliver a point. He was a fierce debater in Parliament. But I perceived a shift from righteous indignation to heart-centred activism in his last years. What signposts indicate that passage? There are many examples of how profoundly Jack touched the nation, and of how he learned, how he spread his wings. He became a statesman, sticking to principles, weaving between being called 'too radical' and being castigated for not being radical enough. Idealism was the carrot that kept him going; enthusiasm fueled him. Optimism may have propelled him as leader of an underdog party through to official opposition status. But Jack was astutely aware of political realities as well, and of the incremental progress that more voters could comfortably support.

The Art of Love.

Jack's love for Olivia and his family and friends dances through this book like a magic wand, connecting disparate groups and far-off places coast to coast to coast in a network of expanding community.

The Symbolic Art.

How Jack could turn things around, turn them on their head like a media savvy magus. His crutch became a symbol, not of infirmity but as Jack waved that cane, it became a baton, a victory sign, with which he danced a jig or conducted his orchestra of supporters. BC painter J Peachy created *Salmon Jack* as "a metaphor of Jack's journey." Jack himself became a symbol of hope. Luba Goy reports that on the day Jack died, one orange hibiscus bloomed on the garden shrine she had set up under his campaign sign.

Over a year later, and I'm still moved by Michael Hollett's article on Jack: *A dream bigger than a lifetime ... Jack was the manifestation of our longing for good and our belief in better.* "I found myself thinking Jack had turned a city into a population of poets, all reaching into plastic buckets to grab a coloured stick and make our affirmations for him, ourselves and our country." September 1, 2011, *www.nowtoronto.com.*

The Art of Respect.

Jack's sense of indebtedness to First Nations was deeply touching and powerful, as evidenced in his family lore. Honouring First Peoples and celebrating, preserving the land, the environment, were strong priorities for him, and are carried on by his son, Michael. Olivia Chow played a key part here too, introducing him to white-water canoeing in the North, although he had always camped with his family.

Applied Jack! Art in Action. Jack's life was based on cooperative, collective principles. That orange glow ignited him in life and surrounds us still. He applied the art of networking, of coming to consensus, to community action. How would Jack have responded to Idle No More, the Occupy Movement, the Maple Spring in Québec? We can surmise, and act accordingly.

Jack himself was a rapid responder. I often delayed writing him because he would answer quickly, usually within a few minutes, and I thought he had other more pressing concerns! When, during the 2007 election, I asked Jack for an arts platform, he responded immediately and set up a policy online. My questions to all candidates included: "What steps would you take to effectively protect and augment arts programs and arts councils? The positive role of the arts in our economy has been well demonstrated. What is your position on the role of the arts in our community? Culture represents ourselves to ourselves ... The lack of response or notice of the arts in campaign rhetoric or platforms is short-sighted, so if you hope to represent us, keep the arts in mind and heart!"

The Art of Artists and the Art of Appreciation.

Jack was energized by the arts. As he liked to remind me, he was a proud member of the Writers' Union of Canada, with several books to his credit: the influential, ground-breaking *Homelessness: The Making and Unmaking of a Crisis*, and his visionary "blueprint for Canada," *Speaking Out*, which was revised and updated as *Speaking Out Louder: Ideas That Work for Canadians.*

Jack respected the arts and delighted in hanging out with artists, sharing a sense of play and possibility: he recognized a similar spirit. He knew how much the arts contribute to community. And so artists responded in kind: writer Thomas King and singer-songwriter James Gordon ran for office for Jack. Journalist James Stewart Reaney, son of the late London Ontario poet Colleen Thibaudeau, writes: "Colleen was proud to show her support for Jack Layton. There is a Team Layton sign visible in an upstairs window facing Huron St. at my parents' house. The image is like one of her poems in the shape of things, simple and direct. I am not sure when mom put it there. I do know she never took it down, election or not. We are proud to honour her wish." When asked to name her hero on CBC's *The Next Chapter*, novelist Emma Donoghue replied that it would have to be "the late, great Jack Layton."

Poet John B. Lee writes about Jack: "I admire what he achieved and what he stands for." Writer Ewan Whyte "always liked many aspects of the public persona of Jack Layton. His concern for supporting the arts and for sticking up for the interests of the common people appealed to many and extended to supporters outside of his political cloth." Poet a. rawlings tells us, "As I came out of the store, Jack Layton swung off his bicycle and tethered it to a metal TTC circle. We exchanged smiles as we passed on the store ramp, and I wondered if I'd smiled with a future Canadian prime minister. Great smile; beyond affable. Came with ease. Summer's end surges a little more crisp in these moments."

Having lived in Toronto's Chinatown for many years, writer Louise Bak recalls volunteering door-to-door with Olivia Chow when she was on local council, observing "something of the visceral milieu that the couple was advancing in the neighbourhood." She describes how Jack and Olivia helped in a family emergency: "I've always been interested in how generations change in that neighborhood – the lingoes, styles and the complexities of choosing political sides. Jack and Olivia were chosen b/c no other recourse legally, politically responded when our world crashed so horribly. I was having such difficulty, trying to help my mom, when everything she knew, built over forty years, was lost. We don't live in a world where there are institutions inclined to help when you fall to nothing. There's no compassion or guidance generally, when there's no material benefit being proffered to assisting parties who are vulnerable. Jack and Olivia helped some in the course of the fight."

Jack would take your calls. He would come up with solutions, or point the way to someone who knew. Problem solving was his forte. We heard story upon story of Jack's willingness to help. Aha Blume recalls speaking to

Jack about "the frustration that many of us youths coming out of university suffer," unable get a job in their field. Jack was eager to discuss the matter.

Jack and the Art of Dying.

Jack manifested his own words: Love, Hope and Optimism. He used his dying time as he lived his life, for social justice and equality. Jack was a model of courage in the face of death. The optimism that came so naturally to him persisted to the last. By not announcing the kind of cancer that recurred and that would kill him, Jack was trying to protect the public. He did not want to increase the stigma for any one particular form of cancer. This was his choice: not denial, but a resistance to spreading the pervasive and corrosive fear of cancer in our society. Jack had faith in the medical establishment. He knew the prognosis. When we talked in the spring of 2011, he straightforwardly explained that the cancer had metastasized, that his hip bone was reduced to frail latticework. But determination kept him going. Political leaders have the right to die in private, in seclusion. Jack's extreme act of generosity was to make his final act, the open letter to Canadians, a public act. Jack's choice was a gift; the famous last words an exercise in courage and inclusion.

Jack and the Arts.

As a poet, I know that making art is a political act. Art allows us to enter the experience of The Other and in this multi-cultural, multi-racial community that Canada is at last becoming, that understanding, that feeling with the other, is essential to community. Art is a kind of communing, entering into collaboration with its audience in a search for and expression of meaning. Art commemorates the moment, the possible futures, the many pasts we might experience. Art articulates what has never been expressed in that particular way. Art moves us to feel more deeply and so moves us to civic-minded action.

How do we actualize our dreams, how do we give them form? The arts are the expression of hope, an act of optimism. The truly despairing do not make art; they are sunk in passivity. Art lifts us out of that swamp of despond. Art stirs the spring blood, inspired, respired, perspired. Art cares. Art rails, sings, dances, lilts, jigs, plays, laments, pleads, scolds, declaims, claims, debunks, funks. Art is fun. Art is the Heart of Community. Spring forth! Write on! Act out!

Jack was energized by the arts. He recognized a similar spirit in artists, for creating art is a political act, exploring what is possible. Jack Layton understood this sense of connectivity to his core. How did he arrive at that conclusion? How did Jack become so much more himself? In the last several years of his life, he seemed to emerge into full-heartedness. This expansive openness is the love people across Canada responded to. In the spring of 2011, Jack even talked to Gavin and me about being spiritual – not a word hitherto in his vocabulary, I would guess. He seemed to us to be transformed, and, despite a realistic appraisal of his medical condition, renewed, living for a purpose outside himself.

"Another world is not only possible, she is on her way. On a quiet day I can hear her breathing," activist Stephen Lewis quoted Indian writer and activist Arundhati Roy in his eulogy for Jack.

How did Jack Layton come to support the arts and in turn to be supported by art and artists? The influences that shape a person's life are always intriguing. Jack seems to have had an innate or inherited sense of fairness that led him to campaign for social justice and equality. Would his role as the eldest of four children have played a part in his wide vision? What gave him, from an early age, such a broad understanding? Growing up in Hudson, Québec, what was his connection to the arts? What was his background? What arts influenced him? I asked his mother, Doris Layton, and his sister, Nancy Layton, younger than he by just eighteen months.

January 6, 2013

Perfect Pitch

Doris Layton, Jack's mother, with Nancy Layton, his sister

The Layton family were musical by heritage. Jack's blind great-grandfather Philip Layton trained in Organ and Piano at the London School of Music. He later emigrated to Canada and began importing pianos to Montréal. All the children sang in church choirs. As a teenager I was included in Sunday Tea at my future husband Robert's home in Montréal. [Doris and Robert met on a blind date in the summer of 1942 so she would have been sixteen. They married in 1948, both twenty-two years old and a year out of McGill.] Tea always ended with Robert's father, Gilbert, at the piano with everyone joining in the singsong, first hymns and then a mélange of favorite tunes. At my home, my mother from Virginia did the same but chose Stephen Foster songs.

Jack was born with perfect pitch and by the time he was three, he was singing everything we sang to him – all the children's hymns and action songs – a nightly ritual at bedtime. Favorite songs included "All in a Row," which the children would sing as they marched off to bed – a Layton family tradition when all the cousins were together too. As the family grew, the grandchildren would join in. Every party ended with a singsong.

When Jack was five or six, I took him to The Young Peoples' Symphony concerts in Montréal – Jack, who never sat still, didn't move a muscle while the orchestra performed. He started piano lessons with a teacher from the Montréal University of Music School and graduated from the Royal Music Academy in Grade 11. Jack sang in the Junior Choir in Hudson Wyman United Church from the age of eight till his voice changed at twelve or so. Later on, he and his brother Rob would play the guitar when teens or the family gathered: any excuse would do.

Olivia's father was an opera singer and taught Jack to sing a Chinese duet with him at his and Olivia's wedding. Her dad had a marvelous voice and it was a way for Jack to connect with him given the language issues.

The Messiah at Christmas became a tradition, particularly in Toronto. A few years ago, the Toronto Symphony was on strike and it looked like the Annual Concert would be cancelled. Jack persuaded them to play for FREE at the Bloor Street United Church. This free concert continues to this day (we all contribute to the cost).

Rosemary Barton of CBC TV claimed that after Jack died she would always remember him as Singing Above The Clouds. She was on the campaign flights and he always had a singsong with the crew and the press.

Penn Kemp: Such a musical heritage doubtless contributed to Jack's sense of music as a strong factor in bringing a crowd to a sense of unity, common purpose, focus and fun. Jack's mother's reminiscences show how natural music was for Jack, how pervasive, and how it influenced his political style of camaraderie. Rosemary Barton's poignant piece is on *http://www.cbc.ca/news/politics/inside-politics-blog/2011/08/memories-of-layton-singing-above-the-clouds.html*, along with the video of Jack leading an impromptu in-flight campfire singalong. Jack's ability to infuse folks with enthusiasm must be hereditary. His father Robert, a Cabinet Minister for Brian Mulroney, believed in the quality so much that he started his own youth group with the self-same name: The Infusers.

"Caring Community"

Herb and Margaret Wonfor

Herb Wonfor and Doris Steeves Layton grew up in Calvary United Church, Westmount, during the same years. Both of them received post-secondary education at McGill University where Bob Layton entered the picture: for Doris, a permanent relationship. In 1961 Herb was called to the ministry in Wyman United Church, Hudson, Québec and was both surprised and delighted to find the Layton family actively involved in the congregation with four children. The oldest, Jack, was a teenager when we arrived.

Bob used his superb leadership skills as he worked with a group of high schoolers named "The Infusers." One of their projects was to prepare and lead youth services for the congregation. This was a time when many folk songs with socially conscious themes were being written and the guitar was the preferred instrument to provide the accompaniment. Jack Layton was one of several youths who accompanied the young people's choir with his guitar.

Bob expanded the experiences of this group of young people by arranging for them to go into the Montréal City Mission a couple of Sunday evenings each year to entertain the clients of the Mission with their songs and stories and to treat them to a light meal which they prepared and served. Years later, when Jack Layton was a member of Toronto City Council and authored a book entitled *Homelessness*, he attributed his interest in this subject to the exposure he had on these trips to the City Mission with members of "The Infusers."

This active group of teens brought honour to their school during this period. Enrollment at the Hudson High School was much smaller than any other school in the greater Montréal high school football league, the division which competed for the yearly football championship. With the philosophy of the "little engine that could," Hudson High fielded a football team each fall. When the teams changed players, hardly anyone playing for Hudson High changed, because they didn't have enough players. Encouraged by community support and by the gifts of their coach and physical education teacher, Doug Steeves, the team succeeded in what seemed the impossible – winning the city championship. It took them two or three years before they got to the championship. Needless to say, Jack Layton and his ilk supplied the heart and soul that made such a coup possible.

As the years passed and life took us to different parts of the country, our connection with the Layton family was limited to a brief message at Christmas. However, memories were rekindled at the gathering to celebrate the life of Bob Layton. One of the most poignant tributes at the service was when Jack sat down at the piano and sang a song, "The Dominion March," that his great-grandfather Philip had written many years before.

More recently at the 100th anniversary of Hudson's Wyman Church in 2007, Jack and Herb were asked to share memories of the congregation during the 1960s. Jack was en route to a political meeting in Halifax, but graciously took the time to spend a Sunday morning with the congregation who had nurtured him in his youth. He referred to the congregation as a "caring community" which responded whenever a need arose, a philosophy which he carried into his life as a political leader.

Penn: In conversation, Margaret Wonfor talked about the Wyman United Church in Hudson where some of Jack's ashes are buried. It was settled by immigrants from Cumberland, north England.

Jack's leadership skills started, Margaret Wonfor commented, when he was very young: "Jack was right into everything that happened. He was so much like his father, Bob. Bob was full of enthusiasm, very outgoing; all the kids loved him. Bob was a model for many of those young people."

Margaret Wonfor continued, "Our youngest daughter Alison lived in Jack's Danforth riding. After the 2006 election, when she spotted Jack walking down the street with an aide, she stopped to congratulate him. He exuberantly hugged her and said, 'What a wonderful influence your father has been. He was such a mentor to me'. That was typical of Jack!"

"The Infusers"

Patricia Bradbury

On a Saturday before Jack died, I was listening to CBC radio. Jann Arden was interviewing the actor, Gordon Pinsent, and talking about obituaries. Although Jann was humorous, her focus made the interview sad. Then something wonderful happened. The eighty-year-old Pinsent, ever the rowdy man, chose an end-of-show song: *The First Time Ever I Saw Your Face* by Ewan MacColl, sung by Roberta Flack. It's not about endings, Pinsent seemed to say. It's really all about beginnings.

That song had personal meaning for me. I heard it for the first time in Hudson, Québec in the basement of Wyman United Church. Mr. Bob Layton, community leader and engineer, the father of Jack, had started a youth group called "Infusers." He had two kids my age, Jack and Nancy, and he wanted to inspire them. In the process, he inspired all of us who made our way to the church on Sunday evenings. We were in grade ten and eleven, which, in Québec, were the senior years in high school.

Bob Layton tried to shake us up. He took us to volunteer in soup kitchens in Montréal; he showed us the film, *Nobody Waved Goodbye;* he brought in organists to play for us upstairs; he talked about social justice. And, one night, he brought in folk singers from New York. The Sixties were happening, but certainly not in Hudson, a predominantly English town with an English Protestant power base. In Montréal, the FLQ were bombing mailboxes but very few of us grasped the Quiet Revolution or the fury building up against the 'Anglos' in Québec.

On this particular night, the Laytons had transformed the dull concrete hall into a coffee house with tables and candles. It was extraordinary that Mr. Layton felt we were so deserving. The lights were low. A young black man and blonde woman, obviously lovers, joined our circle. They talked about prejudice and riots in the south. Then there was a pause. The man played solo guitar chords then began the song of all songs: *The First Time Ever I Saw Your Face*. It was as though the room disappeared for him. He was singing just for her. As we watched this performance, the stillness in the song felt like a prayer. Lyrics and music, love and inclusion: the engine of the Sixties filled me with joy. Did I look around in the candlelight for Jack? I had a small crush on him, so maybe I did.

Not long after, as junior commodore of our English-only yacht club, Jack used his privileges to invite French teens to our members-only junior dance. It seemed joyful at the time, but turned into scandal. Jack was admonished by the board of directors, then, as I recall, was asked to step down.

Bob Layton's efforts found fruition in Jack. Jack felt all of us were deserving. He fought for social justice. He made time for the young. He played a mean piano and a pretty good guitar. He had two great loves: Sally (from Hudson) with whom he shared children; Olivia (from Hong Kong) with whom he shared a career. He never seemed to tire of telling Olivia how beautiful she is. I'm sure he remembered the first time ever he saw her face. Saturday morning, drinking coffee, listening to Jann. Illness and tombstones haunt us all, but love and first times are candles in the dark.

"All in the Family"

Penn Kemp

Such a story gives insight into young Jack and his family's heritage. Jack used to say: "Never turn down an opportunity to serve!" Such a dictum must have been ingrained in Jack from an early age, given his family's political prominence. It has that ring to it. Just as I was writing this introduction, his mother, Doris Layton, emailed me about the motto: "That was a direct quote from his DAD. First used to get the children to clear the dinner dishes but later continued to be the Family Motto. ALL the LAYTONS try to follow that direction in our Private lives – His daughter [Sarah] in her work for Stephen Lewis and Michael in his Political life."

So Jack's mastery of the art of politics is in the family bloodstream, ongoing. Growing up in relative privilege, Jack had the generosity and sense of social justice to use his position to include those who did not – the disenfranchised. He did not abuse that power, the apparently natural power of the white, Anglo male of his time to aggrandize his own. But I believe that he grew up with a confidence that seemed innate. That quality if conscious saves a whole lot of dithering and self-doubt when making decisions.

Life never follows a straight line, but from the wider perspective that we now have of Jack's life as a whole, his trail seems clear. He started, Nancy tells me, as president of the Student Council in high school. He wrote in his year book that he would be Prime Minister one day.

Nancy Layton talks about growing up in a house full of laughter: "My dad loved to tell jokes but he was terrible, either cracking himself up before the punch line or just forgetting the punch line. Lots of groaners too. We also loved puns and the supper table would often end up with us all doubled over in hysterics." A family after my own heart.

Jack's sense of play came as naturally as his sense of fair play. Politics was serious business. The issues were important but Jack's touch was light.

I asked Doris Layton, a librarian, if Jack liked to read as a child or if he preferred the outdoors. She reports: "Jack loved to listen to books on tape as he exercised. He was a very slow reader. When he graduated from high school, his highest marks were science and math, so was counselled to go into science, first year McGill. (Had a university scholarship.) However, after the year was over, he remarked that he didn't want to spend his life in a lab and perhaps should go into LAW. But was concerned about the fact that there would be a lot of reading and he was too slow with it. I suggested that he take a Speed Reading Course during the summer. It began with a test of his skill – He was reading at the Grade 5 level!!! He had managed to get Honour Level marks on his Memory!!! As it turned out, he took the course to improve – ended up going into economics and poli sci – the rest is history – later MA and Ph.D. He never stressed his Ph.D from York – didn't want to be known as one above the fray!"

Jack's son Mike Layton told me a fascinating story about his grandmother's family coming up from the States centuries ago and being helped over their first winter by the Mi'kmaq. He thought Jack felt forever indebted to First Nations because of that crucial and timely aid. Doris Layton confirms the tale about her Steeves family, whose original name of Stieff was later anglicized to Steeves. "The original couple, Rachel and Christian, were possibly Plain People" – Amish or Mennonite. A government offer of land to immigrants brought the couple from Bavaria to Pennsylvania. They soon found Pennsylvania was "not as they had been told and life too difficult there," with land in short supply. Accompanied by eight sons, Rachel and Christian immigrated to New Brunswick from Pennsylvania. Doris Layton writes that they would have starved in the winter if they hadn't learned how to eat and store root vegetables from the Natives.

This tale is such an archetype for the first relationship between many early settlers and First Nation peoples who knew so well how to live off the land, however inhospitable it might appear. How wonderful to celebrate this founding myth in one's own family, and subsequently to honour and acknowledge the obligation and responsibility in return. I can imagine how the legend might have played out, embellished into a grand Romance, in young Jack's active imagination during the late Fifties. What a foundation for Jack's sense of fair dealing. It is a basis for his ongoing respect for First Peoples, and this astonishing land we call Canada.

And the tradition continues. Doris Layton writes that Jack's son "Michael was so touched when his Dad told him about the Mi'kmaqs. Now he is a Toronto City Councillor and concerned about the Native people – lots are among the Homeless. He would like the City to create a Museum of Native Culture and History."

"A Complex Tapestry"

Peter Ferguson

Jack was a warm, caring, dynamic person, who could be bristly and quick to anger, and at other times reflective and thoughtful. (The times he was angry were often justified and stemmed from his love for Canada and his frustration with what was being done by the government – versus what he thought *needed* to be done if we are to build a better, more fair Canada.) A series of anecdotes from a broad spectrum of Canadians will thus present – I hope – a more well-rounded and complex picture of a man who was complex and well-rounded.

My way of thanking you for your book about Jack is, of course, to offer you one of my anecdotes about Jack that I think is noteworthy because it features different views about Jack's youth from both Jack himself and his childhood church minister.

On one occasion when I was chatting with Jack a few months before the May 2011 election was called, I mentioned that his childhood church minister lived in my riding (I was our federal NDP candidate) and that I would be visiting the minister and his wife in a few days. Jack smiled and started to regale me with tales of his youth activities in the church, noting most specifically that the minister had organized a wonderful choir. Jack credited his participation in the choir for instilling the confidence to sing in public and giving him an overall greater appreciation for music that one gets from being a performer. Later when I met with the minister and wife in their home, we chatted about Jack and I mentioned that Jack had just days earlier expressed real appreciation for Herb's role in building Jack's love and appreciation for music, especially as a performer. Herb and his wife looked at each other slightly puzzled, and Herb stated (with his wife nodding in bemused agreement) that while he didn't doubt Jack, he had no memories of Jack as a singer, but rather as a very active athlete who was almost impossible to remove from the pool or the gym – Jack apparently couldn't get enough of the athletic facilities.

Having heard Jack sing and having noted he was not a very large man, but very compactly and powerfully built (he obviously exercised regularly), I had no doubt that, while their shared memories of Jack's childhood church activities did not appear to overlap at all, they are both true. A quirk of human memory is that what we focus on may differ from another who was at the same event, and yet both collective internal memories (and those of others) can be woven into a complex tapestry that reveals something richer, more vibrant, more true of a past event or person.

Thanks again not only for your contributions to the arts but your continued defense of the arts. It's a shame that even the large contribution of the arts to our economy isn't enough to get the Government to increase its support (never mind not making the cuts they made in the 2012 budget). I support the arts for reasons that go beyond any economic rationale. In my essay, "Art for Art's Sake," I mentioned the important role art played in the lives of Jewish prisoners in Auschwitz (as described by Viktor Frankl in his book, *Man's Search for Meaning*), despite the fact they were fighting for survival. Every human starts out as an artist or at least wants to make art (just give a young child a crayon or a lump of clay!). Sadly, our need to make art gets beaten out of too many of us.

The Greatest Prime Minister We Never Had

Donna Lypchuk

The Greatest Prime Minister We Never Had,
      Jeremy Gilbert (Jack! for short!) Layton
Was born in the Atomic Age of 1950 in the "just French enough"
      town of Hudson Québec
A genteel old town full of rose bushes, white clapboard houses
      and middle-class "anglophonies"
Not quite West Mount but close enough to the Gatineau
      to channel the spirits
Of the Fathers of Confederation lurking in the pink quartz
      and tree tops tickling the
Crazy blue sky above the Greek ruins in the home of
      William Lyon Mackenzie King
And near enough to see the gyrating dancers in the pink rays
      of the Fou Fou Electrique
In Montréal where the Greatest Prime Minister We Never Had
      studied political science at McGill.

The Greatest Prime Minister We Never Had,
      Jack ("Back to Jack!" in the 90s!) Layton
Married his high school sweetheart at age 19 and then left
      the haunted rough stone of Old Montréal
For the concrete and glass spires of Toronto,
      where the CN Tower had yet to spear the sky
And where the egg of the Sky Dome had yet to be to laid
      as a stone of Jack's contention
He traversed the windy ramps and damp coves of York University –
      a Master of Poly-Science!
This child of Doris Steeves: the niece of Robert Steeves,
      (the far-from-faint hearted father of Federation)
This son of Montréal PC MP Robert Layton and great grandson of
      Philip E. Layton who composed "Dominion March"
      and fought *for the rights of the blind!!*
Composer of the Dominion March that chimed on the carillon as
      The Greatest Prime Minister We Never Had
      Laid in State under the Peace Tower ...

This Greatest Prime Minister We Never Had
       (Jack for President of Student Council Layton!)
Was elected president of Hudson High thanks to campaign manager
       Billy Bryans. Rest in Peace!
To the sound of Billy's drums on Queen Street Jack Layton
       filled his manifest destiny
To "rise up rise up" to be BE a true idealist like philosopher
       Charles Taylor
Embracing *Canadian Idealism and the Philosophy of Freedom*
       by philosopher C.B. Macpherson
And while Billy played his own version of "Dominion March"
       in the Parachute Club
And The King of Kensington strolled through the market and giant ants
       appeared on the side of the Cameron Hotel
The Greatest Prime Minister We Never Had penned *Homelessness:*
       The Making and Unmaking of a Crisis (Penguin Canada 2010!).

The Greatest Prime Minister We Never Had
       (Jack "Party For Sale or Rent" Layton)
Was a Dad to Mike and Sarah and wrote *Speaking Out*
       and after 14 years of matrimony
Ended it … became a prominent activist who owned a
       Starfleet Uniform and who
Entertained the troops at the Federation of Canadian Municipalities
       with old sixties folk songs
While gay men contracted GRIDS that turned to AIDS
       and then to bathhouse busts
Jack was firmly seated in the futuristic saucer of Toronto Council
       at New City Hall
Beating Gordon Chong and fighting the Skydome
       and the bid for the Olympics and
Then The Greatest Prime Minister We Never Had fell in love
       with Olivia Chow at a fundraiser at Village by the Grange.

The Greatest Prime Minister We Never Had
       Jack the "Fast Talking Auctioneer" Layton
Played Mah-Jong with Olivia's mother and then
       "thanked her for the good sex" after
Failing to learn Mandarin correctly and spending a weekend
       at a cottage with her

Candidate Olivia Chow – whose gaze he first met across the wide
      expanse of teal green water in the peeling pool in the courtyard
      of Ginsberg and Wong just across the street
From the Henry Moore sex sculpture outside the AGO
      made of molten double oculars
"What does it mean?" – running for the House of Commons
      in Rosedale and then after a close race
The Greatest Prime Minister We Never Had managed the mega-city
      as the councillor for the Don River Ward in 1994.

The Greatest Prime Minister We Never Had
      ("Jack Life of the Party" Layton)
Was involved in many charities including the White Ribbon
      and Clayquot Sound Campaigns
Along with Donna Lypchuk (me!), Alannah Myles,
      The Barenaked Ladies and many others
He laughed with us and drank with us and was a man of the people
      and along with
Pastor Brent Hawkes, John Sewell, Bob Hunter those who tried to
Imagine a truly caring world where common objectives could surpass
      individual goals
And while Moe Berg sang out "I'm An Adult Now" and the condo
      towers kept growing like extended middle fingers to artists
      and the poor
And while Mendelsohn Joe blasted opinion from Speaker's Corner
      at John and Queen
The Greatest Prime Minister We Never Had married Olivia Chow
      in a ceremony on Algonquin Island.

The Greatest Prime Minister We Never had
      (Jack) "If I Had Another 4.6 Billion Dollars" Layton
Famous for arriving at City Hall wearing scruff jeans and
      a battered corduroy jacket
Decided to run for mayor as the official NDP candidate and after losing
      to June Rowlands
Traded in his hippie commie style for a suit and contacts and a new
      paternal look
Returned to the ivory tower where the ideals of C.B. McPherson
      and Charles Taylor lived
And rode his bike every day from his home in Chinatown
      to Ryerson University

A so-called Don Quixote planting windmills in the city through
        Windshare and Green Catalyst and then ...
The Greatest Prime Minister We Never Had was finally elected
        leader of the NDP
        at the leadership convention in '03.

The Greatest Prime Minister We Never Had
        Jack "the New Tommy Douglas" Layton
Beat out Pierre Ducasse in 2004 and then took his seat and then
        made friends with
The French by appointing Ducasse as his lieutenant and then
        after attacking Paul Martin
Made friends with the Liberals to avoid a snap election during
        the Liberal minority and
Then in the shadow of the stalled government made friends with Stephen
Harper and Gilles Duceppe for the greater good of all in the spirit of
        idealism and wrote a letter
To Governor General Adrienne Clarkson,
        "Please to consider a three-party coalition!"
And then The Greatest Prime Minister We Never Had walked out
When Harper told the press that he would be King of the Co-op!

The Greatest Prime Minister We Never Had
        Jack "Nobody Knows When You Are Down" Layton
Was hated by the Canadian Auto Workers Union but beloved
        by the Canadian people at 92%
In 2006, part of the only husband and wife team in parliament
        with Olivia Chow
Jack met with President Hamid Karazai of Afghanistan
        to bring our boys home ...
Tried to implement a program to allow conscientious objectors in the
        country ...
Battled the new income trust rules that threatened to impoverish
        2.5 million Canadians!
Told the Conservatives to clean up their act before passing any
        "Clean Air Act"
And then in 2008 The Greatest Prime Minister We Never Had
        lost once again to Stephen Harper.

The Greatest Prime Minister We Never Had
        Jack "darling of the media" Layton

Formed a coalition with the Bloc and the Liberals to fight for the right
        to strike
Proposing a motion of non-confidence and a move to dissolve
        the minority government
Next seen riding on a bank of balloons in the Toronto Gay Pride Parade
Then seen busking on street corner to raise money for the
        Stephen Lewis Foundation
Making an alliance with the Green Party and protesting
        Usage Based Billing
Advising Michael Ignatieff that if he does not show up for work he does
        not get a promotion
And then The Greatest Prime Minister We Almost Had
        announced that he was stricken with prostate cancer.

The Greatest Prime Minister We Almost Had
        Known as "Smilin' Jack Layton"
Doubled the seats in the NDP federal election to 103 – an all-time high
And led the party into the first session of parliament and then announced
On July 25, 2011 ... the saddest day!!! ... that he must leave his post as for
        an unspecified newly diagnosed SECOND cancer
And then on August 20, 2011, wrote a letter to all Canadians:
        "Love is Better
Than Anger, Hope is Better Than Fear, Optimism is Better Than Despair
So Let Us Be Loving, Hopeful and Optimistic and
        We'll Change the World"
And then with family and friends close by ... The Greatest Prime
Minister We Never Had passed away at 4:45 am on August 22, 2011.

The Greatest Prime Minister We Never Had, John Gilbert Jack Layton,
Lay in state in the Centre Block in Ottawa and his ashes were spread
One third in the Toronto Islands, the place of picnics, bonfires and love
One third in the St. James Cemetery where he dressed
        and gave historic tours
And one third in the Church cemetery Hudson,
        Québec where history waits
And Billy Bryans stopped banging his drum and the Autumn leaves
        curled up
And blew away as the October winds howled through the broken heart
        of a country
Who knew they just lost the Greatest Prime Minister This Country
        Could Have Ever Had.

Love Is Better than Anger

Darryl Salach

Jack discovered politics at age 22, while
canvassing for his urban studies professor.
Riding through Toronto streets on his ten-speed bicycle
he would meet a couple of pot-smoking delinquents,
American draft dodgers. They'd learned their
trade as Democrat anti-poverty activists
and headed north to avoid the buzz
of bullets, Nixon and Agent Orange overseas.
They taught Jack about making a difference,
how to stand up to the hypocrisy of self-
serving government. Suits were the enemy
back then, and bushy hair, a faded pair
of denim blue jeans proclaimed his allegiance
to the underprivileged. He led renters in need of a voice
listening to their grievances over draught beer, acting swiftly,
fairly, all in an era where left-leaning sympathizers
were decreed as the sacrificial lamb on Bay Street.
Jack lived among his constituents, not in the towers
overlooking them. He would have applauded the optimism
of the Occupy movement, leading the charge to the Hill.
Your legacy is forever undying, Jack. Hope is better than fear.

"Not the person, but the principles, the goals"

Mike Layton

In early August, 2012, I interviewed Toronto Councillor Mike Layton twice, because the first was inadvertently not recorded. Mike was game to try again, in the interview transcribed below.

"Hi Mike

Penn has just reconstructed your interview before my very eyes. She had to do this because I failed to record it properly, or at all. The failure was of unfamiliarity with a new toy, and I pushed a button once when I should have done it twice.

I hope we can meet in Toronto sometime soon. It doesn't feel right to be at a distance from Jack's family.

For now, I turn this back to Penn.

Love, Gavin"

The piece below is what I recall from the first interview. Such an interesting conversation had its own logic, but I've lost some of the interplay between my questions and Mike's response in an attempt to remember what was said. So I'll begin with a series of direct questions to Mike.

Both you and your dad seem to exemplify the spirit of optimism, of moving forward. What kept Jack going? How did Jack handle feelings of doubt? How was he able to maintain such an indomitable pace throughout the last campaign? I know he was buoyed by crowds. I know he was helped by Nancy's rigorous routine, the hour of daily exercise. What fueled him? What fuels you now? Where do you find your energy, your inspiration? You and Jack seem to have found it in the causes you were working for. You carry that conviction as well. How is Jack still present in your life?

Mike remarks on how much he learned from his father, both directly and indirectly. He would often go to him for advice, both when he was young and more recently as a Toronto councillor. But he also learned from Jack's example as a father and as an activist. Jack's lessons were always in context, not theoretical or patronizing. Jack was not in public service for financial profit nor for personal power. His motive, like Mike's, was to effect change.

The first White Ribbon Campaign, for example, had its office in his bedroom at Jack's house. A year or so after the 1989 Montréal Massacre, Jack and his friends got the campaign going, to stop violence against women and domestic abuse. This campaign was one of the very first to raise awareness of this hitherto mostly unspoken issue. When Mike arrived for the weekend, he would find his room full of papers and flyers concerning the Campaign. Even now he is involved in the still unfortunately necessary White Ribbon Campaign.

As Mike was growing up, Jack spent a lot of time with the family. Mike's fondest memories are of camping trips. When Jack was City Councillor, the kids would attend numerous and ongoing community events with him. They were always involved, always active. Mike must have taken to the life, since he is now repeating the pattern as City Councillor in his own right. By the time Mike was in University, Jack had become a national figure. Their time together was more limited but because of Jack's ability to be fully present, Mike always felt that he had enough attention.

Mike recalls a trip the family took exploring personal historical sites in Montréal. They toured the city, paid their respects at the family plot in Mount Royal Cemetery. They visited Layton Brothers, a downtown store that once sold Layton pianos and now sells electronic and stereo equipment. The owners are distantly related, though the store long ago passed out of Mike's family's hands. Still, the tradition of music-making continues in many forms. Both Mike and Sarah were engaged: Sarah in piano and Mike on the guitar. For Jack, music was another community event, a way of community-building, rather than a personal achievement or endeavour. Mike recalls that his dad could pick up an instrument like the saxophone and play it reasonably well within months. Jack was spontaneous, rather than a perfectionist; he played without self-consciousness or inhibition … even when the kids would ask him to stop! He had enough facility to play without egregious errors and he was generally fearless. Music was a way of relaxing, having fun, and connecting with others, creating a common bond.

Jack's was a life of service. And since there was so much to be changed in the world, Mike, like his father before him, wakes up in a spirit of optimism. What's the next step? What's to be done today? He didn't plan to follow his father's footsteps: in university he started out in biochemistry with an elective in political science. But he felt at home both with the theory and practice of political science. As we talked, I noticed that Mike much preferred the term activist to politician. Like Jack, Mike does not focus on political theory but on direct action and specific cases where he can make a difference to effect change. I noticed in our conversation how often the word 'change' popped up, as well. He remembered very well his grandfather Robert's dictum: "Never refuse an opportunity to serve."

Mike is grateful both to Olivia, whom he considers his mentor, and his mother's second husband. They all spent every Christmas together. That kind of congeniality in the extended family is a sign, I think, of very adept communication and negotiating skill. It illustrates one of the points I find most endearing and important in Jack: that there was no difference between the private man and the public self. He was not out for personal power as in domination or self-aggrandisement, except to change his part of the world. And that arena grew substantially in the last few years of his life to include the entire nation.

I remarked that I perceived a huge change in the last year of Jack's life in terms of how folks regarded him, how he was welcomed coast to coast to coast. Mike felt that it was just that people, other people, began to be aware of Jack's open-heartedness. I expressed my gratitude that Jack would take his dying time, surely the most private occasion in one's life, as a way of reaching out, for the benefit of all those who survived him and were to carry on. What a gift that last letter has been, a solace, encouragement, even a joy. Mike was not part of its writing, as it would have been so painful. But he feels that Jack died the way he had lived, serving the community. There's less sense of lament or grief if you have dedicated your life to service, as Jack had.

Mike's daily practice is to consider policy decisions in the light of what his father would do. He respects Jack most for the principled way he took unpopular stands that he believed in. Mike cites as example Jack's fight against the incinerator in Toronto that was spewing out pollution at Ashbridge's Bay. Now such a stance has become environmental policy in most cities, but at the time, public opinion was very much pro the incinerator as a way of disposing of waste. Similarly, Jack did not, despite public opinion, approve of Toronto's early bid for the Olympic Games, believing, as certainly has been shown to be the case, that the games would be a huge financial drain not easily rectified.

The following interview with Mike Layton about his father was recorded in August and aired on September 25 and December 4, 2012. It is archived on *www.chrwradio.com/talk/gatheringvoices*. I've edited it for print.

Penn Kemp: I'm delighted to talk with Mike Layton, who is repeating his father's footsteps in his own way. He is Councillor for Trinity-Spadina in Toronto and he has been for the last year?

Mike Layton: Two years.

PK: So you're a seasoned activist politician now.

ML: Many years of being an activist beforehand, but just recently as a politician. I saw my dad work on issues that ranged a massive spectrum, first at City Council and then when he moved on to the federal scene. Even the drivers of a lot of his early work were seemingly different types of issues – issues protecting the natural environment and air quality; issues around domestic violence and violence against women. And then there were issues about how we make more liveable cities – we fought a campaign to protect the city's last roller rink when I was very young. But the diversity of different issues all came back to equality, access, to living a good life, a community-based life, and a service-based life and later trying to make the country and the world a better and more fair place. What gets us to that point comes from different directions. Campaigns can be for a lot of different things but all serve that greater good.

PK: I know he had a general view of specific issues. Did he have a detailed view or did he delegate that to those who were experts in their fields?

ML: Some issues he would get into more than others. For some things that really caught his personal attention, he would say, "I'd like to know more about this." The environment in general and climate change in particular were big drivers for him, particularly around renewable energy, reducing greenhouse gases. You know he did many retrofits of his home, putting in geothermal, putting in solar photovoltaic panels, solar hot water heaters, increasing the R-value of the home by factors of ten or twenty. He had a particular interest in the technical aspect of things, as growing up in a house of engineers taught him.

PK: So that was the unexpressed side of him? He also embraced technology very early, like social media.

ML: I remember, it must have been in the late Eighties, when he came home with his first laptop that was the size of a suitcase with a screen that was just about four inches wide.

PK: 156 K, right?

ML: Exactly. But he learned how to use those technologies. And again, as time went on, he was one of the first people that I knew to have a BlackBerry. Then that technology really took off. He stayed right with it and always had some kind of device that was helping him to connect with more people and increase his productivity.

PK: Did he tweet? I was connected with him on email but not Twitter.

ML: He had a fairly solid Twitter following.

PK: He was one of the very first politicians to use social media as a way of reaching out to what he kept calling, in a very positive way, 'ordinary people'.

ML: I'm not sure if he was one of the first or not, but he was definitely an early adopter. It wasn't as common as it is today, right when Facebook was being introduced. But he did pick it up early.

PK: And promote it. He really used it to the max. I didn't realize his brothers were engineers.

ML: His father was an engineer before he became a politician. And one of his brothers was also an engineer.

PK: But you also have music so much in the family.

ML: Yes. Music has played a role in our family for many generations. It all started with my great-great-grandfather coming over from England and becoming first a piano tuner and then making pianos and owning a store in Montréal called "Layton Brothers" which is still there on St. Catherines, I believe.

PK: And they sell stereos now?

ML: And they probably sell some keyboards there. When it was formed, they sold Layton Brothers pianos, of which there are many in the city. It started there and really became part of the Layton family life, to sit around after a meal and sing songs. And so my dad was a fairly accomplished pianist; he knew what he was doing. I think he got it from his grandmother who was a graduate of the Conservatory to a pretty high level. They learned on the Layton Brothers' piano and organ. He learned "The Dominion March," which is my great-great-grandfather's opus of sorts. And so it ended up being that you sang songs when you were with your family. That continued on for every generation. Just recently, we would pick up the guitar and play a couple of songs. Different family gatherings would just end up becoming a bit of a singsong. When you are on the campaign trail, you want to bring as much sanity into it as possible and part of that for him was going back to "What do I do when I'm at my happiest?" That would be for him to be with family and friends and singing a couple of songs.

PK: Sanity and fun, I think it's that sense of uplifting. I really think he used music as a collective community builder.

ML: I think you're probably right. Part of that was Pete Seeger's "Rise Up Singing," the songbook with the guitar chords written in, very easy to read, with every singalong song under the sun. He would buy these books by the case and just give them away to people, if they were over and singing songs, if someone would say, "That's a really great book!" He probably gave away five or six dozen copies of books. They do offer something to do that's fun. It's a community-based activity and it can bring you a lot of good feelings and good memories.

PK: It's a way of connecting. What was his favourite song?

ML: To play? He had this ability to just make up songs and make up words to songs that few people have on any topic, just by playing the three or four chords. The chords he played most often were "Hit the Road, Jack." I think he thought it was kind of funny when he played it. As long as I can remember, he'd grab a guitar. All of a sudden, the lyrics would go in different directions depending on the crowd. They would talk about different political movements or different people in the room. It would make it a little more fun.

PK: Have you carried on that tradition?

ML: I try. I don't quite have the talent he does for making up songs on the fly. But I do the same thing with my friends. We continue to have a singsong with my family.

PK: "The Cat Came Back."

ML: "The Cat Came Back" is one that I enjoyed. It happens to be the same chords as "Hit the Road, Jack," so it's pretty easy to pass on.

PK: Fun. How did Jack influence you as a boy growing up in his household?

ML: Well, I think he exposed me to a lot of different opportunities and a lot of different issues. My parents split up when I was at a relatively early age. A bunch of my time was spent with my father on the weekends or during vacations. During those times in politics, there's always something going on, typically over the weekend and summertime. There's always some kind of meeting going on outside of City Hall or there's a rally or a demonstration. It was interesting because I got exposed to different groups of folks; to tenants living in affordable housing that he was helping organize; or the environmental movement, working to close down the incinerator and through that bringing to Toronto the blue bin program.

PK: The Ashbridge's Bay incinerator.

ML: The Ashbridge's Bay incinerator was still being used, burning garbage, affecting air quality. There was a large campaign to bring down the incinerator and bring the blue bin program for recycling to Toronto. Just a handful of municipalities in North America had the blue bin program. That's probably one of the first memories I have of going to a demonstration, standing on a blue bin and yelling into a megaphone – it was eye-opening when you're a young person.

PK: How old would you have been?

ML: Probably eleven or twelve. It was a pretty early age for me to be exposed to something like that. It helped me realize what was possible and where should I be putting my energies. It wasn't into making money or gaining in popularity. It was into helping communities put up a fight against something that was impacting them or holding them back. And so that opened my eyes a little bit. I still ended up going in a slightly different direction in university, where I was going to study biochemistry. I quickly realized my talents may lie elsewhere and instead followed a public policy, still related to biology and the natural environment, but a shift toward the public policy end.

PK: You worked in the environmental sector.

ML: After university, I worked for many years working around policies to protect drinking water and to bring more renewable energy to Southern Ontario.

PK: So you must have had a direct influence on Jack, enlightening him to the necessity to act for the environment as a priority.

ML: I still think it was a mutual learning experience. I would be learning stuff at my work and when I was in school that maybe was new to him. But then he would be meeting with groups across the country about other policies that were being worked on. He would meet with international leaders. He gained a very close friendship with Tim Flannery, the author of ...

PK: ... the wonderful *Weather Makers*.

ML: ... and just a fabulous global activist for the environmental movement. He would learn from those individuals and come and have that conversation with me. So we had a very lovely relationship in the later years, almost like a policy discussion every time we got together, but one where we were both more excited about telling the other about what we were learning.

PK: Yeah, and who was listening. How essential to keep on growing in that way, to keep on learning. Any one fixed concept may well have been outdated, especially with something like climate change that is so complex.

ML: Well, I recently was given a copy of my dad's platform when he ran for mayor in the Nineties. It was significantly out of date. We've either adopted more of the positions, or become quite a bit more progressive than his stance was. That shows that over time change happens, and you have to learn about the changing times and be ready to change with it.

PK: That's right. He was such an avid biker but all the policies that he must have wanted, like cycle paths, haven't happened. There's a lot more work to be done in that field.

ML: I think he'd be pleased with the progress but not overjoyed. Coming from where it did, we've made some pretty decent moves. But we're not nearly where he had envisioned. He wrote some early policy papers around hundreds of kilometres of bike lanes in the city by the end of 2005. Those were certainly not achieved.

PK: He was always practical rather than theoretical as a policy maker, did you find? Are you the same?

ML: I would say he was practical but he always had some vision.

PK: For sure!

ML: He wouldn't say, "That's practical, so let's make that our goal." He would say, "What is a realistic goal and expectation: what can we actually do?" Then he would work toward the incremental change. He saw, as I do, that incremental change is better than no change. And once you move the yardstick, as they say, you can then just keep pushing.

PK: People get used to one blue box and then we can go to green box.

ML: Precisely. And then we can keep moving forward. If we just take the position that it's an all or nothing game, we end up in a pretty bad state if we lose.

PK: It's too absolute.

ML: Because then where do we go from there? Because you can normally get people to agree on at least taking one step forward. You've built something that can bring you that other step, that incremental change. You saw in his policy later on that to bring people toward a Canada that is more hopeful, loving and optimistic, some people needed to take it in small steps. He tried his best to make those as large steps as possible and pushed as far as he could. He saw that we were still pretty far away from the end point but wanted to get at least some kind of change and some kind of momentum to move things forward.

PK: Everything seems to be a very interesting dance between realism and idealism. He had a very interesting balance in his life as well between fun and work, between keeping fit and working hard in policy. He was a very balanced individual, don't you think?

ML: I think balance would be a good word.

PK: A rhetorical question. I wanted to ask you also, Mike, about his interest in Aboriginal cultures: where did that come from?

ML: You know, there's a history behind my family's relation with the First Nations and then there's what *his* experience has been. He throughout had a profound respect because of this historical relationship but I think it gained as he went to more First Nations, met with their leaders and saw the problems they were facing; learned from them quite a bit about wider problems that Canada and the world were facing. He often speaks of a story when he was up paddling a river with Olivia in the Northwest Territories – they were quite avid canoeists. The elder that was with them was describing how … it would be beautiful lush green hills that were around them. The problem was that they used to be white. He was explaining to them: "we can't hunt here anymore because we don't know how. Because just a couple of years ago, that was glacier and that's the land we live on." And that's a result of global warming. Those personal accounts about the result of global warming I think added to his connection with First Nations. There are stories of the presentation of eagle feathers that fell off a bird right in front of him. That was a sort of spiritual awakening, a connection to First Nations and the land. But it goes back.

PK: What a gift, the eagle's gift!

ML: There's also a historical connection when my grandmother on my father's side was coming up …

PK: This is Doris Layton?

ML: Yes. They were coming up the east coast of North America …

PK: From Virginia?

ML: It was prior to that. They ended up crossing the St. Lawrence at a particular nasty time weather-wise, and were struggling. They were, in fact, cared for by the Mi'kmaqs. And so there was a spiritual connection there because when our ancestors came to Canada, we didn't know what we were doing. We were, in fact, protected and nurtured by the First Peoples of Canada. So there was a very strong connection with my family with the First Nations.

PK: That's interesting because it's so historically correct [I was thinking of how the Puritans were helped through their first winters by First Nations people]. To have it specifically in your family would have the resonance so much more strongly felt.

ML: I believe that he thought that there was an unpaid debt.

PK: For sure. He had a very good relationship with Shawn Atleo. Which I think you've carried on, have you? I've heard of a recent talk you just gave.

ML: I attended the AFN, the Assembly of First Nations, the national body for First Nations across Canada. They were having their annual meeting in Toronto and I had the privilege of going down. I helped to secure some support from the City for their event. As you can imagine, securing support isn't an easy endeavour. We secured some financial support in recognition of the AFN being an incredibly important political body in Canada and a distinct political body that was coming to our city. We wanted to open our doors wide to them.

PK: Congratulations for getting that to happen!

ML: Thank you.

PK: It is very tricky right now.

ML: We had a very interesting encounter with Shawn Atleo, the Grand Chief, when we were at the Copenhagen Conference [Copenhagen Climate Change Conference, December 2009]. After the conference, my flight didn't leave for another day. My dad and Olivia were there as we were waiting for our flight. We were in a little pub on the pedestrian street, just sitting there when all of a sudden, Shawn and his partner came in and sat down with us. We shared a drink and just had a wonderful time chatting with them about issues that arose at the Conference. We weren't pleased with the outcome. So we had a lovely chat and I got to know him a little better and I think we all progressed our relationship over a beer there, on the other side of the world, chatting about issues that we face at home as well.

PK: And yet when it's an outside setting, sometimes you bond together more easily, don't you?

ML: I think so.

PK: What has got you through the last year? It's been such a tricky time, a lot of change.

ML: It's been difficult. There have been some sad moments where I've needed to lean on my family and my partner and to go to them for support. What I've relied on most is that he gave pretty specific instructions about what I was to do with the rest of my time. And it wasn't just me. That letter to Canada was read to the nation at the same time as it was read to me. I could see in it very specific instructions for myself and I think others saw something similar.

PK: Yes they did.

ML: In their own lives, they were to work toward the same goals. I was just fortunate that I was in the position to do something about that in the City of Toronto. So I've tried to do everything I can in my work. Often my job includes dealing with parking and dog off-leash areas but it still affords a significant amount of time to dedicate to trying to bring that message of love, hope and optimism to people and the City of Toronto and hopefully outside. So I've taken that as being what's going to fuel my work and continue to get me to be excited about the campaigns I get to work with, the people I get to meet and the change that we can bring together. I've relied on that for a lot of strength. He wouldn't have wanted me to spend a terribly huge amount mourning the loss. He would have wanted me to Get to Work and to continue.

PK: Move on, move up. Tell me about the *www.dearjack.ca* initiative. That's so moving.

ML: In conversation between family members, his colleagues and other friends in Ottawa, it became clear that something was going to happen on the anniversary of his death, August 22. What could we do to help? We thought about what we expected would happen: we expected people would come and re-chalk Nathan Philips Square. Maybe a couple of small vigil-type things would get initiated in other parts of the country, on Parliament Hill and in Québec. We started thinking. What can we do to reawaken and reinforce the message that he left Canadians, this idea of building a more loving, hopeful and optimistic world? How can we make that the legacy? Not the person, but those principles and those goals. We thought people would try to reawaken them in their own community, so how can we give some kind of apparatus for an exchange of these ideas? Because by continuing the dialogue particularly across the country, we can help bring more life to those words. And so with the help of the Broadbent Institute and other friends, we've put together this platform for pieces on social media, tweets and songs, all in one place. For people to reflect on both Jack as a politician, but more importantly, his message of Love, Hope and Optimism. That's what we were trying to help do through the lead up to the anniversary of his passing. On that anniversary, we'll be doing something here at Nathan Philips Square in Toronto. We suspect there'll be other events that we'll link in over cyberspace. It's a loose framework.

PK: What a wonderful way to give people across the nation an opportunity to celebrate, to feel whatever they're feeling together and to move on in Hope and Optimism.

ML: We just wanted to help facilitate that.

PK: How wonderful. Mike, it's a delight to talk with you. Thank you so much.

Le bon musical Jack

Joan Doiron

My mother supported me in politics since she was an activist, a member of the Waffle movement. After having taught high school English, I was first elected in 1978 as a school trustee for downtown Toronto and continued full-time till 1994. As the years went on, Jack and I would gather for meetings at City Hall when I became a member of the City Cycling Committee. We did not duplicate each other's work; we complemented each other. I was not running in the same political realm; he was a councillor at City Hall while I was a trustee. Olivia became my assistant, creating newsletters, etc. for the area. She then ran with me for trustee in 1980; we never had any trouble being elected. When Jack ran for Mayor, she decided to run for councillor. At election time, we would all work together downtown. In the campaigns, we would have meetings of a hundred or so. Jack would lead us in singing songs in the spirit of *We Shall Overcome*.

One line from that song, "We shall not be moved," was so like Jack: he was determined and happy, encouraging everyone to participate all the time. He would get folks singing and then join them on the harmonica and the piano. At auctions to raise funds for the NDP, he sounded like a professional auctioneer. That rhythm would be going so fast that he gave people no time to think because if they thought, they might not bid; they might accidentally stick their hand up! His voice was a musical, artistic ability in itself. He was really "le bon Jack," generous, open and welcoming. No wonder the NDP succeeded in Québec!

Jack Layton, Last Man Standing

Robert Priest

One day back in the early '80s, I was asked to participate in an environmentally oriented concert. I think it was somewhere on the edge of the old Ontario Place forum. A number of activists would speak and some reasonably high profile singer songwriters would provide the music. And then right at the end, me. We started with a fair sized crowd but slowly as the speeches grew longer and the afternoon hotter, the audience having taken in the more well-known singers, slowly drifted away. By the time I came on there were very few left. The only specifically environmental material I had was written for children and there were no children in the audience any more. Nevertheless, I went ahead with my planned set doing my best not to look too foolish under the three or four sun-scorched gazes left to behold me. I had been asked to do a fifteen minute set and, having practiced earnestly, decided not to cut it short. Perhaps most of those remaining lacked stamina or perhaps they were just slightly embarrassed at the call and response kiddy-tinged content of my songs but by the time I finished, there was only one person left. He had not seemed embarrassed at all. In fact he had participated with good humor in the call and response parts, singing along in a high voice as required.

The sun was so bright I hadn't been able to quite see him but after I finished he came up to me and I saw that he had light sky-blue eyes and enough of a mustache for me to wonder if he might be a policeman. "Great set," he said jovially and shook my hand with a grip of friendly steel. "I'm Jack Layton."

After that I encountered him over the years at a multitude of similar events. In fact, I think he actually saw more of my gigs than most members of my family. Slowly my guardedness fell away and I came to think of him with a mix of love and admiration. He inspired hope in me. And when the times got dark, particularly in the Mike Harris era, I could always find comfort in the thought that Jack Layton was on my side. He was an incredibly hard worker. He could've made a fortune doing almost anything else but he had to do what his social conscience demanded of him. I loved that in him and I felt the love and the drive in him as he went his way in the world championing great and difficult things most of which I ardently believe in. His ease with the arts, his clear attraction to them and the people who create them, his willingness to understand the needs of and the need for artists was just one more strand in the great colourful thing he was.

A Man of Many Colours

Peter O'Brien

Jack is a colourful guy. And like all smart, engaged and compassionate people, his many colours all manage to complement each other and play off each other. In this piece, I use phrases in the present tense that speak about Jack's continuing presence.

I first met Jack in the early 1990s when we were active on the founding Board of Directors of the White Ribbon Campaign, the campaign to end men's violence against women that came into being partly because of the horrific assassinations at the École Polytechnique in December 1989.

Those early days of the White Ribbon Campaign were simultaneously very focused and very scattered. The minutes of the meetings and the various other strategic documents record attempts to build a viable "cross-country outreach," to ensure that we were "consolidating organizational structures," to enlist the support of "all politicians" to endorse the campaign "and to put this support into practice in terms of the policies they adopt," and of course to "appease" our creditors. They also document our expanding efforts and intents as we found our footing – from our first forays into telemarketing, on to our mailer that went out to "250,000" people toward the end of 1992, and further toward our objective "to help stimulate reflection, discussion, and analysis leading to personal and collective action among men to take responsibility for ending men's violence."

Jack was deeply interested in all aspects of the campaign and those early documents record his hands-on involvement. He worked on spreading the word of the campaign and on bringing in new members, but also on the more mundane tasks. "Jack has been working diligently to develop a plan on corporate and union fundraising" says a financial report from February 1992. In the Action Minutes from our December 1992 Executive Committee meeting Jack is noted as working through the details of our finances by reporting on our "invoices and cheques to compare with accounting figures."

A few of us involved in the campaign also played squash pretty regularly in those days, and I can say without equivocation that Jack did not like to lose. Though often sleep-deprived, and sometimes with wonky knees and a sore back, Jack was relentless on the court. He had always been an active athlete. He also had tenacious concentration, as well as a need to not be bested. (I have to add, and I do so parenthetically and somewhat pathetically, that over the course of our many games I do not recall ever beating him.)

Around that time, Jack and I prepared a proposal for then-President of University of Toronto, Robert Prichard, on the idea of "creating Toronto as a full-fledged 'City of Ideas'." We sent a four-page overview of the idea to Prichard in July 1993 and although the idea never came to fruition, it clearly articulates Jack's overriding concerns. Jack always wanted to ensure that Toronto lived up to its potential. In the proposal, we spoke about how the University of Toronto and other universities should remain a "key focal point" of this imagined city, "and all of the attendant artistic, economic, political and intellectual ideas that such institutions generate." We spoke about bringing together "outposts of communication and connection" and of encouraging a "celebration of a multiplicity of connections between the University – in all its manifestations – and the City that bears its name." And we spoke about "pride among the citizens" and the "ideas, solutions, challenges and opportunities" that such a City of Ideas would entail.

As usual with Jack, these were big, colourful ideas – and he was both willing and able to work on them directly.

A few years later I would see him running around the track at the U of T athletic complex with Olivia and I knew he was thinking about the upcoming political leadership position he was about to run for. I imagined him preparing his body, mind and spirit for the upcoming challenges he was to face, as he steadfastly kept to his running and exercise regime.

In 2008, I ran into Jack at a local coffee shop on Roncesvalles Avenue near High Park in the west end of Toronto. By this time, he was fully occupied as the leader of the NDP and the related meetings at which he connected ideas and people together. During our brief exchange, I told him about a new environmental website that I was starting for children, called Arbopals. The idea of the site was that as kids played online, real trees would be planted in twenty-one countries around the world. It took Jack about three seconds to show his support, and he immediately suggested I contact his friend Tim Flannery in Australia, author of *The Weather Makers* and arguably one of the world's top scientists and environmentalists, to enlist his support. Jack was right – I used his name as the connecting force, and Tim was immediately interested, becoming a supporter and endorser of this idea to bring together technology, kids and international tree-planting.

Like everyone else who ever got to spend time with him up close, I was deeply saddened, core-saddened, to hear of his final sickness and death.

In the days after his death, I took my teenaged daughter to the impromptu memorial at Toronto City Hall, and we wandered among the thousands of people and thousands of messages chalked onto the concrete. Through my own tears, I added a phrase from Shakespeare onto one of the surfaces: "Now cracks a noble heart. Good night, sweet prince, and flights of angels sing thee to thy rest!"

I think of Jack as a man of many colours, and like the cosmorama of colours that make up the rainbow (and that also make up people and interests and affections), he was able to weave many of them together. At any one moment, he could be thinking about his young son Mike and how Mike loved to mimic Jimi Hendrix on the guitar, and the academic and intellectual needs of his students, and doing what he could to help end men's violence against women, about his concern for the environment, nurturing friendships, keeping physically active, imagining how new ideas can make our lives better, and helping to improve public policy through people and the governmental organizations we have set up. All of those colours do, after all, complement each other.

Every once in a while, I wander through the electronic address book on my iPhone and delete the people that I am no longer in touch with. A few months ago, I came upon Jack's name and contact information. In that rush of memories – Jack's bristling energy and fertile ideas and core compassions – I could not bring myself to delete his information. He remains.

Jack Layton's Saxophone: A Memory

Tanis MacDonald

In the fall of 1992, several friends and I joined the "From All Walks of Life" walk to support people with AIDS. The starting point that year was in front of the Delta Chelsea Hotel on Gerrard Street just west of Yonge Street in Toronto. The walk started in a mood of political solidarity and ebullience. It was a lovely cool fall day, we were wearing the Walk T-shirts, and we were young and full of energy. I had teamed up with my pal B. to push the wheelchair of a mutual friend with AIDS who could not walk but was determined to participate and be seen. He too was full of such blazing energy that the wheelchair seemed quite light, no trouble at all to push. June Callwood was there at the start, too, and I loved the moment when I said (too loudly) "Wow, there's June Callwood!" and she turned and said, "That's right! And there you are!"

So we started off. The route described a rectangle; we were to walk west on Gerrard to University Avenue, north on University around Queen's Park (with extra chanting and rabble rousing) to Bloor, east on Bloor, then south on Church and west to the party at the start/finish line.

As is often the case with fundraising events that involve physical effort, the Walk began with a rush which diminishes gradually as the walkers spread out and the work gets harder. Our pace slackened after we got to Bloor and we fell far behind the other walkers. The wheelchair presented certain problems at corners that did not have graduated curbs and the work and the logistics of pushing became harder to manage. The morning also heated up in a most unseasonable way. By the time we turned south on Church, B. and I were hot and sweaty and our friend in the wheelchair had started talking about having us just wheel him home rather than finish the walk. It was about 10:00 on a Sunday morning and our fellow walkers were so far ahead that we could barely see them. The street was deserted but for a lone figure standing on the corner of Church and Isabella, holding something shiny.

As we got closer, Jack Layton put the saxophone to his lips and began to play. There were no cameras and no reporters anywhere: just Jack and his sax, playing for us, the only walkers in sight. He played more lustily – and perhaps even badly – as we approached, and he stopped playing only long enough to cheer before playing us away again. We completed the Walk, having taken in resolve with Jack's saxophone notes.

Michael Ondaatje has a poem in which he describes walking into his young son's room to say good night and finding the boy with his arms already outstretched; the poem finishes with a question about how long the child had stood waiting with open arms for his father's appearance. I have that question about Jack and the saxophone. He couldn't know for sure that there would be more walkers coming. But he waited for the stragglers anyway, and played his heart out when we showed up. It wasn't glamorous, and it wasn't recorded, but it was art in service to a cause that he continued to support for the rest of his life. It's important to recall that Jack had lost the race for mayor the previous year, and though he was a city councillor, a new election was not pending. He would go on to play the saxophone on Yonge Street after the Blue Jays' World Series win in 1993, but when I next met Jack – on my front porch when he was campaigning to be the MP for the riding of Toronto-Danforth in 1997 – I mentioned this moment on Church Street to him. He laughed and said the phrase I always associate with him:

"Never turn down an opportunity to serve."

Jack Sax

Algis Kemezys

PHOTO COURTESY OF ALGIS KEMEZYS

This image of Jack is from My Mother's Red Wig Polaroid Portraits. I asked Jack to participate in my project, which was dedicated to my mother who died of breast cancer. He immediately said ... what can I do for her? I said I was afraid it was too late: she has gone to the Spirit in the Sky. It then sounded like he actually cried for a moment as we made arrangements to make the Polaroid, with him wearing her wig that she used after she lost her hair. I thought that was just outstanding and when he showed up with a sax and played a tune for her, I became a fan for life.

Jack Layton could have changed everything. May he RIP knowing we Oh so appreciated his time here playing with us.

Penn: Gavin Stairs recalls seeing Jack depressed only once, when he had lost the mayoralty race. They bumped into each other at the corner of College and Spadina, when Jack stopped on his bike for a light. He was musing on his future. Perhaps this was the one time that Jack experienced doubt. Usually, he would look at all sides of a situation, make a decision, and act.

just jack

Joe Blades

no aide
no entourage
no bodyguard
just jack
at the entrance
to moe's
in dorval
make that
pierre elliott trudeau
airport
catching
a plane or
between flights
and jack goes
to the bar
not a table
like the one
for two i'm
at alone with
mug of beer
and empty
sandwich plate
journalling
while jack gets
a build your own
montréal smoked
meat platter
et un verre
de vin rouge
looking out
over the tarmac
gates and
the endless
movements
of silver birds
international
and domestic

August 23, 2011

Hit the Road, Jack!

Dwight Chalmers

When Jack lost the mayoralty race in 1991, he came over to Toronto Island and played "Hit the Road Jack" on the piano. We were very impressed and asked him to play more. "That's the only piece I know!" he replied.

For Jack's Memorial here on Toronto Island in October 2011, I practiced the song with the guys I play with on the Island who were also friends of Jack's. I asked around a bit if we should play it (how I and others loved Jack's sense of humour!) because I really didn't know how people might respond. And did I ever get a lot of broad grins and a thumbs-up from Olivia! So we had everyone sing along to the adapted lyrics (i.e., "Oh city, oh city, don't you treat me so mean" instead of "woman") and we all had a blast!

A Symbol of Transformation

Ann Lacey

Toronto Island was an important part of Jack and Olivia's life: they were married there in 1988 and continued to visit and support the community. This story was told to me by Ann Lacey as we sat in her lush yard on Toronto Island: it is indicative of the care to which Jack would go on behalf of his constituents, so many of whom became his friends. He loved the community for how Islanders supported each other, and stood up to City Hall and Metro to Save Island Homes.

I had to replace the front of the house because I had only one entrance and the front of the door was a big hole: big garter snakes were coming right into my living room. Though I couldn't get a building permit, friends came over to knock the porch down and start to build. In the nearby wood, we found a huge snakeskin: I knew it was an omen, a symbol of transformation. So for good luck, we brought the snakeskin back and buried it in the concrete of the new footings that support the house. I kept watch out for the building inspector! But he caught us and stuck me with a Stop Work order.

So I had to go to City Hall and lobby for myself. My lawyer was David Miller, who became Mayor of Toronto. Jack advised me throughout. I watched his fluid movement through Council, connecting here and there and keeping a keen mental tally of the balance of favours. The rules were that you could speak to the committee at City Council but not at Metro Council. The way it was presented, I was a poor, single mother. I brought in actual rotten pieces of my broken house in a bag, and put those real life pieces on the committee's table in front of everyone – there was a collective gasp and it was a very dramatic moment!

Jack made the deal in his friendly way. He knew how to hurry the negotiations through before the deadline: I watched the way he was looking at the clock. Jack remarked in an aside to us, "We don't want it to be too clear." Because then Metro Council wouldn't have agreed. But he just poked them and got them to agree to the permit. Then all the neighbours came over and finished the job.

Several contributors have remarked on how Jack worked with people across the political spectrum in coming to agreements: he may have strongly disagreed with opponents' ideas but he continued to treat them affably. He learned to work together toward consensus, toward getting the job done. Jack was always able to distinguish between the person and his/her ideology. He seemed to harbour no resentment or vindictiveness. Even those with opposing views liked Jack as a genuinely warm and caring guy.

As Toronto Islander Bill Freeman writes in *Love, Hope, Optimism* (Lorimer, 2012): "Political parties dominate federal politics. Ottawa is an intensely partisan world where most politicians only socialize with members of their own party. Those in opposing parties are the enemy, scorned and ridiculed — targets of gibes and abuse in the House of Commons.

"Jack refused to participate in that world. He repeated, 'I will work with any party and anyone to further the interests of Canadians'. In his view, he was elected to serve the people of Canada. He was the leader of the New Democrats and advocated its principles and polities, but he would work with anyone to further the interests of the people. That approach had an impact on Ottawa, and after his death it was often remarked that Jack raised the level of debate and helped others to leave behind the bitter wrangling that had characterized the House of Commons in recent years.

"We know where Jack learned that approach. It was at Toronto City Hall and Metro Council that he came to understand that politics was working with people and trying to convince them of the virtues of a motion regardless of their political stripes. As he had pointed out to me, 'In this place you have to work with everyone if you want to get anything done'."

A Conversation with Toronto Island resident, Peter Holt

Peter Holt was an old friend of Jack's from the early '70s and the first one to nominate him for political office.

Peter: I feel like I am still in total shell shock ... feeling so guilty for not adequately expressing my sympathy to Olivia and the kids ... never have I had such difficulty dealing with the death of anyone ... . Be sure to give Olivia her due as an awesome artist too, please..Her paintings and sculpture, her gardening and even her sushi, are infused with an artistic sensibility and competence, fun, casual, organic and passionate. No book on Jack can ignore the fact that those two were one! To do justice to Jack, you have to do justice to Olivia (and she'll never tell you that!).

Sometime when we are together, I will call my place for you and let you listen to Olivia's thank you message for my (very modest) help on her re-election. I am so crazy about her and I feel I have given her and Jack so little back for all they did to protect us all. Jack and I go back to before he became a politician. We were both pool-playing Québec Anglos and members of the Movement for Municipal Reform back in the days of Sparrow and Sewell and Paul Godfrey.

Penn: Ah, Peter, we're still feeling the loss, aren't we. I accidentally deleted Jack and Nancy Layton's duet to my husband Gavin on his April birthday. Keep sending me stories, especially about him playing, singing. Gavin and the brothers used to play Friday night pool but he couldn't keep up!!

Peter: I could give him a good run on the snooker table at the O'Hara brothers' Squeeze Club, though he had the edge. His dad had a snooker table in their Hudson basement rec room ... yeah ... I am still in shock at losing him ... at all our losing him ... and at Olivia being alone without him ... makes me crazy ... Jack's high school sweetheart and first wife Sally, mother of his kids, also deserves every bit of respect shown her ... and lots is and always was, by both Jack and OC [Olivia Chow], and the kids. Sally was, and I have no doubt still is, a trouper ... (an artistic term, as you know, and NOT the currently common militaristic "trooper"). I am sad that I lost \uch with her when she and Jack separated ... will look for a chance to tell that. Thank you for helping me articulate that ...

Penn: The grandchildren help; they always do, but ... I'm listening to Olivia talking right now to CBC!

What about music, that piano, that guitar?

Peter: I seem to remember Jack jamming on the Island ... but those Tuesday night jazz jams were usually a little, ummm ... spacy ... for me. They did house sit for me a few times, and I was always delighted that they, and the kids! had been there ... and for whatever reason, I felt both honoured and comforted by their lively presence in, and their obvious enjoyment of, both my house and the community. What I vividly remember is a sushi party that OC and her girlfriends threw at Grahame Beakhurst's ... omg ... I would never have believed what can be done with sushi .... We should find some of her Chinese bff's and get them to do another ... (PLEASE use my house ... lol)

Penn: Food is art!! When it happens, I'll be right over :)

Art in Action (and other notions of the Carnivalesque)
a vignette

Christopher Pinheiro

Often dressed to the nines in whatever costume the occasion called for, Jack and Olivia were involved in all kinds of civic performances, parades and displays, notably Pride and Carnival. As Olivia comments, "You know he loved to make music and we loved to dance!"

Filmmaker Christopher Pinheiro describes one memorable incident during the 1996 Caribana parade in Toronto. My son, Jake Chalmers, was told of a murdered body on the street ahead of the Star Tribes troupe. From his vantage point as a Stilt Dancer, Jake reported the message to Jack. "Impossible!" Jack reacted. But the police radios were down and Jack was the go-between. Assuming his role as city councillor, Jack intervened with the police to allow the Carnival procession to go on.

His demand in politics for social justice similarly persevered. No matter what, Jack stayed on message. Neither death nor cancer would get in his way. So his spirit carries on in those of us who were so moved by his power of persuasion, by his courage and steadfastness.

"You must come up to the house sometime. Olivia and
I have a whole wall of photographs of us in Caribana,
that I know you'd love to see!"
That was vintage Jack, the original hail-fellow,
well-met kind of guy. I regret I never picked him up on the offer, just for
the pleasure of a visit, because
I already knew the photographs well.
The Layton/Chow pas de deux was the most
famous and favourite couple of Community/Carnival
Arts extravaganzas. And certainly the most photogenic.
Images of this painted pair of rare birds of
exotic plumage could easily constitute a photographic
exhibition, beginning with the aforementioned Chow/
Layton family archive.
In addition to the Summertime Caribana
masquerades of Toronto-Island based Shadowland
Theatre Inc., there was also the Kensington Market
Festival of Lights orchestrated by Red Pepper Spectacle Arts,
led by? You guessed it, Jack and Olivia!

Parliament, the Senate and other corridors of
power were their playing fields, but they also had the
wit to realize that the streets were where the people
were. So they joined the parade, in celebratory mode.
Labour Day, Caribana, Pride, Festival of Lights, the list
is long. Once it was happening, there they were,
not just as spectators, but as fellow festivators. Often
in resplendent regalia. Like they were both born to
wear costumes. Truly this was a duo for all seasons.
One particular year is poignant in my memory.
1996. The Caribana band "Star Tribes." There was a
murder on the parade route. Our troupe was close
enough for one of the Moko-Jumbie /Stilt-Dancers to
spot the bloodied corpse from on high before it was
tarped over. Police immediately barricaded the street
and cordoned off the area. Their first word was that
the parade should reverse its direction, and go back up
the track. A nightmare on wheels, pot boiler from Hell!
That was not the last word for crowd-savvy Jack
and Olivia. Spectacularly costumed in black, white and
blue, they dove into negotiations with the top-cops and
were successful in getting the track opened back just
a crack to allow a single stream of masqueraders to
flow through. Had it not been for their timely intervention,
the riot that was menacing could have
escalated into an ugly incident.
The image of Jack and Olivia, their faces spectacularly
painted, going face-to-face with the cops arrayed in
military gear, will remain with me forever.
And the sound track that's playing sings –
"No, don't stop the Carnival!"

Balm for the Soul

Lorraine Segato

Everyone has a memory of a golden year, a moment when you felt or saw something that was changing. A moment when dreams collided with the right time or the right place and something big happened in your life.

The bubbling, burbling cosmopolitan city that is now Toronto was once a backdrop of Do It Yourself independence and 1980's decadence. Up until the late seventies, Toronto was a deep blue conservative white bread town surrounded by politicians with a powerful moral agenda and prohibition style drinking laws. Censorship was prevalent and the relationship between newly landed Caribbean immigrants and the police force was tense. There were regular raids on bathhouses and gay newspapers – demonstrations in the streets and a burgeoning and gutsy emerging art scene.

I was a part of a ragtag team of artists, musicians, writers, activists who lived illegally in the surrounding warehouses on and around Queen Street West. We frequented a newly minted world music watering hole called The Bamboo Club. It was here I first met Jack and Olivia. They were a young and energized political duo who fit well in the community of artists. Queen Street was a potent stew of art and activism. All of us galvanized around the porn and censorship debates, pro-choice demonstrations, police action against gay establishments, anti-Cruise Missiles testing demonstrations and race issues. The fight for social justice fuelled and created alliances – alliances with like-minded political people who became friends like Jack and Olivia.

Jack is written indelibly into the story of my life and passion for improving the human condition. When he died, so many of us realized that we shared one another's love of this chirpy, determined, committed engagement. Jack really embraced debate, encouraged people to take issue with him – participated with great liveliness of mind and heart in spirited discussions.

I had a lot of first time experiences with Jack. The first wedding I'd ever sung at was Jack and Olivia's. The first political song I was commissioned to write was for Jack's leadership campaign. Jack was the first politician whose idealism and genuine belief in people and mischievous love of frolic and enjoyment of others deeply touched me – and so many. And, then, of course, the first time I sang at a funeral and used my music to say goodbye to someone so beloved.

Let me finish with this observation and homage to Jack. There are few politicians who articulate and demonstrate their commitment to the arts the way Jack Layton did. Jack had a purity and honesty in the way he loved music and the arts – and he brought it to every occasion. I remember taking him to the Junos in Edmonton, and was amazed, and touched by the way in which Jack 'let loose'… here was no requisite picture with the baby, or playing on stage with all the hoke and photo op in the world. Here was a guy who remembered every artist's name because they mattered to him – who laughed and hung out – nothing stilted, artificial or strategic in it – just the pure pleasure of being amongst respected peers. It was a hoot to watch him roll up his sleeves, signature-Jack style, and with a wide grin and infectious authenticity and caring – get to work!

We live in a world where apathy, cynicism and fatigue about 'the good fight' threaten to overwhelm us, and losing one of our most treasured keepers-of-the-faith has been devastating, to be sure. At the same time, one of the things I marvel at is the way Jack's jaunty and weighty mannerisms and exhortations are becoming a part of our public lexicon. The sweetness and gravitas of his parting words – love is greater than anger, hope greater than fear – are a warm, rejuvenating refrain, a restorative and precious melody, a balm for the soul, an enduring antidote to the world's ills, and a gentle, plaintive, resonant note that will usher us all into a new chapter of goodness!

Emails, Jack Layton and Penn Kemp, 2007-08

Penn Kemp and others

From: Penn Kemp <Penn@pennkemp.ca>
To: Layton, Jack - Personal
Sent: Fri Apr 20 17:09:29 2007
Subject: Writers Union meeting tonight

Hi Jack,
The Writers' Union is holding a meeting tonight at our place. The Chair is speaking about Ontario's proposed Status of the Artist Act. Irene Mathyssen has extended her greetings to the group and her support of TWUC's stance for artists, and I thought you might like to as well, if you happen to get this note in time!

Exciting news. Shawn Lewis just called about the fundraiser at Fanshawe Pioneer Village May 26. They're serving food from 100 mile radius (with the help of hydroponics, this time of year!) They are hoping to have you there and Tom King... and they've invited me to perform a couple of poems as well.

Hope it is spring wherever you are... and a spring in your step, as always
Penn

_____

From: Layton, Jack - Personal
Subject: Re: Writers Union meeting tonight
Date: Fri, 20 Apr 2007 18:09:01 -0400

It's very much Spring.
As a proud Member of the Writers' Union and as an MP I fully support the initiative.

Sorry I can't join you.

The 100 km idea is great. Libby and I did that together in Vancouver. It was a breakfast and a big success.

Our new candidate in Québec, Tom Mulcair, the former Minister of Environment for the Liberals there who left Charest's cabinet over disagreements in principle concerning the environment is a huge catch for us. You'll see all the positive reaction on Rabble.ca. It's big news in Québec and adds an immense voice of credibility to our team. He'll also win!!

Best to you and Gavin.
Jack

From: Penn Kemp <Penn@pennkemp.ca>
To: Layton, Jack - Personal
Sent: Wed Apr 23 2008
Subject: Northrop Frye's papers

Dear Jack,
What a delight to meet and hear Charlie Angus on Friday. A wonderful performance, and oration! One of the things I love best about NDP is our individualism, unbridled! SO glad you are in the House! And doing such necessary work.

I've learned that Dr. Northrop Frye's papers have been packed away... Could you please write a letter to the contact below, expressing your outrage? Frye is, of course, a prime Canadian National Treasure!! His influence on Canadian letters has been enormous. I'm asking other concerned friends to write in as well. I feel that Dr. Frye's papers should be in the National Library, or somewhere accessible and open to the public!

Spring flowers to you and Olivia, and thanks again for all you are doing!

At 08:03p.m. 23/04/2008, Jack Layton wrote:

Hi Penn,
Thanks. We do have a wonderful team.
Olivia studied under Northrop Frye at U of T by the way.
I have no idea how such matters are addressed but it is certainly worth finding out.

I recommend that I pursue this through the National Archivist and see what options might exist.
I'll ask Ira Dubinsky, my EA to put together an appropriate letter and we'll keep Charlie posted.

Best to you and your sweetie!
Flowers indeed.
Jack

From: "Layton, Jack – Personal"
Sent: Fri Jul 11 22:28:58 2008
Subject: Fwd: Londoner Recognized by Parliament's Poet Laureate
Subject: Super news

Congrats to you Penn on having your work recognized and appreciated by the Library of Parliament Poet Laureate!
We are proud of you.
Sometime you'll have to come to Ottawa and visit the Library itself - a marvel!

Be well,
Jack and Olivia

At 11/07/2008, Penn Kemp wrote:

Thanks so much, Jack! I was really touched that Irene and Shawn got a press release about it around! Now that got response from my writer friends!!

We'll have to get Tom King into Parliament now! Bet you had a good time in Guelph...

A glorious summer to you and Olivia!
Penn

From: Penn Kemp
To: Layton, Jack - Personal
Sent: Tue Aug 26 2008
Subject: Re: London whistle stop

Hi Jack,

Yes, we were ready to go out at 10:30 p.m. yesterday, and, knowing
your stamina, didn't question the hour!

Peggy Nash and Charlie Angus have been writing great letters, but
I am worried about the cuts to Arts Programs. I understand there's
an emergency meeting of the Heritage Committee today at 1pm: I
hope they get quorum! The arts communities are in a very vociferous
uproar against the bullying tactics of Mr. Harper as he sets the arts
against sports! I think this issue is a chance for the NDP to make
a very firm stand that would ensure the support of arts supporters
nation-wide without alienating sports fans, if funding didn't have to
come from the same Heritage pot.

Meanwhile, all blessings on this election, whenever it happens!!
Penn

_____

On 26/08/2008, Jack Layton wrote:

Absolutely!!
We are on it. We have many artists running for us and we will
present a strong programme and fight like hell to re-establish the arts
funding. These cuts are terrible and wrong.

See you on the campaign trail and keep on fighting the good fight.
Jack

_____

From: Penn Kemp
To: Layton, Jack - Personal
Sent: Fri Aug 29 2008
Subject: Re: protesting arts cuts
Hi Jack

I think my orange slip is blatantly showing! I'm so glad for the great response to our huge letter blitz from two NDP MPs... the ONLY political response so far!!!!!!! so of course we've posted them on my Facebook group: Save Prom-Art: Promote Canadian Arts and Culture..

And of course I'd love you to write a note of support re protesting Arts Cuts... maybe just what you've said below? Let me know if I may post your note on our group and myspace.com/pennkemp. It will then reach at least 7,000 folks immediately.

I know you're just a tad busy, what with meeting the P.M. this weekend!

Here's to stamina. The NDP has such a strong position all around. I'm so proud to belong.

Here's to you!
Penn

————————————————

Date: Fri, 29 Aug 2008 2008

From: "Layton, Jack – Personal"
To: <penn@pennkemp.ca>, "Monk, Kathleen"

Hi Kathleen,
Can you get a letter from me on behalf of all MPs and candidates sent to Penn asap. She's one of our artistic treasures and her grassroots work is superb. Let's be a part of it.
We could mention some of our candidates and MPs who have arts backgrounds. Tara has a list.
J

Ps thanks Penn!

Date: Sun, 31 Aug 2008
To: "Layton, Jack – Personal"
From: Penn Kemp <penn@pennkemp.ca>
Subject: Re: I'm a member of the writers union

I've been getting incredible response to your letter that I posted just this evening.

No other party is responding to the arts cuts the way the NDP is. May I suggest you use that momentum to stand up for the arts, representing us vociferous artists :) ?

The Town Halls are meeting on Sept. 3. What better time for a press release from the NDP, following the one from Charlie Angus?... Or even a press conference?

Especially as a member of the Writers' Union, you are so well placed to speak to and for the arts... and TWUC was one of the first organizations to protest the cuts*. I'll send further info about the Town Halls on Sept. 3 to Kathleen. I'm trying to arrange for Irene to speak at the Town Hall meeting in London.

Thanks, as ever!
Penn

And could Arts be included in Issues on ndp.ca?

*What is it about Canadian culture that frightens Stephen Harper?
AUGUST 12 , 2008
"The Harper government has shot another arrow into the side of Canadian culture," Wayne Grady, Chair of the Writers' Union of Canada, said today, referring to the announcement last Friday that the Conservatives are axing another arts-funding programme, this time the Department of Foreign Affairs, Industry and Trade's tremendously important PromArt.

On 02/09/2008, Office of Jack Layton wrote:

Dear Penn,
On behalf of Mr. Layton and as requested, please find attached the NDP statement on the funding cuts for the planned September 3rd Town Hall meetings.

All the best,
Rosalie Boutilier
Co-ordinator, Leader's Outreach Unit
Office of Jack Layton
NDP Leader

_____

On 05/09/2008, Kathleen Monk wrote:

We will get the statement translated and get it up asap.

_____

From: Penn Kemp
To: Layton, Jack - Personal
Sent: Sat Sep 06 2008
Subject: Re: NDP protests arts cuts, http://www.ndp.ca/ under Statements

Hi Jack,
I am so impressed that Kathleen got the statement up so fast! We need to make the Arts cuts an election issue, and this is such a great article. Gavin has printed dozens of copies and we will distribute them wherever appropriate. We distributed many more copies today when I was reading at a Rally and when I was a panelist for the Town Hall meeting on the Arts at Museum London.

I brought copies to the Museum London Town Hall, and they were gobbled up, along with a great letter that Irene Mathyssen wrote. She was the only MP or MPP there, so in my presentation, I pointed that out and compared the NDP fast, articulate response to other parties' responses, or non responses. We had good press for the Town Hall beforehand in the London Free Press and today in James Reaney's column; we're now the Department of Culture, London. I've posted both letters in my blog on www.myspace.com/pennkemp as well as on my Facebook group. Olivia kindly mentioned this group in her Newsletter too! As well, I sent your letter round to my listservs, including TWUC. So the word is going round!

We're so delighted the CAW president is backing the NDP once again! YES! And we're glad Nancy is there to help with everything. Who better! Have a wonderful run, Jack... it's looking good! Thanks again, and see you on the Trail!
Penn

From: "Layton, Jack – Personal"
Sent: Sun, 7 Sep 2008
To: <penn@pennkemp.ca>

Great news all 'round. Nancy and I (and the national media) landed in Calgary and we're going into the heart of Harper's riding to tell Canadians that we're goin' after his job!

The Art of Jack

Gavin Stairs

Were it not for my brother's great good fortune to marry Jack's sister Nancy, I doubt I would ever have met him. We moved in close but separate circles, growing up in Québec, working in Toronto. The first time I met Nancy, I knew we were from similar families, and brother Joe had made a good move. I met Jack, Olivia and Jack's two children, Mike and Sarah, at Nancy and Joe's wedding in 1996. I don't remember much from that meeting, except that Jack's children were astonishingly beautiful, and that Olivia's smile could light up the sky.

After that introduction, I was accepted as an auxiliary in the Layton brotherhood, and became for a while a fourth in their regular monthly meetings in Jack's Toronto neighbourhood near College and Spadina. They, Jack, Dave and Rob, would bounce around the local bars and hangouts playing pool and whatever was on offer, with a beer chaser. I only lasted a few outings. Clearly, the Layton level of activity was too much for me.

But that was Jack: high energy and active all the way. Olivia is the same. Jack and Olivia participated fully in the community parties and celebrations while they were city politicians, dancing, singing and engaging with the people of the city, enjoying it all to the fullest. And whenever the opportunity was afforded, Jack would lead whoever was around in song, accompanying with guitar or piano, singing altered versions of the lyrics of familiar tunes. And that was the art of Jack: he would participate in whatever activity was going on, always leading people in upbeat and joyful activity together. Jack was not an artist in his own right, but art, particularly participatory art as in music and dance were an indispensable part of his life. He turned art to service of his central ideal. He loved artists for their engagement and action, and for the joy and insight they bring to the public arena, and for their life.

I think that this was his centering device, his mind clearing, his restorative. During that marathon of double campaigning, he also continued regular workouts with Nancy as part of his physiotherapy and I've no doubt that was an important part of the mix as well. Nancy is an athlete and Phys. Ed. teacher who became a private school head and a champion amateur golfer as well. She was his amanuensis through two election campaigns. Not only to provide the fetch and carry of personal items, but also to spend time together as a sister and a friend, and to make certain that Jack would be able to follow his physio routine daily. Nancy and Jack were very close, and this was, as it turned out, a blessed final time together for them both.

I am also certain that Jack not only continued learning his political art all his life, but also became more clear and mindful as well. This became most evident during his last campaign, while he was simultaneously fighting an election and his prostate cancer, and winning both. It was evident to those of us who were observers that he was growing stronger through the campaign, which is very unusual. Then in the Québec campaign, it became evident not only to us but to all of Québec that a true phenomenon was at play: *Le bon Jack* appeared, and stayed. Penn and I watched in astonished joy as a very rare thing happened before the whole country: a politician became a spiritual being before us. And the people of Québec responded as never before.

The transformation continued after the election. As it became evident that Jack's cancer had returned, it was also evident that Jack was not fading in spirit: just in body. He was exhausted, as he must have been earlier as well, but he was reaching out to people around him, as well as across the country, spending his last energies to pass on a message of hope, love and compassion. That last letter was his last gift to all of us. The whole of his last few days was an inspired and inspiring ritual. A piece of theatre from a master of political theatre, and a truly inspiring being.

Jack and I had conversations about politics and activism over the years, and he, being Jack, was vehement about the necessity of action. He has demonstrated how to be an open-hearted activist. In India, they might call this *nishkam karma* (selfless action), a high ideal. I don't think Jack thought in such terms, though. He might have thought of his illustrious ancestors, particularly his father, who also served the country and people in political engagement. It is also what he saw in Tommy Douglas and why he came to the NDP. I suspect he thought of himself as just a guy who loved to work for the benefit of the people. What he demonstrated was that there is love and joy in what we call compassionate action. Those qualities are worth emulating. Let Jack live in the hearts of the people, and let us change the world.

Friends, Jack would say, it's not about Jack Layton. It's about Hope, Optimism and Love. Compassion. That is what I came to love in Jack, and what will endure.

It's a No-brainer!

Daniel Kolos

As natural as sunshine: Support the Arts! Why? Let's start with basics. Stephen Harper, the MP from Calgary Southwest, who happens to be the leader of his party, sings and plays the piano. He may have taken lessons at some point. A tuner worked to bring his piano in tune. A group of people, individually or collectively, supported his musical development and can continue to support him on his occasional forays into performance. It would not take Harper too much imagination to realize that, in order for him to make his living from musical performance, he would have to rely on some form of government support. Instead, he chose a career where he requires full time government support.

Jack Layton played the guitar. His guitar went with him everywhere, and he consorted with the kind of laid-back, easy-going people who either played a musical instrument of their own, or easily burst into song when a guitar and a drum made their appearance. Layton was a populist musical player in the same way that, while Gwendolyn MacEwen became an establishment poet and a darling of academia (and deserved every word written about her), her gruff ex, Milton Acorn, became the first "people's poet."

Today, no one questions the place of music, poetry and the arts in Canada's cultural life. Walk through Stephen's Harper's office, or his temporary home in Ottawa, and there will be paintings hanging on his walls. Painters toil annually preparing heavy portraits for the walls of Parliament. The Government, however much any particular party tries to deny it, supports the arts one way or another. Would the Conservatives, for example, admit that they support establishment artists but not emerging ones, fledgling ones who have yet to reach a wide enough audience to become well known? Layton did not have a problem choosing between establishment or populist artists and musicians, amateurs or professionals. He was surrounded by both! In spite of being a party leader like Harper, he was not an elitist. He had no trouble acknowledging that the arts were part of Canadian Culture: an integral part of it!

Why support the arts? Every form of art, no matter how influential or fleeting, has traditionally been the subject of support by various patrons. This need for support is not a unique Canadian problem. It is the nature of the arts themselves. Jack Layton found this need self-evident. There are indications that the Canadian Government at times forgets that Canadian Culture reaches right down into the grassroots artists who rise from farm-houses and city apartments and contribute the immediacy of their context to the greater culture. Jack Layton was such a contributor, always ready with his guitar, ready to hand out his song-sheets, bring music and lyrics into his surroundings, whether that was family and friends, or political meetings and public appearances. Support for the arts, for Jack, was a no-brainer.

Jack and The Art of Politics

Bernie Koenig

As a musician, a philosopher who has written on the importance of the arts (*Art Matters*, Academica Press 2009) and a long time New Democrat who worked for Jack, I would like to talk about both the importance of the arts and the relationship between art and politics. In politics, as in contemporary art, we have developed a two-tiered view. On the one hand we want to present abstract principles such as social justice and fairness to voters, but all too often voters don't understand these concepts or at least they don't see how those concepts affect them in any direct way. So we have to find less abstract ways to get our message across.

The same thing happens in politics. All too often the NDP did not do as well as we should have because we presented our views in a too abstract manner so people did not get what we were saying. You can't expect people to get Bach when all they know is Metallica. By making connections between so-called high arts and pop arts, we break the divide and open up people to all levels of art.

And this is where Jack comes in. He knew how to speak to people in terms of how the issues affected them directly while showing them that NDP policies would actually be better for them. Jack was able to take our big picture policies and show how they translated into everyday bread and butter issues. What Jack did was to talk about two specific issues that affect consumers: ATM and credit card rates which were gouging us. In so doing, he directly challenged the concept of "market forces" without mentioning it. And after canvassing, Jack would sit around singing songs with political themes. In these ways, he bridged the gap between abstract principles and practical applications, and showed that he mastered the art of politics.

The Two Mr. Sweets

Silence Genti

I grew up in Harare, Zimbabwe; my street adorned with forty tiny, asbestos-roofed houses on either side of a lean strip of rough-tarred road. The children spent a lot of time playing on the street, usually around the drainage hole that ran on one side of the street. The women who spent their late afternoons talking were early YouTubers, using their words to create viral visual experiences of the goings-on in the neighbourhood – who got married; who just bought a new car; new eligible bachelors.

One of the most favoured subjects in this well-oiled gossiping (or perhaps broadcasting) system was one short man with the gift of a good heart. There were many theories on why he was single and even more theories on how to ensnare him.

Every weekday around 5 p.m., this man, with a purposeful, calm stride, made his way from the bus stop, about a kilometre away, to his house at the eastern end of the street. Despite being noticeably tired, a smile enveloped his face every time he crossed paths with a neighbour. He would spare a minute to ask about the health and family and then continue his walk home. He knew everyone by name.

Once in a while, he would cause the biggest mayhem on our street. His employer gave him several packets of candy (we called them sweets) every couple of months.

"Amasweeeet, Amasweeeet!! (Mr. Sweets, Mr. Sweets!!)," we would shout when we saw him carrying the candy.

Some weekends, he would sit in his backyard, the peach tree his only cover from the scorching midday sun. Dressed in short sleeves he would tell a group of us stories. Stories of travel, of dreams still to be realized.

And he would always smile – rather proudly, I always thought – when he saw me carrying the morning paper. "You are gonna work for the newspapers when you grow up," he would say.

In so many ways, Mr. Sweets reminds me of the late Jack Layton.

When Jack walked the streets, he always had a smile ready for the next person. Colour or social station didn't matter. He would embrace others with no restraint. Many have said there was no aftertaste of being played when one spoke to him.

"Ideas matter. Democracy matters, because all of us need to make a difference," he wrote in his book *Speaking Out Louder*.

An advocate for social justice, Jack has an authenticity that is not common in politics. My friend Precious saw the inside of a polling station for the first time in May last year. "He makes me believe," she told me afterwards.

Even my friend Sam, who has zero knowledge of politics, knew of, and liked Jack Layton … "He was a great guy," he said rather laconically.

That was Jack's greatest gift. He was a guy. Politics was the vehicle he used to change the world. He could be marching in Gay Parade or Chinese New Year or debating in the party leaders' debate. He still looked and sounded like an ordinary guy, not a politician.

Jack personalized politics. Like Mr. Sweets telling stories in his backyard, Jack Layton could enthral audiences, redefining what was possible and igniting hope.

A friend of mine once joked: Canada would be flooded with immigrants if Jack Layton was the welcoming party at Pearson.

I did not know Mr. Sweets' real name and I never physically met Jack Layton. But both men stand out in my mind.

Mr. Sweets will be remembered by some of the kids for his "candy parties," and I will particularly remember him for providing me intellectual stimulation at a young age. There are many things that have enamoured me to Canada. John Gilbert "Jack" Layton is one of them. As a Canadian far removed from his childhood home in Africa, I will remember Jack for his power to embrace others, his belief that cultural differences were to be celebrated. As a father-to-be (in years to come), I will remember and applaud his unshaken belief in a better Canada – because that's what I'd want for my children.

When Nelson Mandela said: "A good head and a good heart are always a formidable combination," one could be forgiven to think that he was talking about Jack.

It's Not a Parade, Jack

Gianna Patriarca

Gianna Patriarca writes that Jack was a presence in her neighbourhood
(College and Grace in Toronto) for more years than she can remember. Jack
loved that neighbourhood, his home turf, and he could often be seen biking
to work.

another good Friday
in my neighbourhood
theater and culture
all pruned for spring
statues dusted
the priests all clean
a thousand women ready with
hymns and tears and beads
and tiny cameras seize the moment
in time.

just behind the last Jesus
and the brass band
there's Jack and Joe and Olivia
little giants of my neighbourhood
striding slowly to the missed beats
along with the mayor, the banker
the top cop
the smiles, the waves
the necessary presence
my history now
thirty three years of Good Fridays
on this downtown street
and they still don't understand
Jack
it's not a parade.

but i will miss not seeing you there
next year Jack
when that last Jesus will fall
without a sound
among the infidels
and the tourists in the crowd.

The Compass

Eugenia Catroppa

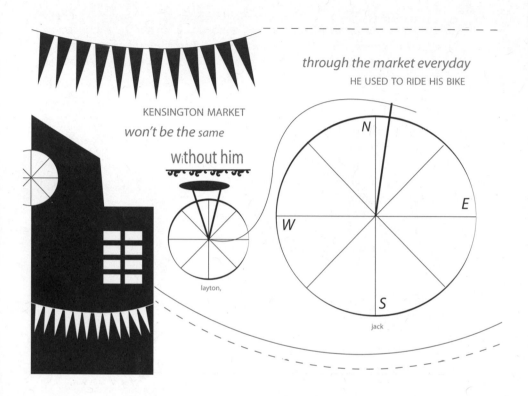

through the market everyday
HE USED TO RIDE HIS BIKE

KENSINGTON MARKET
won't be the same
without him

layton,

N

E

W

S

jack

Annexing Flowers

Lisa Richter

There were always two signs on our front yard around election time: my mother's orange NDP, and my father's blue Conservative. It was confusing to our Willowdale neighbours, who questioned the presence of the former and validated the latter by placing blue signs of their own on their suburban lawns, but it made perfect sense to me. What my parents lacked in solidarity they made up for in tolerance of difference, at least some of the time. My mother, the daughter of Montréal Jewish communists, former hippie, artist, writer and amateur bodybuilder, was a staunch supporter of all things New Democratic. It was not until many years later, long after we had lost everything, lived in too many furnished rental apartments to count, that I had the fortune of encountering the man who would, for so many people, embody this very tolerance. "I like your flowers," the cyclist said.

In the spring of 2007, the Annex side streets of Toronto were alive with intermittent cyclists and the fragrance of new green things. Stopping at the corner, I looked up from my bike, whose basket I had decorated with an assortment of dollar store plastic vines, silk birds-of-paradise, African daisies. The fortyish, pretty Asian woman on the bike next to me had similarly festooned her own basket; we smiled, as if sharing a private love we both understood and nurtured, in a cross-maternal sort of way. Her partner or husband riding alongside her leaned over to compliment me on my bike decoration as well. He squinted at me in the luminous, leafy sunlight of a spring afternoon. His eyes were nearly colourless in the haze, a silver-mustached man in a white shirt and tie, sleeves rolled up past his elbows, everything in his posture and demeanor neighbourly, fit and kind.

"Thank you, Mr. Layton. Olivia." I tripped slightly over my words, feeling a brief shock of embarrassment over addressing the leader of the NDP more formally than his MP wife. "It's nice to meet you both. I've voted for both of you."

We all rode off, leaving me with a flustered mix of awkward regret over what I'd said and how I'd sounded, all the while wishing I could have said more. Jack Layton and Olivia Chow were visible and accessible in a way that politicians normally weren't. Skeptics scorned this visibility, but I was thirty years old, working as a teacher of English as a second language, writing poetry and prose when I could, living on the third floor of an old Victorian house on Dupont Street. It seemed fitting to me that Layton and Chow would be the kinds of people who would cycle around the community, who would appreciate the beautification of an ordinary, utilitarian object like a bike basket. They liked my flowers, and took time to tell me so. And I, in return, admired theirs.

"He was there in every cause or campaign"

Tina Conlon

I did not realize how much his death has affected me because I have not really worked directly with him.

Following the 1995 FAO 50/50 conference held in Québec City, Québec, I worked on the formation of a coalition of civil society organizations across Canada in preparation of Canada's submission to the World Food Summit. Following the WFS, this coalition, together with various government representatives, wrote Canada's Action Plan which was launched at the World Food Day event I organized in Toronto in 1998: *http://www.agr.gc.ca/misb/fsec-seca/pdf/action_e.pdf* – Canada's Action Plan for Food Security (1998). In the middle of that celebration, Jack Layton approached and congratulated me. I wasn't that happy with the plan and told him that it was more of a compromise plan. He reassured me that this was a good start and again congratulated me on my work.

A few years later, I approached then councillor David Miller to advocate a campaign I worked for to ensure that the City of Toronto source its garments from fair wage labour. David was not yet thinking of running as our mayor then until during a May 2002 debate where I was present at council chambers, Lastman yelled at Miller, "You will never be mayor of this city because you say stupid and dumb things!" After the initial discussions with City Administration, we submitted some pretty strong deputations in June, 2002. Jack Layton again approached me and congratulated my work and then asked if Olivia could also help David in the initiative. Of course! Olivia was an ally in council for this initiative. We ended up being the first municipality to have strong language on this. City of Toronto Council directed that the Fair Wage Policy of the former Municipality of Metropolitan Toronto be adopted for all City Departments, Agencies, Board and Commissions, with the intent to enhance the reputation of the City for ethical and fair business dealings, *http://www.toronto.ca/fairwage/policy.htm*.

It's funny that even if I did not work with him directly, I would often brush against him as he was there in every cause or campaign I've worked on, fighting against homelessness, advocating for the environment, green roofs, food security, bike lanes and the White Ribbon Campaign that advocated against domestic violence. His last letter was a very thoughtful piece that mirrored a lot of what I have been reflecting in my faith in the last few months:

> promise, as in justice, not grasping;
> deliverance, as in prayer, not resignation and
> sustenance, as in hope, not scarcity.

Art, AIDS and Jack Layton

Gale Zoë Garnett

The following piece demonstrates just how much Jack "was there in every cause or campaign."

I first met Jack Layton at an arts-activist event in Toronto's Harbourfront Centre. We were on a panel re: AIDS in the arts. 50% of the people I knew were either dead or dying of this plague, and I'd been AIDS front-lining since 1981. Politicians, fearing stigma connected to what was erroneously seen as "only a gay disease," tended to avoid being identified with it. Not Jack. He vigorously and eloquently joined the fight, whether involving gays, straights, men, women and/or children. In general, Jack was good at being front and centre for what he believed: in 1993, Jack was the only Toronto City Councillor to show up in support of "Artists Against War," an all-day arts event in Toronto's Nathan Phillips Square, opposing what proved to be the homicidal folly of the Iraq War.

From 1981 to his untimely death, fighting AIDS was on Jack's "A List" of commitments. When medical advancements (principally "the cocktail") turned most AIDS from a terminal to a chronic illness, he joined many of us in the fight against AIDS in sub-Saharan Africa, regularly marching and speaking, donating both time and money, as did his beloved partner in love and public service, Olivia Chow.

One of the last times I marched alongside Jack and Olivia was at The Grandmothers to Grandmothers event created by Ilana Landsberg Lewis, Executive Director of The Stephen Lewis Foundation. We were marching with Canadian and African grandmothers (who were raising their AIDS-orphaned grandchildren, after the 'middle layer', their mothers and fathers, had died). The African Grannies filled the air with that wonderful sound made by African and Arab women. I'd always wanted to make the sound, but my voice was too low, or my skill-set insufficient. Turning to Jack, I said, earnestly, "Oh, I wish I could ovulate." "That may be true," Jack replied, laughing, "but I think the word you want is *ululate*." We giggled intermittently from George Brown University to Nathan Phillips Square. Every time I saw Jack after that, he would smile and inquire as to how the African Ovulation was coming along.

"Courage, mes braves!"

Penn Kemp

So many of the NDP politicians I have spoken to about this project across the country credit their entry into politics to Jack. He tapped them on the shoulder, encouraging each one individually to run. In engaging women in politics especially, Jack had an enormous effect. This support has been one of his secret weapons. When women demurred, saying they weren't qualified, weren't ready, didn't have the experience or the knowledge necessary, Jack didn't take no for an answer. He would answer each argument with a rebuttal until they gained the confidence to run ... and win. After all, much of the learning involved in politics is on the spot. Jack didn't leave candidates stranded, either. During his cross-country campaign tours, despite his schedule, he would take each person aside, with specific tips on how to run successfully, how to handle the media, etc. His mentorship continued whether they won or not. If they did not, there was always the next election to consider. The result is an increasing number of women in both provincial and federal Legislatures. The quality of these outstanding, progressive leaders is exceptional, and they all began as leaders-in-training. So now we have quantity as well as quality in the Legislature, at least in Opposition! And yes, there is strength in numbers. Quantity does matter in that it builds a measure of solidarity, people have your back and glass ceilings are shattered.

Writer and communications consultant Carolyn Gibson discusses the necessary process of empowerment in her talk, "Women and Political Engagement: A Democratic Imperative." "Study after study shows that when we have more women in elected office, politics looks different: the manner in which business is conducted is different; the policies and issues that get prioritized are different; and, the role model effect that is sent to our future generations is different." There is something about inclusivity that makes people feel better about government when it's more diverse. Her talk explores the main barriers and obstacles to explain: "Why don't we have enough female candidates?"

In a recent talk at London's Brescia University College, Carolyn Gibson compared the entitlement men might feel to running for office to the historical lack of confidence women professed. When asked to be candidates, women often felt they had to be better educated, better informed and more experienced before taking the leap into a higher profile in public. There remains the problem of childcare, for as Carolyn remarked, women are still generally expected to be responsible for their children as well as working and performing well outside the home. Who, for example, was going to take care of Johnny or Jill if the child fell ill? NDP policy would of course ensure that good childcare was provided for all.

Jack's encouragement of women candidates was essential to the Orange Crush win in 2011. In caucus or out, Jack would not allow disparagement or put-downs based on gender, race, or any other stereotype. As Hillary Clinton told Vital Voices' Women's Global Leadership Summit in New York City: "Research shows the presence of women raises the standard of ethical behavior and lowers the corruption." Will the number of women politicians now engaged as MPs change the antagonistic atmosphere of Parliament? Can we look forward to women-friendly forms of engagement? What form would this take?

Listening to Women

Sylvia Fraser

Jack Layton loved strong women.

At age seventeen, he became leader of the opposition in the Québec Older Boys Parliament. This was a big deal since members of this church-based group got to spend an expenses-paid week in Québec City and to argue in the province's legislative assembly. Jack's party's first bill proposed that the "Older Boys" mock parliament change its name to "Youth" parliament to allow females to participate. He added this cheeky invitation, "If any of the government members wish to join us to pass this bill, we have young women ready to participate this very week."

The premier and his party were gobsmacked. Half their members crossed the floor; the bill was passed, and Jack's party formed the government with a contingent of eager young women. Now, as the party in power, Jack's team challenged the Older Boys in other provinces to follow suit. All this happened in the 60s before the word "feminism" was in popular usage.

During a kitchen-table conversation I had with Jack Layton in his Toronto semi-detached home filled with art and books, he told me that his belief in female equality began with his parents – Doris, a librarian, and Bob, an engineer whose main credo was "never lose an opportunity." After dinner, the elder Layton typically asked his four kids, "Who wants the opportunity to clear the table?" The result, of course, was a collective groan, and while there's no evidence that Jack was more nimble than his siblings in volunteering, a lesson was implanted.

Jack's marriage to Olivia Chow involved the wooing of two strong women. Olivia's mother, Ho Sze, sternly disapproved of him on four solid grounds: he was a divorced father with two children; he was not Chinese; he was not a doctor or a lawyer; worse, he was a politician.

For two years, Jack and Ho Sze lived in the same co-op complex with Olivia dividing her time between their two apartments. Even when Ho Sze passed Jack on the stairs, she refused to acknowledge him with so much as a word. Then, in a sudden turnabout, Ho Sze invited Jack to her place for a meal. With her mahjong partners lined up on the couch assessing him in rapid Cantonese, Ho Sze served him ever more esoteric dishes, from curried tripe to candied duck feet. Expertly wielding his chopsticks, Jack consumed plate after plate with gusto. As he triumphantly reported, "I ate my way into Amah's heart!"

Once converted, Ho Sze became one of Jack's staunchest supporters, and her care of the Layton/Chow household was key to allowing their charismatic partnership to flourish.

After fourteen female engineering students were killed by a lone gunman at Montréal's École Polytechnique on December 6, 1989, Jack proved he was, indeed, a guy in touch with the female spirit. Though at first he saw this as the one-off act of a crazy person, that changed when traumatized women friends began confiding their personal experiences of male violence. One notably strong woman, who was struggling with fragmentary nightmares of a brutal act she had blocked from consciousness, further horrified Jack when she confessed that she felt guilty that this experience might have been her fault. He was left to ponder: *What kind of a society causes women to feel guilty when men abuse them?* After Olivia shocked him with revelations of her own nasty experience of male violence, Jack began to feel that most of the women he knew had been victimized by men simply for being women.

This was unacceptable.

He decided that it was time for men like himself to speak out in support of their sisters, partners, mothers, daughters, colleagues. Jack became a founder of the White Ribbon Campaign in which a white ribbon signified that its wearer had pledged that he would never commit, condone or remain silent about violence against women. When the WRC was officially launched in 1991, one hundred thousand Canadian men wore white ribbons. This made-in-Canada campaign later spread to some sixty other countries.

In the election of 2011, Jack Layton fulfilled his destiny, foretold at age seventeen, by becoming leader of Canada's official opposition. If the NDP should ever form the government, it would partly be due to the strong women Jack welcomed into its ranks.

Author's Footnote: I did not know Jack Layton personally, only as a journalist. Before his death, I would have thought it presumptuous to write about him as "Jack." After all of Canada embraced him on a first-name basis, it would have felt odd to do otherwise.

The Kindness of Jack Layton

Kathy Figueroa

For many years I worked in the film industry as a technician. Eventually, I wrote a feature-length screenplay and decided to make my own film, so put all of my time, effort, expertise, and savings into writing the screenplay, and then shooting the film. Eventually, with the actual shooting nearing completion, I applied to the Film, Photography, and Video department of the Ontario Arts Council for the November 1, 1990 or 1991, deadline. The next night I was brutally attacked on the street, by persons unknown, and hurt very badly. It took a long time to recover from the injuries that I received and was left unable to work and unable to focus on my film project. My grant application contained many offers of distribution for my completed film, which was part of the criteria that the application had to meet. Also, it contained my screenplay and a video trailer comprised of footage that I'd already shot. Anyhow, after some time had passed, it came to my attention that it looked like the material contained in my grant application was utilized by someone else, who had made a movie which appeared to be a derivative of my work. It appeared to be a very serious case of 'intellectual property copyright' infringement by the spouse of an employee in the Film, Photography, and Video department of the Arts ouncil.

Trying to get justice seemed like an exercise in futility! People just kept telling me, "Hire a lawyer," which was very hard to do when you're reduced to collecting disability welfare and lawyers weren't allowed to work on a contingency basis, back then. I was very demoralized and scared. No one in the film industry offered any support because of the power that the filmmaker in question, and the members of his clique, wielded.

One day, when I was walking along the sidewalk in downtown Toronto, I met Jack Layton, back when he was still a municipal councillor. He'd been cycling and had his bike with him. We started chatting and I ended up telling him all about this horrible situation that I've just described, here. He listened intently and was sympathetic. He didn't doubt, for a moment, the veracity of what I had told him. This was very important because a lot of people seemed to prefer to indicate that they thought that I was a liar, rather than believe that the filmmaker, in question, would do such a thing as plagiarize someone else's work.

Jack Layton didn't hesitate to offer to speak out on my behalf. He provided moral support when I really, desperately needed it. He also offered to draw attention to my plight, publicly, but, because all my efforts to get some sort of justice had been futile, and I had been feeling so defeated and demoralized, I didn't take him up on his offer, which I now regret. I think that Jack was a wonderful person. He genuinely, sincerely, cared about my situation. I've always thought of him as a saint. He was one of the good guys.

When Private Meets Public

Silvia Langer

From 1996 to 2002, I worked for Greenest City Environmental Organization in Toronto, while Jack Layton was a City Councillor and for a period, the Chair of the Toronto Atmospheric Fund. Jack was actively and enthusiastically involved both in his activities and also those he supported. Two standout episodes come to mind, though there were many.

I remember seeing Jack Layton and Olivia Chow at various environmental group fundraising events or after-parties. It always seemed that given both Jack and Olivia's busy schedules, it was only late at night at these events and parties that they ever got a chance to see each other. They may have felt they were there under some social obligation to attend these events, the way that friends are kinda obligated to support their friends or maybe they thought they were going to socialize with friends – but when Jack and Olivia were in the same room together, all they did was kiss and coo.

Once, Jack rode his bike, as usual, from downtown City Hall to a school at Yonge and Lawrence, to speak to a group of grade-schoolers on behalf of one of GC's programs, Active & Safe Routes to School, about the benefits of active transportation. He was a little late to the meeting, so the small group of young children, parents and teachers were already assembled outdoors awaiting him when he pulled up. Jack didn't even dismount, gave an enthusiastic 5 minute speech from his bicycle seat pulpit and then said, "and now I'm afraid I have to leave you to go to a council meeting at City Hall." And off he went with a smile and a ring-a-ling of his bicycle's bell, leaving many smiling faces behind. He turned to look, to smile, to wave again, before he disappeared around the corner.

Jack was true to his word: he walked/biked the talk literally and figuratively.

Jedi Jack

Shawn Lewis

In 2002, I made the decision to finally join a political party, signing up to be a part of selecting a new leader – what Jack Layton offered was appealing to me – and building a party that could start to work toward earning the opportunity to serve as government to the people of our nation.

I have served in numerous campaigns, including breakthroughs that saw the election of London Ontario's first-ever federal representative in MP Irene Mathyssen, and most recently successfully helping the NDP win London's first ever "double orange" riding with the election of MPP Teresa Armstrong. In a decade of activism, I've served in many riding association executive roles at both the provincial and federal levels, including more than five of those years working full time with the amazing MPs in our NDP caucus. I've invested a significant amount of my life into building the New Democratic Party

Jack's job as NDP leader meant a lot of time spent on the road going from event to event. It was one of the benefits of my volunteering with the London-Fanshawe riding association that I was usually the person who got to pick up visiting MPs or MPPs at London airport and be the chauffeur de jour. I loved doing this, for the opportunity to meet and talk with some pretty interesting people. In 2004, Jack was still fairly new to the leader's job, well before we had a New Democrat MP in London and before I'd started working in politics full time.

I drove Jack on one of these occasions, after a day full of events. Amazingly, Jack had no calls to make or emails to respond to – this was before we all lived on BlackBerries – and the political conversation had pretty much run its course. Jack had been asking about me – what had brought me to the party (funny enough, it was the chance to help pick a new leader, and my pick was Jack), where did I work, what my other interests were. Jack was always genuinely interested in the people helping build the party. I remember saying, "You'll probably laugh but ... ," starting to talk about my love of comic books and science fiction, and that's when I learned Jack was a fan of good science fiction stories too.

We talked about good books and movies of the genre, and naturally, as sci-fi fans will, the talk at some point reached the "*Star Wars* vs. *Star Trek*: what's your favourite?" question. For me it was easy. I liked both, but at the end of the day the original *Star Wars* trilogy had so strongly shaped my childhood – I saw the original movie in London, Ontario in 1977 as a five-year-old and the whole experience of a visit to "the big city" and the hustle and bustle of the downtown only added to the impact – that it had to be *Star Wars*, no contest.

We talked about this all the way to the London airport, how *Star Wars* had become a modern day mythology – pulling together the excitement of the space age "what's out there?" imagination with equal parts of mythological archetypes akin to Arthurian knights or ancient Greek heroes, with a dash of Americana; the idealistic youth, the wise old mentor, the princess (in not so much distress. Jack had a laugh at my *Star Wars* geek observation that Princess Leia never missed when she took a shot). The dashing rogue, the faithful companions, and the epic quest which was both a rite of passage and a saving the kingdom tale.

The sci-fi trappings of the *Star Wars* trilogy offered a way for Jack and me to connect on the subject. But our talk that afternoon was about more than that. It was about the love of a good story, and how some of the best stories are the old stories recycled and re-invented for new generations. I remember commenting that one reason I so loved comic books was the continuous re-inventing of archetypal heroes like Batman for each generation. Ever the supporter of Toronto in all things (except hockey – but that is another story), Jack put in a plug to visit the Silver Snail, a great comic book shop there. We talked about the important lessons the stories I loved had taught me: Spiderman, "with great power comes great responsibility." Spock was right: "the needs of the many outweigh the needs of the few or the one." And of course that important *Star Wars* lesson: even in the face of overwhelming odds, when people take a stand against oppression, there is always hope.

Jack understood the importance of storytelling to who we are as human beings, whether in word, in verse, in song or in pictures. He understood that a good story can be a well-deserved escape from the burdens of our regular lives if even just for a short time, and he also understood that a good story can inspire someone to reach for new goals. He understood the value and power of words and images not just as tools of communication, but in expressing ourselves as human beings.

Jack and I talked many times about many things in the time I knew him. Mostly it was work related. After all, we both had a lot of work to do trying to make the world a better place, but that fifteen to twenty minute drive and the purely personal conversation we had that day was the one that always stuck in my memory because it was all about the shared love we had for a good story from a long time ago in a galaxy far, far away.

It was a terrible day when we lost Jack. I woke up to the BlackBerry buzzing much earlier than usual. When I saw the subject line, I knew the news was bad. Yet for the next few days, I had a scene from the original *Star Wars* movie running over and over again in my mind's eye. It was the light saber duel on the Death Star between Ben Kenobi and Darth Vader. Over and over, I heard Alec Guinesss saying, "If you strike me down now, I will become more powerful than you can imagine." ...Through those days leading up to Jack's funeral, Ben Kenobi's voice became much more Laytonian in my head. Then I heard Olivia saying how some of Jack's final hours were spent watching *Return of the Jedi*. Of course he was. It was the final movie, the end of the story, where the Empire is defeated and oppression overthrown, where love, hope and optimism win the day.

Merci, Jack. May the force be with you.

PHOTO: JOE WILSON

"King of the Road"

Peter Haase

A few years back, as a long-time member of the NDP, I helped with a fundraising/auction event at the Legion Hall on Salt Spring Island on a warm July night. Jack Layton and his wife Olivia were present, and it was also Jack's birthday, so the local NDPers decided, as well as a fundraising auction (in which Jack was the auctioneer), we'd throw a party for him with some of the folks baking him a huge cake. Jack and Olivia specifically asked to be seated with the young people in the crowd who had arrived to perform a song for him. I was also asked to sing a couple of tunes on stage with my guitar as I'd played the club scene decades earlier and was enthused to do my small part on Jack's big day.

As the auction began to slow down, I suggested we keep the ball rolling by asking the audience how much they'd bid as a donation to see Jack and me sing a tune together on the stage. An offer here and there arose and stopped at fifty bucks. Jack and I had never sung a note together before. We were about the same age so I scratched my head and said, "Hey Jack, do you remember 'King of the Road'?"

Sure enough, he was game. Never one to dodge an unexpected challenge, he said, "I know the tune, but you'll have to lead with the words." I didn't know if he was joshing me or what, so we got started and really got into the groove. After all, Jack was a groovy guy. There was not a foot that wasn't tapping and hands were all clapping in time, with the usual help from the audience on the chorus. When it finished, we had a good laugh over it – boy what a gas!

I later mentioned when we were all leaving the Legion Hall and heading home, "Jack, lad, you should use that tune on your campaign. It's catchy and maybe you could change the words a wee bit to suit the need?" To my delight, a few months later, I caught a news clip on the tele, and there was Jack singing "King of the Road."

And he was just that.

Politics and singing always go well together, for sure.

Well done, ol' chap, you sure could hold an audience, and we all loved your great leadership, singing voice and big heart.

You were a gift to us all.

PHOTO: JOE WILSON

"Poetry Makes Nothing Happen," Says Auden. True or False?

Susan McMaster

In January 2003, I read on Parliament Hill, this time to thousands, and by accident not plan.

"United States Declares War on Iraq"

Winter news. Deep, frozen. Of course the war was coming. It's been coming for months now, but even so I'm seized with anger, and fear for what's to come ... A few people I vaguely know, peace activists, Quakers, Raging Grannies, artists, writers, politicians – have sent out a joint email to say that if the war starts, gather on the Hill. So that's where I'm going ...

In my bag is a printout of *100 Poets against the War*, gathered on the internet in just one month by Canadian poet Todd Swift. My poem, written two weeks ago, is in there. The anthology has attracted thousands of submissions and will soon be published by Salt, an Australian press. A similar volume will appear from a British publisher later this month. Another internet project has gathered 10,000 peace poems just this week. There's been lots of publicity. None of it has stopped the war ...

We haven't joined the war yet, maybe the Prime Minister can be persuaded to hold out. The Peace Tower looms overhead, so much larger than it appears from Wellington. So gothic, so fanciful in our practical hard land. And yet it's alive with all the words that have been spoken and shouted on these steps that lead to its feet. The gargoyles that are its eyes and ears seem to bend down to listen.

Closer, I can hear better with no distorting boom. It is a widely varied range of community voices coming to the microphone, from unions to politicians to activists to artists. Some shout and thump. Others talk firmly of hope. The Raging Grannies sing.

Suddenly I realise that my poem in the anthology in my bag includes the line, "reading this poem on Parliament Hill." Here I am. How can I ignore this?

"Oops, excuse me."

It's characteristic of Ottawa that no one tries to stop me as I sidle gingerly up the side steps to the platform, and that, once here, I can introduce myself to one organizer, who finds another, who finds another. Steven Artelle is introducing the speakers. We've never met but it turns out he's heard my name.

"I promise I'll use no more than thirty seconds. What I want isn't exposure for myself but a chance to represent the 10,000 and more poets world-wide who have contributed to peace publications in the weeks just before this. I have the first printout of an anthology –"

"Is that *100 Poets against the War?*" he asks. "Yes, I've seen it on the Internet. I think we could just slip you in after this speaker if you keep it really short."

Steven steps in front of politician Jack Layton.

"We have one poem to do first, if you don't mind." Jack steps back.

"I'm here to represent 10,000 poets…"

The microphone booms, the faces look up.

> *Against the war I'll refuse*
> *to be insulted today.*
> *Against the war I'll recite this poem*
> *on Parliament Hill,*
> *drive my car not at all,*
> *gossip about love…*

I'm reading to thousands of people, more than ever before, but it's not about me and I'm surprised to find that my voice is steady.

> *… Against the war I'll act*
> *today, as I can, for peace*

Jack Layton nods at me, and steps forward into my place. On this bitter winter evening, I wonder if anyone beyond this gathering is listening to any of us.

Layton went on to succeed Alexa McDonough as leader of the New Democratic Party. Eighteen months after the event on the Hill, he walked alone and down these same steps on a fall day to accept a poem and book from me as part of the national project, "Random Acts of Poetry." Did he remember me, is that why he came? I was too flustered to ask. But I did notice that the poem he chose for me to read is a poem about being too often away from the one you love. And that he listens well….

And it turns out that Jean Chrétien, at least, did listen to those many Canadians who were on Parliament Hill on that black, January day in 2003, urging the government to stay out of Iraq. Chrétien may even have heard me read the poem, and noticed that it came from a Canadian anthology.

Random Acts of Poetry on the Hill, Part i

Susan McMaster

In October 2004, the poets selected to perform Random Acts of Poetry in the National Capital area were asked to present poems to as many politicians as possible.

I arranged to meet Jack one day and read him a poem. He walked toward me alone, without entourage or TV cameras: no agenda to be served. He just listened. Closely. And smiled. Told me he would share it. Jack's work has made it possible to share our poetry and art with each other more widely across Canada and beyond, and to be richer for it. Thank you.

And he may have remembered receiving a peace poem three years before. According to Sandra Stephenson, writing for Sam Hamill's *Poets Against War* internet newsletter in fall 2006, "It could be that a contingent of 52 poets under the name 'Convergence', who hand-delivered peace poems wrapped in original art to Ottawa Parliamentarians in 2001, who held a reading at the National Arts Centre four days after September 11, swayed the vote that kept Canada out of Iraq at a time when public opinion polls claimed that Canadians favoured war." Whatever the reason, the Prime Minister and the Parliament of February 2003 refused to join the war against Iraq. I won't forget that.

Jack Layton was that extraordinary thing: a passionate, honest, dedicated person who worked as a politician, not for fame or power or thrills, but to make life in Canada and around the world better for us all. He could have been a teacher or social worker and have affected the lives of hundreds or thousands. He chose instead to become our political representative and affect the lives of millions.

But it was not a thoughtless or sentimental dedication. Jack had definite views about how to achieve a better world, through specific social and legal actions, and, notably, through institutions and structures to actively support and strongly encourage the arts. He held that the arts gave us a shared voice and a shared empathy and vision that went beyond our immediate place and time, and allowed us to reach across history and geography and into each others' hearts as human beings. He said that without a shared and strong culture, no society could be called civilized or hope to transcend the petty brutalities of greed and war.

Random Acts of Poetry on the Hill, Part ii

Ronnie R. Brown

Here's how Ottawa poet and writer Ronnie R. Brown remembers that encounter, a Random Act of Poetry in the fall of 2004.

Among those few politicians who actually welcomed us was Jack Layton. We met Jack on Parliament Hill beside the Eternal Flame and Susan McMaster read him a poem from her collection, *UNTIL THE LIGHT BENDS*. The poem entitled "Still Enough" speaks to the ability some things have to make us happy even after long periods of time.

Margie Martin, a young journalism student from Carleton University who was covering our Random Acts for Carleton's *CHARLATAN*, noted that "Layton was visibly moved." Before he bounced off back into the House, Jack turned and told us, "That poem makes me feel wonderful. When I get home I'm going to read it to my sweetie, Olivia," and in those few words he encapsulated what Random Acts (and poetry in general) should do for people. How lovely that Sue and I had a chance to make the man who brought hope to so many feel "wonderful" that October afternoon in 2004.

Two Picnics

Heidi Greco

Aside from all-candidates' meetings, those public Q & A sessions we voters rely upon, I'm not often tempted to attend social events for politicians. Over the last few years, I've attended a grand total of two. Both were picnic-style affairs, much less threatening to me than any sit-down dinner in a hall or a restaurant. Both took place on beautiful summery days, with sun and breezes and sweet smells on the air. But that's where the similarities ended.

The first was a potluck supper style picnic that was held in a beautiful garden on August 3, 2008 in Mission, BC. The tables groaned with an assortment of homemade salads and berried desserts, a cornucopia of fresh summer fare. Kids, grandparents and all sorts of in-betweens wandered about chatting and laughing – and in the midst of the party, Jack Layton. Dressed maybe not quite as casually as the laid-back BC locals, he smiled, joked and chatted with everyone. Even though it was clear that his back was bothering him, he looked you in the face and gave an answer to whatever question you asked. No evasiveness, just forthrightness. Heck, the guy practically reeked integrity.

But then, this summer, there was another such event, this one sponsored by my local Member of Parliament. He (er, we the taxpayers, I am sure) provided hot dogs for the crowd, not quite the proverbial loaves and fishes he might have wanted us to think it was. Still, it was food, and people seemed happy to eat it. As with the Layton event, all ages were in attendance. So, you're asking, What was so different?

Where Jack had been open, talking with everyone freely, my MP managed to find himself a spot where he could be conveniently surrounded by a phalanx of his faithful – not quite a full-on barrier, but effective nonetheless. A burly fellow in a red T-shirt hovered nearby. Maybe I'm wrong, but he appeared to be nothing more than a thinly-disguised security thug, there to ensure that the supposed "representative" of our riding wouldn't be annoyed by anyone (like me) who might deign to ask the wrong question. You know the kind: something about habitat, or one of the many entanglements in the omnibus budget bill. Or worse, a question about their infamous crime bill.

Open to meet with constituents? Not a chance. It was as if you needed a ticket in advance to even get near the guy. Grinning? But of course. The omnipresent smile that says Vote for Me – about as real as the bits of cheese inside a jar of Cheez Whiz. Although they're from different parties, my MP certainly could have learned from Jack. But since he clearly hasn't, I can only commit myself to being sure that I have. And really, political stripes have nothing to do with the qualities embodied by Jack – above all, the ability to listen. How else to be compassionate, if not by hearing and understanding? How else to go forward toward a goal of common good?

As Jack reminded us in that remarkable letter of farewell, he *listened* to our "… dreams … frustrations, and … ideas for change." You'll remember the conclusion of his letter to Canada: "Love is better than anger. Hope is better than fear. Optimism is better than despair." Good guidelines to live by in anybody's book. And somehow I don't think he would mind my adding to that list – something I have learned from his actions: Openness is better than being aloof.

On the Fridge

Michele Girash with Emma Girash Bevan

I am fortunate. I have many stories and memories of Jack as I was one of the lucky folks who worked with him. For this piece, I sifted through the stories – anecdotes of driving him in a souped-up Mustang because it was the only union-made car the rental company had. Of more than one Sudbury Saturday Night. Of the last conversation we had at the Vancouver Convention in June of 2011.

The stories that are most poignant for me, however, are older ones from long before I worked for the party. In 2002, I was a delegate to the Cooperative Housing Federation of Canada's AGM. I had heard of this Toronto councillor named Jack Layton and knew that he was named as a possible candidate for leadership of the NDP but hadn't met him. I had only put early thoughts into the leadership race. Jack was a plenary speaker at the AGM. He spoke eloquently and passionately about housing, about his and Olivia's challenges with attacks from folks who were ignorant about what co-op housing really was, about homelessness and poverty. I was hooked. That speech, however, didn't even approach the admiration I felt a short while later.

The AGM was held at the Hamilton Convention Centre. It was one of those stifling southern Ontario summer days – unbearable humidity, burning sunshine and no breeze. The walkway from the hotel to the convention centre was shaded and thus several folks who had nowhere to go were sitting in the shade. Some were panhandling. After his speech, and after lunch, Jack looked at the huge bowls of ice holding cans and bottles of juice, water and pop. He then looked around the hall and asked for help bringing them outside. At that point, I knew that this was no ordinary talking head … action was what this guy was all about.

The next year, Ontario was in a general election. I was working as the E-Day organizer for Irene Mathyssen who was making a provincial bid. Now at the time, I was a single mom with three kids, aged seven to twelve. I lived in a wonderful co-op that had welcomed me when my separation first happened. I was VP of my co-op board. During that campaign, this new leader, Jack, was coming to London to support Irene. He would spend the Saturday talking about housing issues. My co-op was on the tour and so the responsibility fell to me to host the event.

I woke up early on Saturday, thinking that I needed to get my ten-year-old daughter Emma to *swimming*, clean the common room at the co-op, pick up refreshments, make a few more phone calls to ensure a turn-out and be ready for early afternoon when Jack arrived. My boys were away for the weekend so it all seemed doable, at least until Emma woke up. She ran down the stairs, crying and snuffling out, "Mommy, my bunny – something's wrong with my bunny." Now, this was a geriatric rabbit but she loved him to bits. I checked and obviously the rabbit was ill. He tried to hop but went in circles and fell down.

So, swimming fell from the list while I phoned through every veterinarian in the city to find one open on a Saturday that looked after rabbits. We then drove across town to a vet in Hyde Park and the rabbit died of a heart attack in the office. Devastated, we returned home. My amazing wee daughter offered to help with the preparation for the afternoon and stayed quite close to me.

The time came when Jack was to arrive. He was a bit late and we waited in the parking lot – Emma literally clinging to my skirt. When the entourage appeared, media in tow, I greeted Jack and we headed to the common room. As the tour was late, people were rushing us in but Jack noticed this wee child beside me with red eyes and a sad, pale face. He stopped, bent down and introduced himself. He handed Emma his business card and took the time to explain why it had Braille on it. What a gorgeous moment. Here was this busy fellow, on his way to make a speech, being handled by others who wanted him to hurry, and he took the time to make a little girl's day. Because really that's what it's all about. Looking after each other – taking the time to care. The business card went on our fridge.

Emma is now nearly twenty and in 2nd year University studying English and Art History with a bit of Political Science thrown in. We have moved since then and had two different refrigerators. The business card is still there. The day we heard that Jack passed away, Emma pulled down a box of photographs and found one from that day – Jack, Emma and me, walking from the parking lot to the common room – a white business card in her hand. Now that picture is on the fridge too.

PHOTO: SIMON BELL.

Jack with Tom King, who was running as an NDP candidate in the 2008 election, and an admirer

Listening: Specialty of the House that Jack Built

James Gordon

Singer/songwriter and MLA candidate James Gordon writes about improvising with Jack in his story.

I first met Jack Layton not long after he had won the leadership of the NDP. He was out doing a summer barbeque tour drumming up support in a time when the party was pretty low in the polls. He arrived here in Guelph alone, by bus, and wandered unannounced into the apartment building courtyard where a rally was supposed to take place. I had been asked to provide some music before his speech. He came over and introduced himself and we talked music for a while. He tried out my electric piano while I tuned up my guitar. We looked out as things were about to get underway and saw that there were probably only about a dozen people gathered, the old party faithful. Preaching to the choir. If it were me, I would have been pretty annoyed to have made the trip from Toronto for that. Jack seemed totally unfazed, though I was quite embarrassed. He said a few inspiring words to the not-quite-a crowd, then turned to me and said "Let's play some tunes." We jammed for a while – he took the lead on "Hit the Road Jack (And dontcha come back no more!)." Come back he did, though; we stayed in touch, and with each returning visit you could see momentum gathering around his message and his power of connecting with people.

Each time he came back, there was always music involved. Once he came to support our mutual friend Tom King who ran federally in Guelph for the NDP. Tom and I both have first nations ancestry, and take part in a big drum circle. The singers and drummers were there for the occasion. I took my spot in the circle and I could see Jack listening and responding with pleasure and appreciation. I gestured to the circle leader to see if it was OK to invite Jack in. The invitation was extended and Jack seemed quite surprised and honoured to be asked. (He didn't seem to know that he was JACK LAYTON!) He appeared to be quite transformed by the experience. Most other politicians would have considered this a 'cute photo op' and after a few moments would have returned to schmoozing. Jack stayed with it and afterwards expressed gratitude at having been given that opportunity. He said that he was able to really feel the connection that circle made with the ancients, with the wisdom of our elders.

The connection that he felt in that circle is the same one that so many grew to feel through Jack's passion and commitment towards his country and his community. In the same way that the big drum gave a voice to the First Nations' elders, we learned as a nation to entrust Jack to being a voice for *us*, lending a heartbeat rhythm to the flow of connection, the collective shift in learning and consciousness that he was helping to create right across Canada.

That guy really knew how to listen! To me, that's the greatest skill one can bring to any musical interaction: truly listening to the other musicians around you, to your own inner muse, and to those for whom you are performing. Jack could do this, and of course we have learned how important that quality of listening became as he built a trust, a sense of collaboration, with all those who shared the values and the possibilities that he was describing to us with such eloquence and heart.

When I became a candidate for the Provincial NDP here in Ontario, largely on Jack's urging!, we were sent to "candidate camp" in Toronto for a weekend. One of the workshops was about relating to the public in a way that was genuine and effective. The facilitator mentioned that Bill Clinton, also a musician!, was the best example in recent political history of someone who always came across as someone who cared and who was listening. One fledgling candidate asked, "What was his trick?" The facilitator responded, "The trick was that there WAS no trick. He REALLY DID want to hear your story and he really did care about you. He apparently could remember the name of everyone he had ever met. How did he do this? Apparently he DID have some mental exercises that aided him in this feat, but mostly it was because he REALLY was listening when he heard you."

Jack could do this too. I've often heard people relate that they met him twice up to twenty years apart and he'd remember their name and the situation in which they met. This takes a deep openness to connecting, to hearing, to really listening, much the same way that a jazz musician will help create an ensemble improvisation: by staying in the moment with true presence and at the same time drawing on their technique and experience to make that solo or that interaction a meaningful one. That sense of 'improvisation' in the arts is akin to the kind of responsiveness and fluidity that I witnessed in Jack's grass-roots style. This approach is going to be necessary to engage our citizenry in a major collective shift in how we live and how we relate.

On another visit to Guelph, Jack had asked a number of "culture workers" to gather in a restaurant for a brain-storming session that was meant to help create the NDP platform on arts and culture. If I may boast about my home town for a moment, I should say that for a small city Guelph has an incredibly rich, diverse and extensive arts scene. In that room were visual artists, choreographers, writers, composers, musicians and theatre people, all with local connections and national reputations. Jack introduced the proceedings with very few words. He said that he was there to listen. Specialty of the house that Jack built. Listen he did. The conversation was stimulating, and there WAS a common sense of urgency about the threats to culture under our existing government. Jack seemed to ENABLE the quality of the discussion by hardly taking part in it. He thanked us for our time, and left us without many closing words, and with a feeling that we had TRULY been heard.

Jack seemed to learn, as I have, to use music as a real connector. I remember seeing pictures of him in his last campaign, handing out songbooks to the press and supporters at the end of his long day on election trail, then pulling out his guitar and leading a singalong. When the press first reported on this, it was with a certain amusement at this kind of unorthodox "flakey" tactic. Obviously, that same press started to get into it as the campaign wore on. He had helped to create a more relaxed environment for them. He had, in a way, given that group of tired workers a sense of community through singing together. And as we all know, Jack was all about creating community. His lasting legacy, I believe, is that so many more of us, through his example and his leadership, have learned the value of finding that sense of community. In turning to one another for support we've learned that indeed "love is better than anger, that hope is better than despair." Those of us who became inspired by his message and the honest, open, inclusive way that he delivered it will soon, I am sure, find ourselves, largely through his efforts, in a place where we can really effect change and create the kind of world where we all are surviving and thriving.

When Jack called to urge me to enter the political arena myself, he spoke of the value that he could see in bringing an artist's perspective and sensibility to a system of governance that has too often become insensitive and dehumanized. He was often working from that artist's perspective himself, I believe, and that perspective helped give him a unique voice that so many, across all party lines, have come to respect and admire.

Like others I felt numbed by a sense of loss when Jack died. My way of dealing with that grief presented itself quickly. His last letter to Canadians that has been so often quoted since, read a bit like a song lyric to me. He DID write, I think, with a musician's sense of timing, rhythm and poetry. Sitting with my guitar I was taken back in my memory to the first time we had met, when we "just jammed" together and quickly made a connection that lasted. Listening closely just the way a first nations drummer does to his or her ancestors, and the way Jack did, a melody appeared right away, and the words of his letter became a song almost instantly. It felt like a true collaboration between the two of us. I continue to be inspired by the man, and I continue to ask, "What would Jack do?", when I find myself wondering how to be effective and authentic in any interaction.

Here's the song, "Jack's Dream:" a dream that I believe will become reality in the not too distant future.

Jack's Dream ...

Love is better than anger. Hope is better than fear. Optimism's better than
     despair.
So let us be loving, let us be hopeful. Let us work to build a world that is fair.

Our system excludes many from our collective wealth.
Too many homeless, too many in poor health.
But if we carry his passion and his values you and I
Can make sure Jack's Dream never dies.

Love is better than anger. Hope is better than fear. Optimism is better than
     despair.
So let us be loving, let us be hopeful. Let us work to build a world that is fair.

With our commitment we can shift society. We can face climate change
     and poverty.
We will succeed together if we try.
We can make sure Jack's Dream never dies.

Love is better than anger. Hope is better than fear. Optimism is better than
     despair.
So let us be loving, let us be hopeful. Let us work to build a world that is fair.

Let us honour that dream, finish the good work that's begun.
Don't let them tell you that it cannot be done!

Love is better than anger. Hope is better than fear. Optimism is better than
     despair.
So let us be loving, let us be hopeful. Let us work to build a world that is
     fair.

Hear the song on YouTube at *http://www.youtube.com/watch?v=TQSdJz5Uu34*.

Apprenticeship with Jack

Joe Wilson

During the time I worked with MP Irene Mathyssen (NDP, London-Fanshawe), I had the great pleasure of helping staff Jack Layton during several of his visits to London. Each occasion gave me insights in to what a special man Jack was.

1. When we worked with Jack's office to build the visit's agenda, Jack invariably insisted that time be scheduled for him to work out. During a visit in 2008, it turned out the best possibility for Jack's workout was early afternoon at the Goodlife Fitness Club in downtown London. Being a Goodlife member, I volunteered to take Jack. Knowing he just wanted some quiet time for his daily workout, I kept this as low key as possible. However, as soon as I signed him in on a guest pass, two young female staffers fluttered in to welcome Jack, ask him if they could help in any way, and offered to show him to the men's change room. I commented that *I* never got this sort of personal escort, but they weren't listening to me!

After leaving his starry-eyed escorts (who stopped short of the change room!), we managed to slip into the gym unnoticed, and Jack did an hour on a cross trainer. He explained to me that daily workouts seem to enable him to keep his energy up and waistline down. Afterwards, he washed his quick-drying workout gear in the shower, and soon was packed up and ready for the rest of the busy day we had planned for him.

Jack was famous for the high-energy approach he brought to everything he did. Part of this was his innate enthusiasm, unfailingly positive attitude and strong personal connection to the world at large. But part of it also was careful planning, daily dedication, and hard work. Maybe few people shared Jack's natural gifts, but probably even fewer worked as hard and as smart as he did. Any time I need to give myself a boot in the rear, I think of the day I was Jack's gym buddy, and saw close up an important part of what kept him going.

2. During another of Jack's visits, we ended up at Western University in the evening, where Jack was to spend time with the UWO New Democrats. He clearly loved being around enthusiastic and socially-committed young people. Part of my job was to make sure we rendezvoused successfully with the driver hired to get Jack back to Toronto that evening. On top of a day

filled with events, he had a two hour car ride before he could escape the day's pressures and return home.

However, none of us had eaten. Jack bought me a beer, and he, MP Irene Mathyssen and I shared some food with the students. They were extremely excited by this informal chance to meet Jack, and talk with him – at length. Jack never short-changed anyone: no quick work-the-room-and-leave for him! I called the driver and said we were delayed – maybe a half hour or so.

But, even after the food and planned meet-and-greet were finished, Jack wanted to spend more time with these obviously energetic and focused young people. Clearly keen to succeed, they talked with him in depth about planning, organizing and getting more people involved. I called the driver and said we were delayed another half hour.

On leaving the UWO Student Centre, after saying good-bye to the students, we were accosted by a UWO faculty member, who invited Jack to drop into a UWO post-conference reception. Here was a room full of academics and community members who were delighted to welcome Jack, and engage him in conversation on a range of subjects. He was just as delighted to meet with a new group of bright, energetic and committed people. I called the driver and said we were delayed another – well, I'd call him when we left the building.

Later, Irene, Jack and I strolled through the empty university campus to our rendezvous point. There was quiet discussion about a day well spent. Here was a public figure who truly enjoyed engaging with people, who didn't see the many events we had planned for him as something to endure and get done with. Rather, he was fully involved in all of them. We delivered Jack to his driver, for his two hour drive home to Toronto. I suspect most of it was spent not in a well-deserved rest, but on his cell phone.

3. Jack could accomplish the seemingly impossible task of being highly demanding while also being very supportive. Over dinner during a busy day of events in London in 2008, he asked MP Irene Mathyssen and me, Irene's campaign manager, how preparations were coming for the soon-to-be-called election. We had been working hard, and I proudly reported on our progress. I was particularly proud of the money we had raised, in a riding where fundraising is difficult. Jack said it was not enough and we had to do more.

Here was a man who had grabbed the NDP by the neck: a federal party which often seemed content to be a third or fourth place "conscience of

Parliament," but certainly never official opposition or government. In the face of nay-sayers, complacency and seemingly insurmountable challenges, Jack was making the NDP a force to be reckoned with. You listened to Jack, especially if you were serious about succeeding.

What was most remarkable about Jack's criticism of our efforts was that it didn't feel like criticism. He recognized we were a hardworking and successful Riding Association that was capable of doing more. It was worth challenging us, because we would respond positively. It was a professional courtesy from someone who knew we were as keen as he was to succeed, and would do whatever it took. It was, strangely, a compliment from a man who was both our peer, and a great leader. We redoubled our efforts. We won that election, and the next one, and last year also won the seat provincially.

4. In 2007, Jack was the star attraction at London-Fanshawe's "Midsummer Madness" fundraiser held at the home of MP Irene Mathyssen. To make sure he had the chance to meet everyone, he joined the food crew and served out hamburgers and hot dogs. Later, to spur the fundraising, he took over as auctioneer. Who would have thought Jack Layton was a professional-quality, rapid fire auctioneer! The bids just grew and grew! My older daughter, Jessica, had brought our new grandchild, Julie, to the event. Jess's auction contribution was a 'onesie', an infant sleeper to which she had applied the NDP logo (Julie was also wearing one!). Jack auctioned the sleeper for almost $100.

I have a picture of Jack holding my new granddaughter with a rapt look on his face. I have another picture of him on stage, holding my daughter's NDP infant wear, beside my wife, Kathi, and Jess and Julie. Jack with three generations of NDP women! Those pictures are Wilson family treasures.

5. Jack loved to teach. On one of his London visits, I had arranged for him to visit a picket line in Woodstock on his way back to Toronto. It was a very bitter strike, and shortly after we arrived management tried to get a van full of scabs into the plant. The air turned blue, and things became very tense. Jack's assistants were clearly unhappy that I had helped put our national leader into a volatile situation. I could see my career as an NDP organizer becoming a very short one.

But Jack took it in stride, and we worked our way back toward his car. When we got across the road, he took time to explain to me what he was going to do to make sure he was able to engage the media in a positive fashion as he was leaving. A valuable lesson for a new organizer! And a gracious gesture for a man who always looked for a way to help people do better.

On a later occasion, at an NDP Leader's Levee, I introduced him to our 2011 provincial candidate, Teresa Armstrong. Jack was always eager to meet a new NDP candidate, and rather than just chat with Teresa, he started to give her a quick lesson on how to be an effective candidate canvasser. Part way through his mini tutorial, he was called to the front to address the crowd and the media. But first, he finished his conversation with Teresa. He invariably treated people with consideration and respect. When he was talking to someone, he was truly engaged with that person, and wouldn't cut them short.

Teresa, now our NDP MPP in London-Fanshawe, learned a lot that evening about becoming an effective candidate, but also about how to continue being an authentic and gracious person after entering public life.

Jack certainly had flaws and shortcomings. However, it is very telling that those who had the privilege of working with him, even sporadically and briefly as I did, became all the more loyal and connected to him. He was genuine, passionate, and considerate. He dared to truly care, and to work hard to make his caring matter. He was extremely intelligent and capable, but not in an elitist manner. He was realistic and perceptive about people, but never demeaning or dismissive. He was intensely human. Perhaps this is what so many Canadians came to realize – to feel – about him during the 2011 election. "Le bon Jack" indeed. Jack was the one great man I have had the privilege to know personally. I miss Jack every day: Jack, the great Canadian, and Jack, the fine human being.

The Day I Met Jack

Teresa Armstrong

I always admired Jack from when I met first him. He was the kind of person you wanted to have a coffee with and you felt like he would listen. He had a way of making people feel like they were part of something that could change the world. He was a heroic champion of social justice; his thoughts, visions and inspirations are still reshaping Canada's political landscape. His personal and professional commitment to all Canadians was realized by all generations. Seeing Jack Layton take the time out of his busy schedule to come out to a London-Fanshawe blue collar home to sit with a family over tea, discuss life and politics, in itself showed his genuine care for Canadians and the type of caring spirit he embodied. He truly left a legacy for all Canadians and his memory will live forever.

I was a first time candidate in 2010, for the London-Fanshawe Riding, and the first provincial candidate nominated in Ontario. As a first time candidate, I experienced many firsts which in their own way were all very special to me. But my most memorable and distinct memory as a new candidate was the day I met Jack. I am saddened to say it would also be the last time I would meet him.

It was on a cool night when Joe Wilson, my campaign manager, and I were attending a Toronto leader's gala event. I was a little nervous, especially since Joe said he would try to introduce me to Jack. My opportunity to meet our charismatic and energetic national leader! I had hoped to meet Jack, but somehow in the back of my mind I had my doubts. After all, he was a very popular man and always the centre of attention. So why did I think I would have the honour of taking up some of his time that evening?

As luck had it, Joe and I managed to make it through the crowd to get close to Jack. It was not hard to find him because he was the most popular man in the room, surrounded by many vying for his attention. Would I get the chance to say hello to him? As the moment got closer, my palms started to sweat as I wondered what I would say to him. Me, a first time candidate meeting our National Leader and the next Prime Minister of Canada!

Finally, the time came, and Joe said, "Jack, I would like you to meet our provincial candidate from London-Fanshawe, Teresa Armstrong." When he heard the word "candidate," Jack's face lit up and he looked me straight in the eye. He was very engaging as he immediately offered advice to a new candidate on how to engage with voters. He showed me his special hand shake, where his index finger was extended and touched the other person's wrist, and of course he explained that I should always make eye contact. I asked when I should release my grip, and his surprise answer was, "You don't, until you move on."

Before Jack could finish his mini-tutorial with me, he was called up on stage to speak to the crowd. But he did not rush off and excuse himself in mid-sentence. What made an impression on me that evening was that he did not cut our conversation short, but rather he finished what he had to say to me – me, the unimportant rookie candidate!

Jack had a way of demonstrating to everyone that they were important to him, mostly because they were. And when you spoke to him, you knew he was genuine, a real person and not "just a politician." I learned a lot from Jack in our brief conversation. It goes without saying that Jack truly was the people's politician.

Heart in the Asides

Sandra Stephenson / Czandra

Jack showed up late for dinner. The local NDP riding association awaited him for the Vaudreuil-Soulanges pre-campaign dinner. It was spring 2004 and I was secretary of the riding association, though my loyalties were divided almost schizophrenically (how Canadian). I had run as a candidate for the Green Party in the 2002 provincial elections. Jean Charest, the Liberal party leader, was a Conservative in provincial clothing who led the federal PC party until he gave up on getting a majority after Mulroney and moved shop to Québec. Trying to erase the conservative streak, I campaigned for the NDP, donated to the Greens, and voted Bloc.

Jack's team had been in Montréal meetings so when he arrived at Mon Village restaurant in Hudson, he looked end of the day used up. Jack had begun his first campaign as party leader in the Montréal area, meeting and reconnecting with people from the riding where he went to school. He hoped for a chance here, had recruited one of his high-school buddies from a respected family of artists and business people to represent the NDP in Vaudreuil-Soulanges. The Conservative Party kept tossing in obvious decoys to beat out Liberal candidates. Their men (no women) were like skeets at hunting season – an astronaut and a spend-thrift later appointed to the Senate despite being elected nowhere – lame targets in a riding they didn't know. The Conservatives underestimated Jack's one-time hometown and its surroundings, whose people were not bought by flash. The seat had been going to the Bloc for honest local involvement, and Jack was ready to pitch it to the NDP.

After a short sit and a few sips of beer, Jack perked up and playful banter began. His presence had me in a pleased kind of thrall, but one look he shot me struck with that "bingo!" quality – it spawned my conviction that if ever the working class could field a winner in hypertrophied politics of the 21st century, it would begin with this man. In the melting deep-freeze on "communism" and increasingly dogged adherence to outmoded economics to explain away the unconscionable, Jack was it. His unconventional sense of convention convinced listeners to rethink. His perception of himself included the absurd, a combination that took time to grow on the public.

The look Jack gave me that spring evening in Hudson was at first a mixture of amazement and reprehension, then he fixed my eye, a twinkle passed between us, and he let rip a great moustache-rippling belly-laugh.

He had been autographing books, his newly released *Speaking Out Louder* (Key Porter, 2004). Flipping briskly to the front page of a copy proffered by an acolyte beside me, he asked, "So what's the name? How do you spell it?" Without thinking, I slipped in blithely: "J-A-C-K L-A-Y-..." at which he looked up to see if I could be serious.

The electric eyeball connection, then, "T-O-N!" I finished with a flourish and grin. Jack Layton's cheerleader in less than a heartbeat. And it stayed that way, though his genuine anger in debate sometimes shook me. I replay that laugh in my head: how quickly he gratified my childish enthusiasm with humour, the heart of healthy discourse and sound loyalties. In Parliament, which he attended more religiously than any other leader, it sometimes looked as if Jack took things more seriously than the Prime Minister, but people who met him could feel the ripple of laughter, the camaraderie of a darn good sport.

Beams of Light

Laura Bird

I was inspired to compose a song after Jack died but the subject was not what one might expect considering the words he left behind for all of us. I was truly inspired by the love he shared with Olivia and particularly moved by one of the many stories included in *The Toronto Star* the day after he passed. (I also loved hearing how the newspaper reporters enjoyed traveling on the campaign trail with him because after a long day, he'd crack open the guitar case, hand out the *Rise Up Singing* books, and have a good old fashioned singalong!) The front page of *The Star* that morning was filled with that beautiful shot of Jack and Olivia kissing. My intention was to record the song and gift it to Olivia. When performing the song live, my intro goes something like this:

It's a year now since Canadians lost "the best prime minister they never had." It's been said that Jack Layton loved music equally as much as he loved politics, but I think we all know he loved Olivia more … . During their first meeting at a Mount Sinai Hospital fundraiser, he was the auctioneer, she the Chinese interpreter. He said he fell in love in four nanoseconds. According to Olivia, she took a little longer: it was over their first dinner date. Years later after Olivia had been diagnosed with thyroid cancer, she found herself being treated at that same hospital. She could look down and see their home from her hospital window. And as Jack gazed up toward her, he would aim his "beams of light … ." I have envisioned that beautiful smile on Jack's face. When I perform the song live, I invite the audience to sing "beams of light"… and their voices sound lovely.

The mp3 of "My Olivia" can be heard on *www.laurabird.com.*

My Blue Canoe

Christian McLeod

Our Medicare is the blue canoe which we all ride in and must continue to paddle to stay afloat … Blue represents the medicine of modern man. We share the canoe, we love the canoe, let's take care of the canoe … This is what Jack Layton and Tommy Douglas and June Callwood represent. Jack carried on Tommy Douglas's legacy. He continued to build the canoe, the blue canoe. 'The Montréal' style canoe is the largest and holds us all in our journey, the man, the icon, the ideas and the will to act. Jack loved canoeing, and the tradition/lineage …We all know that if asked what to do for the summer holidays, Jack would be happiest paddling the Nahanni River. And as he paddled I'm sure his mind was building a better world as he slipped across the water. Mr. Layton worked tirelessly for all of us his entire career. One of his mentors was Tommy Douglas, a man from whom Mr. Layton re-shaped ideas for all Canadians. To Jack Layton: you worked and smiled and worked some more for all of us!

ILLUSTRATION: CHRISTIAN MCLEOD

My Blue Canoe (Our medicare is the blue canoe which we all ride in and must continue to paddle to stay afloat.)

MEDIUM: ACRYLIC ON CANVAS
SIZE (INCHES): 48 X 36
SIZE (CM): 120 X 90

You Know the Facts

Robert Banks Foster

Forestry Notes For
Arundhati Roy: *The new earth is coming, on a quiet day I can hear her breath.*
and Jack Layton: *Always have a dream that's longer than a lifetime.*

Part I

You know the facts, I know the facts:
as the puddle fills with poison
at first the tiny bit around the edge
hardly shows for the longest time
when at last you notice
well it's only creeping inward
then well, it's crept more
you turn around twice and it's half full
& you blink or stammer
all dead, all gone.

But does it change mind
this sustainable last death?
The dark wood becomes the poisoned wood.

Reduce uniqueness to utility.
That's what we call sustainable.

Part II

Half through the journey of our life
I lost my way in a dark wood.

At the rally someone said, *We are the forest.*

The leaves of the trees are for
healing of the nations.

Part III

What can I do?
    Gather.
    Listen.
    Study and listen.
    Hear the wind in the leaves.
    Wait.
    Share.
    Wait until you and others must speak.
    Hear the wind in the leaves.
    Become visible so all see you.
    Become vocal so all hear you.
    Share, study, and listen.
    Hear the wind in the leaves.
    Feed others, share, study, and listen.
    Hear the wind in the leaves.

    Begin.

With thanks to Michelle Mungall for inspiring Part III. I was in a very small group with her here and she gave a beautiful response to a question I asked. She's our NDP MLA.

"Jack let me know I could change the world"

Michelle Mungall

When looking back at my first few encounters with Jack Layton, I have to conclude that Jack was inspired by the idealism of youth. I was active in the NDP's youth wing in 2002/03, and like many of my peers, had all kinds of ideals that fell under the heading of changing the world. Since then, some of my perspectives have changed, others have expanded, and others I hold onto very tightly. But what I will always remember is how Jack responded to me and my peers, and how his approach allowed us to grow into our own potential with confidence and conviction.

Rather than attempting to temper our idealism, Jack encouraged it. He was unique in his ability to motivate us to think creatively and strategically. He didn't hold back if he disagreed with us, but engaged us in thought-provoking debate without any doubt that we were his equals. He recognized we had a thought process and he was curious to understand it. All this while, we drank beers in his backyard.

In the summer of 2002, I was exploring the idea of running for City Council in Nelson BC, a small but vibrant and politically active community. Many responded to me with pat-on-the-head style comments. Jack, on the other hand, had full confidence I could win and took the time to strategize with me. In just a few minutes I learned more about winning with integrity than ever before. These life lessons are dear to me and I hold them close.

As Jack became Leader of the NDP and a Canadian icon, I continued on my path in politics. Every time I saw Jack at a convention or fundraiser, we would say hello and briefly chat. The last time I saw Jack in June 2011, we were at the back of the Convention Hall. We bumped into each other as he was heading up to the media booth. He gave me a big hug and said, "I am so proud of you."

Jack was proud of all of us, and he was never afraid to show it. He knew our potential and asked us to reach for it. There is art in everything and culture is forever in the creation phase. Jack's contribution to the art and culture of politics was one of integrity, inspiration and solidarity.

A Jack We Barely Knew

Larry Sakin

Jack Layton had just been voted in as leader of the New Democratic Party in 2003 and as a Member of Parliament in 2004. It was auspicious, because Layton rode a wave of NDP politicians who flooded parliament that year. In the spring of 2004, my friend Norla Antinoro invited me to write a political column for *MyTown*, an online Canadian magazine. She told me the magazine had a progressive bias, many of the readers identifying themselves as supporters of the NDP. As an American, my focus was on the ineptitude of the GW Bush administration, so the NDP was new to me. I needed to understand ultra-progressive Canadians to gain credibility with them, so researching the NDP became a priority.

What I didn't expect was how this man and his political party would personally affect me. It became apparent that America had a lot to learn from her neighbor to the north, and I from Jack Layton. The whole saga of Layton's rise to leadership of the NDP was inspiring. This former Toronto town councilman pushed ahead, working to lift the NDP to the position of Official Opposition in just seven years while consolidating his party's success. At the time, no one could imagine a day when the name 'Layton' would be said with the hushed awe reserved for the Canadian political elite. However, Layton and his party had an ambitious plan for reform which they started on quickly, creating a budget for the nation that provided enhanced services for Canadians, including better public healthcare.

In the United States, few politicos commit themselves as wholly to their constituencies as Jack Layton had. American politicians work mostly with corporate attorneys and lobbyists to fulfill *their* own agendas. But Layton embodied a selflessness within the political arena that is all too rare in public life, and went about improving the lives of Canadians without the hubris that has become common in the US. He and the NDP rarely let Canadian progressives down even when the weight of progressives' dreams might have been difficult to bear. I did not know Jack Layton. And yet, he stands among my greatest mentors. Layton taught me the importance of staying with what you know is right, no matter what others may think, that leadership is about commitment to bettering our communities, and how one can go about the business of change with the courage of quiet fortitude.

My activism has expanded since writing for that Canadian magazine. I am currently working with people from all over the US to expand the list of candidates voters can choose from in primary elections. In many states, independent voters can only vote for a Democrat or Republican candidate in a primary and in other states independents can't vote at all in the primary. Under the Top Two system we are advocating, voters are not limited to the major parties as their choice. They may vote for whomever they wish. The two candidates with the most votes move on to the general election. The system has been implemented in Washington State and California, and there is a citizen's initiated proposition for Top Two on the Arizona 2012 ballot. It's the kind of activism that Jack Layton would have approved of wholeheartedly. His balance and sense of fair play would have led him to it.

Layton's integrity guides my conscience and motivates me to make incremental, consistent steps towards a goal. His example of consummate political action and the principles of his party remind me that community should always be the first beneficiary of our actions and that keeping the promise of integrity is the greatest reward one can know. My hope is that the light that shone from within Jack Layton continues to inspire others as it does me and all leaders can learn from his example.

"Jack Layton changed my life"

Gina Barber

That may sound dramatic, but it's true. Jack Layton inspired me to run for the NDP in the general election of 2004 although I had maintained for twenty-five years that I would never be a candidate. But run I did and when another election was called in 2006, I ran again. I was proud to carry the banner of a party with Jack Layton as its leader.

His optimism, energy, and commitment were compelling. He was always up to the challenge, embracing whatever opportunities came his way.

I first met him at a Leadership Debate that some of us had organized for London. Since London wasn't on the "official" leadership tour, we had considerable leeway in the format. We decided that we would add interest to the event by asking each of the leadership hopefuls to entertain us after the debate. Not every contender was enamoured of this; several found reasons to regretfully decline. Not Jack, though. He used the occasion to demonstrate his auctioneering skills and to sell his book on homelessness as a fundraiser. Then he delighted us all by accompanying himself on a keyboard to a hilarious rendition of "Hit the Road, Jack." He didn't take himself too seriously.

He did take the issues seriously, however, and wasn't afraid to take some heat or cold when taking a stand. The second time I met him was on what was the coldest day in January of 2003, in front of the John Labatt Centre, rallying with others against the invasion of Iraq.

Then there was Jack, the family man, doting on his wife Olivia, cherishing his mother-in-law. At the leadership convention, I got to see Jack at a hospitality event, entertaining his supporters with lots of back and forth repartee, but immediately giving over the stage when Olivia joined him. The chemistry between them was palpable, each empowering the other, with not a hint of competitiveness. Later, after he had won the leadership of the party, Jack introduced with pride his mother-in-law who had worked for thirty years in the laundry department of the hotel where we were celebrating.

By then, I was thoroughly enchanted. With Jack at the helm of the party, anything seemed possible. He had a vision and a plan. It would take a while, but it would happen. So I decided to run in 2004, and Jack came to campaign with me in Wortley Village. He was a great hit with the community; I was proud to be seen with him! I didn't win, not then, nor in January 2006. But it made possible my successful run for Board of Control later that year. As the results came in on election night, Jack called to congratulate me. I treasure the memory.

Jack changed my life and he changed politics in Canada. He proved that nice guys don't have to finish last, that courage, honesty and caring still have a place in the hearts of Canadians.

Time for a Friend

Irene Mathyssen

Time is one of the greatest and most precious gifts we can give each other. Jack Layton had many talents and many gifts but the way that he offered his time and attention made people feel valued. Supporters and admirers would gather in great anticipation to hear Jack speak and he never disappointed them. He would wade into the crowd with energy, exuding a real sense of camaraderie, to meet with the people who just wanted to talk to him, touch him and to be acknowledged. Jack not only understood that; he embraced it.

I remember hundreds of rallies. Some however stand out in my memory, along with some members of the audience. There is a young New Democrat in London, Ontario who never missed a chance to see Jack. Bill is non-verbal, confined to a wheelchair and profoundly challenged. When Jack came to town, he was always able to spot Bill in the audience, find him in the crowd and speak to him by name. Even when Jack's press secretary or tour manager was trying to hustle him off to the next event or press conference, Jack would take the time to reach out to people like Bill. He always had time for the people in the crowd who needed to connect. All they wanted was a kind word, an encouraging response, a hug or a handshake. And when Jack reached out to them, it was magic. This simple gesture told all those people that they mattered to Jack. He was a Rock Star, a Rock Star who showed respect and humility and genuine caring for all those who needed his time. And we loved him for it and for giving us all that precious gift of time.

"The house that Jack built includes us all"

Joyce Balaz and Bill Hiltz

We write this piece from the perspective of Bill Hiltz, a person living with differing abilities who most people simply ignore, and Joyce Balaz, who supports Bill and connects with him on many different levels. Bill has an active support circle of friends that assist him with planning and advocacy. Although Bill cannot express himself by voice, he has deep insights about life that need to be heard and honoured. Joyce uses her knowledge and experience about disability issues to educate others and help them understand why changes which assist persons living with disabilities will assist society in the future. Together, we work tirelessly to advocate for full inclusion for everyone as each and every one of us has strengths and gifts with which to build a better community, country and world.

We were ecstatic to read that Jack included a commitment to the UN Convention on the Rights of Persons with Disabilities in the last election platform, specifically the call to end the reservation on Article 12, an issue so dear to Bill's heart. From the first time that Irene Mathyssen introduced Bill to Jack until the very last encounter with Jack at the NDP convention in Vancouver in June 2011, it has been clear that Jack whole-heartedly embraced inclusion. There was not a time when we were at an event with Jack that Jack didn't go out of his way to speak with Bill, be it at a rally, at a dinner event, a fundraiser, a convention or just on the street.

Jack had been speaking with Ed Broadbent when he noticed Bill and said very nicely, "Excuse me, Ed. I must say hi to my friend, Bill!" and promptly gave us both such a warm embrace. That hug reached deep into our inner spirit and was indeed a life-changing moment. That warmth lives on in us today! Later that evening, Bill was dancing in his wheelchair at Jack's party. Jack came onto the dance floor, leaving his jacket and cane on the stage and started dancing with Olivia. When he noticed Bill, he promptly came over and danced a few steps with Bill. Bill acknowledged Jack's efforts with a hearty vocalization and big smile. Jack would greet us whenever he saw us with, "I knew you would be here! You are one of my best supporters." And Jack was right. It didn't matter how Bill was feeling – if Jack was in town, Bill would be there to meet him and show him his support.

Bill was at camp when Jack passed away, so I called and asked the director to let Bill know. When details about a candlelight vigil being held in London the next day were posted on Facebook, I was not surprised to hear that Bill was coming home from camp to attend. That is how much Jack and Bill connected.

During the week of Jack's passing, Bill felt an urgency to work on a message of thanks to Jack. That message came in the form of a very large card with the words THANK YOU in large orange letters. In that card, Bill included some pictures of Jack and Bill as well as one of Bill's Olympic Torch Run and his message of thanks to Jack. Once finished, the card was express posted to Jack to arrive on Friday. Along with the pictures, Bill reminded Jack of the last encounters we had had together at the Vancouver Convention.

It seemed only fitting that Bill would leave camp Friday evening and head to Toronto to be one of the lucky people to join in the celebration of Jack's life on Aug. 27th. That celebration was a true testament to Jack's vision of inclusion and we knew that we could continue to build on the foundation of the House that Jack built. A while later, we could not have been more thrilled when Raffi, Bill's idol, put Jack's words to music for all to share. Today, we will once again travel to Toronto to share with those at Nathan Phillips Square as we celebrate the life of our friend Jack Layton. We are Jack's legacy! Jack's words to Canadians will live on in our hearts forever as we continue to advocate for Jack's vision of inclusion for all and a Canada where no one is left behind!

August 22, 2012

Irene Mathyssen, Jack and pensioner.

Jack and His Locus of Control

Kathleen Dindoff

Jack Layton was a man of strong values and commitment, driven by intellectual curiosity to make an enduring difference in Canadian society. He was an enigma – a thinker and conceptualizer as well as an activist who fought to achieve his thought in everyday reality. His vision and values compelled him to transform society and eventually to touch the lives of individuals in a deeply personal way. In an interview with Penn Kemp, his wife Olivia Chow says that she taught Jack to listen. It was this gift of attentive listening that captured the hearts of Canadian men and women, young and old, rich and poor, from diverse backgrounds and persuasions.

As an executive coach and psychologist, I have helped business, academic and social service leaders to be more effective. It is from a coach's perspective that I would like to examine Jack's gifts as a powerful leader. To many in Canada, Jack Layton was an "overnight success" when he became the leader of the Official Opposition in May, 2011. What was it that catapulted him into the forefront of so many minds and hearts, and tore at the fabric of our emotions and hearts with his declining health and death just a few months later?

Jack was the epitome of a charismatic and transformational leader. The key markers of such a captivating and energizing style include expertise, likeability and a strong and clearly articulated vision. The fuel that ignites such a leader's success is an ability to communicate to others their unique importance, called "individualized consideration" in leadership theory. Jack did this by listening, as if his audience of one or thousands of individuals were the only people who mattered to him, and who mattered as individuals. He communicated a message of optimism and inclusiveness in an age when the .01% of income earners command a third of economic gains in Canada and the world, when the just society of Trudeau's vision now seems to favour those who can most afford justice.

The overnight success Jack achieved was gained with a lifetime preparation. His fight was borne of observational learning at his father's knee, dedication to learning the science of politics and political action that culminated in a Ph.D., and a commitment to the disenfranchised in Canadian society that spanned individual outreach and action. His three books on homelessness and the power of political action show this commitment. Jack was indeed what Penn calls a "J'Acktivist" in the best sense, one of those rare leaders who creates a powerful and activating vision of inclusiveness and empowerment. He inspired Canadians to participate in the creation of a social order that embraces diverse voices and contributions. His synergy of vision, voice and action compelled our loyalty and actions to achieve the possibility he articulated for us, *all* of us, young and old, rich and poor, able-bodied and -minded and challenged, female and male, immigrants and natural-born citizens and First Nations and Inuit peoples.

Jack started as a moral leader and angry intellectual who campaigned against the injustice and discrimination that degrade our collective potential. Along the way, he learned to hear and embrace the voices, hearts and spirit of all of us, at our best and at our worst. Slowly, Jack developed the character of a leader who demonstrates the path to our own greatness. He remained true to his longstanding vision of Canada – as a professor and City Councillor in the largest and most diverse city in Canada, head of the Federation of Canadian Municipalities, MP and leader of the Official Opposition in Parliament, and voice of the voiceless who are so necessary to the full evolution of our multicultural society.

His magic was the result of several well-executed cognitive-behavioural processes like internal locus of control, goal setting, self-efficacy, and resilience. Jack developed a strong internal locus of control that was self-motivated and self-directed. He understood that unless he took personal ownership for results he wanted to achieve, he would wait by the shore forever for the winds and tides to swing in his direction. He was the self-efficacy poster child for the little engine that could. He set goals, broke them down into small steps, and worked tirelessly to execute those steps to achieve his vision. Finally, he embodied resilience – the flexibility to adapt his behaviours and goals to achieve the ends in which he believed so strongly.

Leaders like Jack are rare, and his passing has left a void that calls on us to achieve the Canada he envisioned for us. Each of us now has the opportunity to develop our own way to fulfil this powerful vision.

Jack Layton's Legacy Isn't What You Think

Glen Pearson

When he planted a big kiss on my cheek, everyone roared. The Opposition Lobby of the House of Commons isn't used to such charged non-partisan moments, but on this particular day things were destined to be different.

Then a Liberal MP from London, I had written a blog posting titled "You Don't Know Jack," in which I spoke of my observations of his fight against prostate cancer and how his grace in adversity had assisted the House of Commons in finding a few moments of respect and non-partisanship.

When he had first stood in the House to announce his challenge with cancer, the air was still, the emotions charged. With aplomb he spoke of how he would follow all medical advice in hopes of continuing his life with his family and his place of leadership in the House. When he concluded, the chamber emptied as MPs from all parties lined up to shake his hand. Speaker Peter Milliken halted the regular proceedings and looked on with a smile and respect.

Then came "Movember" – an initiative started by MPs that had men growing moustaches in Jack's honour as he battled his cancer. Thousands were raised for cancer research.

Then came my blog posting. The day it was published, I had a lengthy conversation with his mother Doris. Jack later told me of how the blog had surprised her because it was praise coming from someone from another party. In tears, Doris spoke to me of her fear in the moment, of how the very word "cancer" had challenged her emotions. She thanked me profusely for the effort and commented that her son was a true fighter – a prescient and prophetic observation.

Jack met me in the lobby just before Question Period and embraced me in a bear hug. Everything around us stopped. "I can't tell you how much that meant to her," he said, a tad emotionally. Then came the kiss. It stunned us all and had people from all parties dashing for their cameras. He pulled back, hands on my shoulders, and muttered a quiet "thank you." Then he was out the door and into the House, prepared to give one of his animated speeches.

Jack Layton's passing stunned us all. But there is something different about it, something very human. In an age where politics has turned elitist and partisan, people are more removed from government than at any time in recent memory. People are frustrated at the collective sense of isolation. Yet there was something about Jack Layton that transcended all that. He was the champion of the oppressed, of the marginalized, of the lonely. Because voters were feeling that way themselves, they found in him a connection, a desire for grassroots politics that mattered to communities. They found in Jack much of the personal respect for politicians they had lost.

To London-Fanshawe NDP MP Irene Mathyssen, my friends in the NDP, and Jack's family I offered special condolences. This was an unusual passing because a common man in a charged political setting had passed away and left a whiff of the common touch at his departure. His death will be honoured and grieved by millions because, in truth, he never forgot them. And for me, I'll always remember that kiss as a passing of affection from a truly great public servant to one not nearly his equal. Politics will now be diminished with his departure. May he rest in peace and accomplishment.

On the day of Jack Layton's death, I was asked to do a number of interviews regarding his passing. Though I was a former Liberal Member of Parliament, Jack and I often conversed about public policy and we got along well. So, of course, I agreed. The interviews coalesced around the former NDP leader's legacy. Almost by default, the interviewers themselves were assuming that his greatest accomplishment was attained on May 2, when his party won big and he became the leader of the Official Opposition. I reminded them that only political types think this way. What politics giveth, it can also take away, suddenly, and often with brutal results. For Jack Layton, his legacy will be something far more important and vital to the Canadian context.

Think of the groups or issues that have been largely ignored in the past number of years and you'll find Layton consistently championing their causes. The environment, Aboriginals, unions, those struggling in poverty, women, the unemployed, social justice – Jack and his party fought faithfully for these issues and often suffered a lack of strong voter support as a result. For years they remained the third party because Canadian voters appeared far more interested in the economy than they were in those struggling at the margins. Yet year after year, often with mixed election results, Jack Layton soldiered on, reminding Canadians that any society that overlooked the importance of such issues wasn't functioning as it should.

In my view at least, this explains a portion of the remarkable appeal the NDP leader had with the public during his final days and those leading up to his funeral. Canadians are a good people, even if they at times forget those being left behind, and they recognized in Jack Layton a champion of both public service and humanity. We inherently respect those who struggle for the "little guy," and God knows there has been a shortage of supply of such action coming out of Ottawa in recent years.

It is no small irony that, while Canadians grow increasingly frustrated with political partisanship and its damaging consequences, that Jack Layton was one of the fiercest partisans on Parliament Hill. Years of being largely ignored by the other larger parties in Parliament had understandably turned many NDP members against their political foes with an animated fervor. But if you looked up in the visitor gallery on any particular day the House was sitting, you would see advocates of the forgotten causes cheering on the NDP. There is something to be learned from this for all political parties: go for power all you want, but Canadian citizens are smart enough to discern the difference between power and public service and Jack Layton had turned that into an art form.

Politics is supposed to matter because it's designed to protect and resource Canadians to be all they wish to be. Sadly, under the present political structure, there are too many citizens that lie outside of that promise. Jack Layton, despite his partisanship, never forgot them and in the end Canadians didn't forget him because of it.

Jack's mother's greatest fear was that she would lose a son to the disease and she would be left alone. Well, it happened and our hearts and prayers are with her these days. But Canadians are now suffering something similar. A good man, a hearty public servant, is gone and we are left in our grief. That sadness would surely become easier to bear if future political leaders ushered in all citizens to the Canadian promise and not just those who can swing votes.

As I now embark on my own odyssey of chemotherapy, I can only hope that I carry it through with as much grace and fortitude as Jack did. But more than that – much more than that – I pray that throughout my journey I will always work for those who are marginalized and left outside the system. That's a lesson I learned once again from Jack.

"The ability to do the right thing despite challenges"

Rupinder Kaur

In my six years of working for him as a Press Secretary, Jack Layton was more than just a political leader, for me he was a mentor and a good friend. He insisted we call him Jack – just Jack.

I know many Canadians feel sadness about his death, especially the Sikh community, both in Canada and across the Diaspora. He took up many of the concerns and issues raised by Sikh Canadians from recognizing the importance of the Five Ks by introducing a motion in the House of Commons; standing with the community on calls for justice in India on the 1984 pogroms; demanding answers as to why divisive and controversial people like Kamal Nath were allowed into Canada; calling on the Government of India to reconsider the death penalty against Prof. Devinderpal Singh Bhullar; and generally fighting to end the racism and discrimination faced by the community. He was our voice in Parliament and an activist who stood with us shoulder-to-shoulder on the ground.

I fondly remember one of the first occasions I worked for him. In Toronto for an event, he suddenly decided to hold a press conference on the outrageous and ballooning gas prices. I was taken aback by the unexpected issue thrust on my plate. I was a novice then, and new to the vagaries of my job because I had yet to gain experience pitching stories to the media and executing media events.

"No problem," said Jack. He sat me down at his kitchen table, gave me a telephone and a list of local media outlets and told me to call them and sell the story. Now I was double-stunned! I had to sit in front of the leader and urge the media to show up at an impromptu press conference! Maybe I was lucky or maybe it was a slow news day, but that press conference was a success with a great media turnout. At the end of the day, Jack gave me a high five and congratulated me on the "good work." I learned a valuable lesson that day: don't undermine yourself when others believe in you.

The very first press conference I had the opportunity to organize for Jack was in 2007, when the NDP called on the federal government to apologize for the *Komagata Maru* tragedy of 1914 where the Government of Canada denied the docking of the ship on the shores of Vancouver, which carried 376 passengers from colonial India. He was appalled to learn of this dark historical episode and was committed to pressing for an official apology in the House of Commons.

Even the World Sikh Organization presented him with a beautiful Kirpan as a sign of thanks and in appreciation of his consistent, continued commitment to justice and fairness for all Canadians. He was very moved when I explained the significance of the Kirpan to him: the ability to do the right thing despite challenges blocking your progress.

Jack was fearless. He was courageous. He had leadership and vision. I would joke and tell him that he's really a Sikh inside because of his social justice work, and he would smile. Whenever I would meet with him, he greeted me with a "Sat Sri Akal" and his "Waheguru Ji ka Khalsa, Waheguru Ji ki Fateh" was always impeccable and perfect.

I had the privilege of accompanying him to the annual Vaisakhi Khalsa Day parades in Toronto, Vancouver and Surrey. He was quite taken by the generosity of the community, from the warm welcome he would receive, to the heaps of delicious food the community would serve at the various stalls. The most recent one we attended was April 2011 in Toronto and we were both astonished at the rock star reception he got as he walked through the crowds. I knew he was respected by the community but this outpouring of love really touched him.

I would draft his speech for these parades and add one simple line at the end, something to the effect of "Aap sabh nu Vaisakhi di lakh lakh vadhaaee hovey ji" [may you all have great joy during Vaisakhi] and he would demand I add more Punjabi – not only because he wanted to share his sincere wishes with the community, but also he knew it would set him apart from the other politicians who only did it as a chore. It would amuse me to see the positive reaction of those listening to his speech and I was delighted when members of the Punjabi media would give me thumbs up for Jack's performance and delivery.

He wasn't just a champion for my community – he was one for all Canadians. He played an instrumental role in convincing Prime Minister Stephen Harper to apologize on the floor of the House of Commons to the First Nations and Aboriginal communities for the residential schools and forcible removal and conversion of their children. He worked with local Tamil leaders in coordinating and pressuring the Government of Canada to intervene and work with the United Nations for a peaceful resolution to the conflict in Sri Lanka. His political goals included dignity for seniors, lifting people out of poverty, ending homelessness, ensuring Canadians had access to doctors and proper medical care. He was a true fighter and it's hard to believe that something like cancer would ultimately beat him.

I've had the honour to travel across the country with him and I was always amazed at how down-to-earth and friendly he was with everyone. I was often questioned by people, "What do you do for Jack Layton?" and I would state, "Oh, I'm just a Press Secretary." He once overheard and said: "No, Rupinder, you're not just a Press Secretary; you're my colleague." I'm really proud that I had the opportunity to be a part of his team. Under his leadership, we worked hard to go from fourth-party status to become the Official Opposition in the House of Commons, with a historic number of NDP MPs representing the entire country. I remember when people used to laugh and say that the NDP would never amount to anything significant, and Jack would always say, "Don't let them tell you it can't be done." That's another lesson he taught me and one I'll keep close to my heart.

In a farewell letter to Canadians, Jack concluded by saying: "My friends, love is better than anger. Hope is better than fear. Optimism is better than despair. So let us be loving, hopeful and optimistic. And we'll change the world."

He would even sign-off his personal emails with a quote from Tommy Douglas: "Courage my friends, 'tis never too late to build a better world." Now we must carry on his fight to make Canada, and this world, a better place for everyone. Over the years working for him and the NDP, Jack instantly became my mentor and a good friend. Reflecting on the one year anniversary of his passing, I realize that it was a tremendous loss for all Canadians, no matter where one's political allegiance lay.

Jack, I never got a chance to tell you this in person: thank you. Your words of love, hope, and optimism will guide me.

Thank you for teaching me to have courage when all I want to do is run and hide.

Thank you for showing me that it's more rewarding to walk the walk than talk the talk.

Thank you for reminding me that it's never too late to build a better world.

Piano to Piano

Clark Bryan

I had the great pleasure of spending some time with Jack a few years ago during a 2006 municipal by-election in London, Ontario. A rally was held at Aeolian Hall and in preparation for this event, Jack spent some time preparing and resting in my teaching studio on the ground floor of the hall. He greeted me warmly and to my astonishment, he seemed to know everything about Aeolian Hall and me. We spent some time chatting about art, culture and especially music. I discovered we held similar global beliefs about life and creativity.

Many pianos and a harpsichord adorned my studio during those years and Jack and I started playing music for each other with great excitement. I remember him being drawn particularly to a square grand piano built in 1885. He reminisced about his own grandfather's piano factory in Montréal. I found out that Jack and I shared a great love for the music of Bach and I played my favourite works for him. He played some of his favourite pieces as well, Bach and a pastiche of things from folk music to jazz.

All of this happened when he was supposed to be getting ready for the rally. After his aides interrupted us, he quickly went over his speech and then went upstairs to the hall, filled with energy. When he walked out on stage and the capacity crowd roared, I knew I had met a unique spirit and felt very inspired by the pathway Jack had chosen.

This was a turning point in my life. I had become quite active in social issues in those years and how art and culture can be a catalyst for positive social change. My conversation and experience with Jack that day really crystalized how I might continue to develop this relationship between what I was doing at the Aeolian and how it might be used to educate, inspire and connect people in community. Community is the foundation stone upon which we build a beautiful world; a world which cares for its most vulnerable. Jack knew this.

When Jack died, Gina Barber organized a memorial event at Aeolian Hall during the telecast funeral of Jack. We felt so honoured to draw many Londoners together to celebrate his life. Our front sidewalk was adorned with epitaphs in chalk that day. A testimonial to a great man whose life continues to remind us of the work we need to do and the values we need to live by.

Six String Nation: Reflection on Jack

Jowi Taylor

I first met Jack Layton when I was a DJ at CKLN FM in Toronto. It was a listener supported station and every year we'd do a fundraising drive both on the air and with various special events. When those events included an auction, Jack was invariably our auctioneer – a role he seemed to really relish and that I saw him perform many times for CKLN and for other organizations. And we'd encounter one another from time to time at various functions – though I wouldn't have thought that he knew who I was.

In the autumn after my Six String Nation project made its debut on Parliament Hill (on July 1st 2006), I was pretty much on the ropes financially (Bev Oda, once the Conservatives came to power, having reneged on some modest support promised by the previous Heritage minister) and what had until then been my annual pre-Christmas party took on elements of a Six String Nation fundraiser. I know that my publicist at the time had done a little bit of work to get the word out about the event but I really expected it mostly to be family and friends gathered at the Lula Lounge to play a little music, eat tequila jello and generally support me and the project. I didn't personally invite Jack but – as I said – I wouldn't really have expected him to know who I was.

All of sudden, there's Jack at my party at the Lula Lounge! And because the Leader of the NDP was at the Lula Lounge, so was CityTV. Jack came and spoke to me in his warm and personable way and I wondered why I had ever imagined he wouldn't have known me. Along with all the other guests, he came and posed for a series of portraits with Voyageur – the guitar at the center of the Six String Nation project. This guitar has been held by tens of thousands of people in every province and territory of Canada – though most people who take the opportunity aren't actually players; they simply want to connect with the history and stories of the country, with the Canadian musicians they know and love who've played this guitar and with the community of others who have had their portraits taken with it all across the country. This was a process and an impulse that Jack understood perfectly – with the added bonus that he also knew how to play the guitar quite well (one of the handful of politicians pictured with the guitar of whom that can be said to be true). Later in the evening, I turned a corner to find Jack talking eloquently to the CityTV camera about my project and its value to Canadian identity. He really got the project, all the points of view that it takes to really get it.

The following year, Peggy Nash and Gerald Keddy had jointly sponsored a Six String Nation photo session with Voyageur in a conference room in the South Block on Parliament Hill. Jack returned for another round of portraits (these ones with Peggy, Paul Dewar and Charlie Angus – who had played the guitar at an event in Cobalt already) and I'm quite sure that the presence of some of the other politicians who showed up for the session (Alan Tonks, Peter Mackay, Peter Milliken and others) was due to Jack's power of suggestion.

I do a presentation about my project at schools, conferences, festivals, corporate and public events. There's a section where I show a series of politicians' portraits – usually to a round of guffaws from the audience, after having seen a series of well-known musicians look a bit more natural holding a guitar. But I end the series on one of Jack taken at the Lula session – one where he's really engrossed in playing – and it always prompts a collective sigh from the audience, whether that audience is a group of students or a conference of tourism professionals or teachers or land surveyors or credit union managers. And more than once, it has prompted members of that audience to come up to me – often holding back tears – to tell me how much it meant to them to see Jack with the guitar. It matches how much it means to me that he recognized both me AND my guitar for what we had to offer.

PHOTO: DOUG NICHOLSON, COURTESY OF SIX STRING NATION

Bob, Bob Bobbling Along

Irene Mathyssen

In early 2008, Paul Hallet, a novelties entrepreneur, came to see me about what he said was an incredible fundraising opportunity. He said we could raise ten grand without any risk. I didn't know Paul and was a tad skeptical about this "incredible fundraising opportunity." After all, it's never easy to raise money and like so many New Democrats, we have always had our challenges in London-Fanshawe. I did agree to talk to him; talking never hurts. I expected to thank him and then go back to our tried and true, if ever challenging, fundraising methods.

Paul presented me with a Jack Layton bobble head; he believed they would sell like hotcakes, given Jack's national popularity. He also said that he had created and tried to sell the bobble heads of the other federal leaders: Stephen Harper, Michael Ignatieff, Gilles Duceppe and Elizabeth May but wasn't getting much interest from the other parties; and it was Jack's bobble head that looked most lifelike because Jack was so incredibly photogenic. Paul also said that for a mere $10,000, we could have a thousand of the bobble heads. My first reaction was that the investment of ten grand was out of the question; and as popular as Jack was, a thousand bobble heads was a great many to try and sell. This, however, was a time to consult and consult I did. I asked some staffers and volunteers to have a look at the bobble head. The more I looked at the tiny statue, the more I liked the idea and the more I thought it just might be possible to use them as a fundraiser. The response from everyone consulted was appreciative laughter and genuine interest in this crazy idea. We contacted other ridings to gauge interest and resources and decided to take the chance. After all, wasn't Jack the one who said we had to be willing to take risks and to get out in front of every opportunity? And didn't we have a country to save from those other leaders!

The first installment of the thousand bobble heads arrived and the fundraising committee wanted to present Jack with the first official Jack Layton bobble head doll. Jack had not seen the bobble heads and, in fact, was unaware of what we were up to. I took the bobble head to the next caucus meeting and announced that I had a gift for Jack and that caucus members were welcome to purchase replicas of the gift in any quantity they desired. When I unwrapped the bobble head, Jack stared for a moment, seemed unsure of how to react and then started to laugh. I guess it's one thing to be immortalized in song, poetry, bronze and legend, and quite another to see oneself captured as an eight inch bobble head doll. Jack did however take it in his trademark classy style. And soon we were both bobbling at each other. They caused quite a sensation.

Of course, there were the usual clever quips from caucus about Jack's new stature; some ordered a bobble head for their offices; others even ordered enough for their entire staff. I hoped we were off to a positive start for our venture, particularly when, despite the Commons prohibition rules, bobble heads started to occasionally appear on NDP desks in the House of Commons. Jack, of course, took it all in stride and was once seen to bobble his way through a particularly irritating answer from the PM. Their bobble heads are real, however. Ours are statuettes. You do have to have a sense of humour … .

The riding of Toronto-Danforth ordered a box of bobbles. Rumour has it that the little statues were seen in a number of businesses and store windows in the riding. People instinctively loved and admired Jack. The bobble head was tangible evidence of Jack's good humour and the trust and faith constituents had in Jack. They just wanted him around, even if in a miniature form with a propensity to wobble at the neck.

Since then, the bobble heads have graced the homes of supporters, been given as gifts; cherished by recipients and the many people who loved and admired Jack; and appeared at NDP Council meetings, Conventions and fundraisers of every description*. We long ago sold all of those 1,000 original bobble heads and have since sold many thousands more. The bobble head gave us the idea to set up a web store and we can now offer the little statue at *www.ndpstore.ca* to ridings across the country, maybe even to admirers around the world. After all, entertainers have their Emmies, Genies and Oscars, the Queen her stamps and currency, Prime Ministers their portraits and we have our Jack Layton bobble heads.

*There is now a Tommy Douglas bobble head available from The Douglas-Coldwell Foundation.

Jack Layton, the Personification of Grace and Courage

Anne Lagacé Dowson

On August 4, 2011, Anne Lagacé Dowson wrote a column about "pillow talk" with Jack in *Bloke Nation*. In 2008 she ran for the NDP in a by-election that was cancelled to become a general election, in Westmount-Ville-Marie.

There is a bitter standing joke to cover up the meanness and duplicity that swirls around so much of the underside of Canadian politics.

"If you want a friend in politics," goes the line, "get a dog." That was half true when I ran a double campaign for the NDP in 2008.

Except for Jack Layton. Now that his life is threatened, it's time to tell some stories out of school. Based on seeing him up close, Layton is every bit the "bon Jack" that we see and so many have taken to their hearts.

There was merriment at the beginning. I was negotiating an unpaid leave of absence from the CBC to jump into bed with Jack to run in a Westmount-Ville-Marie by-election. The bed part came in lawyer Julius Grey's Westmount home. While a fundraiser was unfolding in the living room, Jack and I headed for the only quiet space in the house – the master bedroom. I sat at the foot of the bed. He got comfortable at the head. I was accompanied by my guy Brian. Jack was aided by the party recruiter, the talented and funny Rebecca Blaikie.

To reassure me about the NDP, Jack's pillow talk was unexpected. He told me how, for party headquarters, they had bought a building in downtown Ottawa, which continued to appreciate rapidly in value, and by renting out some of the prime real estate, the party was able to get their headquarters virtually free of charge. He wanted to reassure me that the NDP was fiscally smart. As I listened to his spiel, what was seductive about Jack was the enthusiasm and energy that shimmered off him.

There was a powerful precedent to what the NDP was planning in Québec in the summer of 2008. After shopping himself around to various political parties, provincial Liberal Tom Mulcair had mysteriously switched to the federal NDP, after blowing up all his bridges with the Charest Liberals. Burned by the sponsorship scandal, the federal Liberals were as vulnerable as a piñata, even in the traditionally Liberal fortress of Outremont. The NDP ran a classic door-to-door campaign, and aided by Mulcair's black Irish political smarts, they captured Outremont.

Now the NDP sought a repeat of that Outremont by-election win, in Westmount-Ville-Marie. I signed on. Jack was at his best during the by-election. No standing on ceremony. The leader of the federal New Democratic Party did kilometres of killing door-to-door, up and down stairs in apartment buildings. He attended every event he could muster. He sent in senior members of his caucus and staff. Nothing was spared.

Nothing gets the measure of a politician better than the way they handle money. Pierre Trudeau was legendary for never carrying cash. In the harum-scarum of the campaign my bag was stolen. They took everything. Wallet, ID, cash. Jack got wind of it. He reached into his pocket, pulled out $60 saying, "Here, take this, and don't worry about it. Get something to eat. Take a taxi home. I get paid way too much, anyway."

Campaign polling showed we were passing Liberal Mark Garneau in that 2008 by-election. Then Harper dropped his hammer, turning the by-election into a general, completely disregarding his own fixed term rules. Up against the Liberal brand in English Montréal, we were done. But we still managed the best result the NDP ever scored in Westmount-Ville-Marie. Some say it was a harbinger of what was to come … .

Meanwhile, I search for words to describe Jack Layton. Hemingway defined courage as grace under pressure. So there is courage, in abundance. Once, Jack Kennedy was asked if he was happy. He said he was, quoting the Greeks: "Happiness is the full use of your powers along lines of excellence." So Jack must be happy too.

Finally, there is a light that emanates from Jack, a brightness burning. In the July 25 news conference announcing his illness, he said:

> "We *can* be a force for peace in the world …
> And we *will* work with Canadians to build the country of our
>   hopes
> Of our dreams
> Of our optimism
> Of our determination
> Of our values …
> Of our love."

May that brightness light up our country for many years to come.

Hang in there, Jack. I owe you 60 bucks.

In August 2012, Anne writes us:

"There was a buzz when we went door to door with the leader on a cool evening in NDG [Notre-Dame-de-Grâce] during the by-election of 2008. Layton took the stairs of the apartment buildings and houses two at a time joking and telling stories. Going up and down the treed streets, he told me that he realized that it wasn't enough to be against, you had to be *for* something. Not to just oppose, but to propose. That has stayed with me.

"Jack Layton was disarmingly honest and graceful. His life's work was proof that ideas and politics are a human project, not just numbers and messaging. That a positive approach and perseverance could win out. His most winsome and winning trait was his sense of humour about it all."

PHOTO THANKS TO LUBA GOY

Jack Layton and Luba Goy at the state dinner with Gov. Gen. Michaëlle Jean for Ukrainian President Viktor Yushenko.

Riverdale Share

Susan Baker

There is certainly no shortage of stories about Jack and his rise in the Canadian political scene, but it's the very human stories about his special relationship with people in general that have always touched me.

I run a non-profit organization that produces the annual Riverdale Share Concert in Toronto. Jack was one of our biggest supporters, always there to lend a hand and missing only one show in 19 years.

One of the most endearing relationships for me to witness was the warm friendship that grew between Jack and my long time cleaning lady, Lolita. Lolita is a strong and imposing, yet warm and loving Jamaican woman in her 60s who had been working with my family for many years. She held the fort at the Riverdale Share after-party and before the throngs of performers and volunteers arrived, she would take several slices of the spiral-cut honey-basted ham along with a nice selection of side dishes, lovingly wrap it all in foil and place it in a warm oven.

There was a huge demand for Jack's attention when he arrived. He'd get engaged in one conversation after another, sometimes disappear into an empty room to do a phone interview and then end up at the piano singing songs – usually tunes you recognized with lyrics changed to fit the current political climate. The buffet table would be well picked over by the time he got there. But he'd wander into the kitchen where Lolita would take his plate from the oven and he'd eat his dinner with her and ask about her family. She'd always say that none of her friends believed that Jack Layton was her friend and that one day she was going to have a picture taken with him to prove it.

This week we will produce our 20th Anniversary show and Jack's presence will be greatly missed. In tribute to Jack's memory, I asked Steven Page to perform Leonard Cohen's "Hallelujah" as he had done at Jack's funeral. Steven said he couldn't count the number of times he has been asked to sing the song since then but that he has always said no. That he felt it would somehow take away from the specialness of that day. But since Jack was so intrinsically involved with Riverdale Share, he decided to say yes.

Jack's daughter Sarah recalled that her Dad had always said that he couldn't wait for his granddaughter Beatrice to be old enough to come to Riverdale Share. This year will mark Beatrice and Solace's very first Riverdale Share.

Memories of Jack

Luba Goy

Memory of Jack at Riverdale Share Christmas

I live in Jack Layton's Toronto-Danforth riding and would often bump into him at various neighbourhood functions. He was a great supporter of our yearly community fundraising variety show, "Riverdale Share Christmas, " this year, celebrating its 20th and the first year without Jack.

Jack would attend the concerts and run up onto the stage and enthusiastically encourage the audience to be generous with their donations to help those less fortunate, even though times were tough for all.

I'm a shutterbug, and would stand in the wings taking photos of Jack firing up the audience. I'm so glad to have those pictures now.

One year the fellow who was to play Santa became sick and there was a mad scramble to replace him. Someone said that Jack often played Santa at various functions, and even had his own suit. The organizers were relieved when Jack accepted the gig – he was going to be there anyway, as usual. Jack's Santa looked super fit, despite the extra padding they stuffed into his suit! The audience had no idea that the man coming down the aisle to sit on Santa's Throne was Jack Layton, until they heard that distinctive voice. Their delight became quite obvious, with much applause and laughter. That year, the Happiest Santa Ever delighted the children at the annual concert. Jack's genuine enjoyment of life was always clear to all who met him.

However, it was an Election Year, and the committee received an irate letter from a Liberal concert goer, saying how dare they use Santa for Political Gain! When, in truth, they were simply relieved to have gotten someone to replace the sick Santa.

At the Performers and Volunteer Party afterward, Jack would come to sing carols with the improvised band of musicians, and carve the giant ham at the table laden with delicious food. It became a yearly ritual for us to wait for Jack to carve the ham before we started to eat. His participation somehow made the feast taste better!

I was surprised, but delighted to see Jack at the last concert, as we knew he was very ill. Always loyal to his riding and the community, Jack stayed after the concert as was his way – talking, listening, giving and receiving hugs from the many people who loved him dearly. There was no concert the Christmas after Jack's death.

Memory of Jack's message on my machine

I came home from an *Air Farce* rehearsal to a message from Jack on my answering machine. "Hi Luba, it's Jack Layton. I need some jokes for tomorrow night's Annual House of Commons Talent Night!!!" I called him back and left a message, "Jack, leave the jokes to *Air Farce*. Just do what you do best – play your guitar and be the great NDP leader!" I sort of felt badly, knowing I could have provided Jack with some comedy material, but thought, "Hey, why fix things, when they ain't broke?!" CBC News showed a clip of Jack singing and playing his guitar at the Talent Night on the Hill. We thought he was very funny, and used the clip on *Air Farce*!

Jack loved music and was a terrific piano player. At Marilyn Churley's* wedding reception, he jammed to jazz with the groom, Richard Barry, who was playing the saxophone. I hoped at the time that someone was making a recording of this wonderful duo. I took photos of Olivia lovingly watching her husband attacking the keyboard with joyful abandon, while the saxophone happily wailed next to him. They entertained the wedding guests for an hour! It was such a memorable and exciting part of the wedding celebration. Jack was a very special person, who had music in his soul, and was never afraid to play his heart out.

*Marilyn Churley represented the riding of Toronto-Danforth in the Legislative Assembly of Ontario from 1990 to 2005.

Memory of Jack on *Air Farce*

Jack was one of our most delightful guests – he came to the rehearsal with his effervescent exuberance, he knew his lines, was relaxed and had the best time and more fun than any of the performers. I took photos of him backstage watching the monitor while a sketch was in progress in front of our live audience. It was a political sketch in a log cabin in Alaska, involving Presidential hopeful John McCain (portrayed as a forgetful old fart) and his running mate, Sarah Palin.

Jack was laughing out loud, completely enjoying the outrageous humour. What amazed me at the time was how he could be so relaxed, when his sketch was the next one up?! I would have been looking at the script, getting into character, and having some pre-performance jitters. No butterflies or nervousness was evident with Jack Layton. When his sketch was up, Don went out as Jack, and Jack surprised and delighted the audience with his appearance. He nailed his lines, got great laughs, and at the end, the Two Jacks rode off the set on a bicycle built for two. When they took a bow, Don turned to Jack and said, "I can do something you can't!" "What's that?" asked Jack. Don ripped off his moustache – the audience roared with laughter. But that night, no one laughed harder than Jack!

The Two Jacks

Don Ferguson

My best Jack memory is the time he appeared as himself on one of our final *Air Farce* shows. I was playing Jack, one of several politicians it was my job to impersonate – what a great job, everyone should have as much fun at work as I did – and the setting was Parliament Hill, with Jack answering questions from a group of off-camera reporters. One of them asked for an explanation of NDP economic policy. Naturally I couldn't help, as NDP economic policy has always been more opaque than the Vatican's method of electing a new pope, so in my Jack character I called offstage for expert help – and the real Jack wheeled in on a tandem bicycle to huge applause from our surprised studio audience.

The routine went brilliantly, Jack's timing was bang on, his delivery confident, and he got every laugh there was to be had in the script. When the sketch was over, we bantered a little bit in front of the audience and then I told him there was something I could do that he couldn't. "What's that?" he asked. My response was to grab my moustache and tear it off my face. "Your turn," I said, and the audience roared, as did Jack. It was one of the few times he was even momentarily speechless. I still have the moustache; it sits in its own tiny plastic make-up box in my office.

A second memory is far less dramatic and shows another side of Jack. A couple of years after the *Air Farce* series ended, we ran into each other at a Breast Cancer fundraiser. I mentioned to him that I'd hung on to my Jack Layton tie, the one I always wore as part of my Jack Layton costume, and asked if he'd like to have it, perhaps as something that could be auctioned at an NDP event. "Tell you what, Don," he said without missing a beat, "you keep it for a fundraiser that you're doing, call me when it happens and I'll come by and help *you* auction it off." I don't know whether Jack had to be careful because of some obscure political fund-raising rule or if he instantly realized that appearing at a non-NDP fundraiser would be more useful to him politically than appearing before a gathering of the faithful, or if he knew that no NDPer would ever pay more than $2.00 for a necktie no matter what its provenance. In any event, I kept the tie and that was the last time I saw him alive. I still have it, but have never had the heart to auction it.

PHOTO: LUBA GOY

Jack and Don Ferguson on Air Farce.

"Great Taste!"

Nancy Loucks-McSloy

It was a beautiful sunny day in November, 2010. In addition to the great weather it was a very special day for me. Jack Layton was coming to my home. Jack was coming to visit as he wanted to talk to people in the area about the impact the HST was having on families. I felt so honoured. To me Jack Layton was real: he put the people of Canada first and he was a great leader.

My husband and grandson were raking leaves and cleaning up the front yard. Young Matthew came in the house and said, "I am going to have a quick shower and get changed before Mr. Layton arrives." Shower and change he did! Just as the car pulled up, Matthew came out of his room. I looked at him and for a minute mortification set in. He had changed into a black t-shirt with a huge marijuana leaf on the front and a picture of Peter Tosh embedded in the leaf. I thought of sending him to his room, but when a child is eighteen years old, grounding probably would not work. So rather than having a battle of wits I quickly decided to suck it up and deal with it.

Within a minute or two introductions were being made. What happened next reinforced to me what a great and real person Jack Layton was. He walked over to Matthew, shook his hand, patted him on the back and said, "Great taste in music, Matt." The next several minutes of the visit were spent with Jack and my grandson talking about music legends such as Peter Tosh, Bob Marley and so on. It was a great visit. We sat around the dining room table for about an hour. Talked about living in an old house, talked about our aquarium and fish … I will never forget that day, nor will Matthew! After the visit, Matthew and Jack corresponded several times by email. Matthew said several times, "You know I am going to be able to tell my friends at some point that the best Prime Minister in history visited me."

PHOTO: SIMON BELL

Svend Robinson, Jack and Olivia in Gay Pride Parade, Toronto.

How often Jack and Olivia were seen on their tandem bicycle on the streets of Toronto – a good metaphor for their ongoing work together.

"Do what needs to be done and do it harder."

Olivia Chow

This piece is excerpted from an interview with NDP MP Olivia Chow about Jack. It aired on August 28, 2012, and is archived on *www.chrwradio.com/talk/gatheringvoices*. How poignant and appropriate that Olivia so often refers to Jack in the present tense. His spirit lives! Throughout this book, many folks remark on how close a listener Jack was. When I asked how she had influenced Jack, Olivia replied: "I think he learned to ask questions a lot and he listened more." So we have Olivia to thank for his attentiveness!

Doris Layton reminded me to ask Olivia about her own art. She wrote: "Forgot to mention an obvious detail – He Married an ARTIST – OLIVIA."

Penn Kemp: Hello, this is Penn Kemp for Gathering Voices. I am thrilled to introduce Olivia Chow to you, not that she needs introduction. She is the MP for Trinity-Spadina in Toronto. She is well-known in her own right and she is also the widow of Jack Layton: it is in that respect that I am interviewing her. Welcome, Olivia!

Olivia Chow: Hello, Penn.

PK: I wanted to know how you two met …

OC: Ah! We met fundraising in an auction for a local Toronto hospital, Mount Sinai.

PK: And you got married on Toronto Island?

OC: Mmm-hmm, a beautiful hot day in 1988. Lots of people and right by the waterfront. We had three separate parties that went on till very early hours the next day.

PK: The Islanders would love to celebrate that and celebrate you. The Islanders were great proponents of both you and Jack because you were both so supportive of Save Island Homes, ongoing.

OC: Islanders are a very loving and caring group of residents, very much part of a community and they support each other. Creativity is right in the heart of the Island community. It is almost like a second home for Jack and I because we spent a lot of holidays there. I was just there on the long weekend. I swim in their beaches. So, lots of fond memories for Jack and I over on Toronto Island.

PK: And just recently last December, the Islanders put out a book, with Bill Freeman, celebrating Jack.

OC: A labour of love that gives the history of the relationship with the Islanders, his political work, his fundraising work even to the extent of auctioning off his pants for the Island Public School auction. He would auction over a hundred items, hours trying to raise for the school kids. Lots of memories all captured in that beautiful book.

PK: My kids went to the Island school and they still live there now, as do my grandchildren.

OC: Ah, perfect!

PK: And arts … How are you an artist, Olivia?

OC: Oh … me? Jack is the artist. He's an amazing singer, plays guitar, plays piano and harmonica; loves the Blues and jazz, Beatles and Bach. He grew up listening to Chopin. Loves Chopin's piano pieces. I'm on the more visual arts side. He's more musical. I am a sculptor and painter.

PK: What kind of art do you have in your house?

OC: Very eclectic. Jack collected many Inuit sculptures. We would buy paintings from time to time. I have one piece of my relief on the wall and some Aboriginal work.

PK: How did he get into Inuit work?

OC: He was travelling in the North quite a bit. There would be stone carvings he would order and they would be sent to Toronto.

PK: And Aboriginal work in the same way?

OC: Yes.

PK: What is your relief?

OC: I have several. Hard to describe.

PK: You have to see it and we can't do that on the radio!

OC: Exactly.

PK: Has painting been helpful over this really difficult and very emotionally filled year? How has art helped you?

OC: I did a painting for a friend of mine that was very therapeutic and then I did a sculpture. That was also very helpful.

PK: Just to be able to get the feelings out onto the canvas or whatever medium...

OC: On clay. I was doing clay.

PK: Lovely. Did you find that it was a cathartic process?

OC: Very much so.

PK: How has the last year been for you? It must be very mixed.

OC: I was doing a lot of work on the political front, trying to push through the national transit strategy so we can have fast, reliable and more accessible transit, more funding for infrastructure. Also I'm doing some speaking engagements regarding cancer, palliative care, celebrating nurses – the amazing work they do, caring for other people. And I took some time for a holiday in a remote part of Canada, a northern river trip, a mountain river.

PK: Were you canoeing?

OC: Yes, I was. I continue to swim and run, that kind of thing.

PK: It was such an interesting decision that Jack and the family took to not reveal the nature of the second cancer that eventually killed him. Nancy Layton told me that it was so that people wouldn't find that particular kind of cancer ...

OC: Too scary. Yep, that's true.

PK: Is that the only reason?

OC: Absolutely.

PK: I found that his giving of his dying time to the Canadian people through the letter such an astonishing gift because I can't imagine a more private time than that.

OC: Well, I think it's important to leave behind some values that are eternal, whether hope, love or optimism. Those values are eternal and if we can live by them, then the world would be a better place.

PK: It sure would be. You seem to, like Jack, live love and optimism through the practical. You live your idealism through your step by step action. Has that always been the source of energy for you?

OC: Well, that's the only way, I think. If we believe in something, we should take action. If not, then that belief is empty.

PK: So it's in the action that it becomes real, becomes realized.

OC: That it translates.

PK: Is that your spiritual practice, would you say?

OC: We could call it spiritual; it could be called any number of things. I'm less interested in naming it than in seeing the impact it has.

PK: Exactly. Tell me about Jack in relationship with other cultures. How was he received, for example, in your family?

OC: Very well. My mom loves him, loved him.

PK: She certainly loved to cook for him.

OC: Yep, yep. She spoiled him!

PK: Well, he didn't get fat at all!

OC: That's because of all the exercise he did, all the bike riding.

PK: What role did exercise play in the balance that you and Jack seemed to achieve between work and play?

OC: Keeping your body in good shape means that you can work longer hours, be more energetic, so that's what we did.

PK: And it sharpens the mind as well, toning the body.

OC: Absolutely.

PK: Did Jack have a gift for languages? He certainly spoke French.

OC: He spoke some Cantonese. He could communicate. He could order a meal in Cantonese and auction in Chinese.

PK: So he knew the important things, like numbers and food.

OC: Once you learn how to say what you want to eat, I think it goes a long way.

PK: How did music communicate? I know your father was an opera singer. How did they communicate?

OC: Jack loved to play the piano. There were always songbooks in the house. Jack would be giving away the songbooks so there would be a singalong afterwards.

PK: *Rise Up Singing!*

OC: He ordered many boxes. It's absolutely precious to be able to sing together and to come together through songs.

PK: In my mind, music transcends. It goes beyond intellectual difference and it creates community the quickest way possible, perhaps.

OC: Yes, absolutely.

PK: Did you inherit singing from your father?

OC: No. Gosh, no. Nope, that stayed with my father.

PK: You have a lovely voice.

OC: I think you're being kind.

PK: Jack encouraged so many people, including myself, to move from being an artist for art's sake into political involvement and to take action for causes we believe in. That was extraordinary and I think you do the same. It's the way of effective action that makes the difference, doesn't it? You carry that conviction too.

OC: Artists are supposed to reflect the reality or to transform reality and to teach people how to see. In order to see, you have to feel what is happening around us. Artists are usually the most sensitive to the environment, whether it's people suffering or what is happening to society. Whether it's Goya or Käthe Kollwitz or any number of artists, they've expressed in different forms, either the yearning for peace or the brutality of war or injustice. Art and politics, I don't believe can be separated. If an artist is true to what he or she sees, the way that it comes out could be in Abstraction or the Dada movement or it could be Existentialism or Surrealism. That is a commentary of the times so, of course, it is political.

PK: Very much so. And it's a shifting and an opening of perception.

OC: Yes, I think that's important. When a culture changes, then we have political change.

PK: Right. Also, Canada is by definition a mosaic rather than a melting pot. I think that all the different cultures that Jack so valued, and you as well, add different voices and such different perceptions just through the language alone, each with a different world view.

OC: It opens up connections with others. Canadian culture is always evolving. We are unique in that there are so many different connections transforming each other – so the music and the art are influenced by where the forefathers or foremothers come from. It's a unique way of pulling together different aspects of different heritage and culture into a Canadian form, which is what makes Canadian art exciting and unique.

PK: The variety and the diversity. How did Cantonese as a language affect your own perception? Can you articulate that?

OC: No, because Cantonese is just a dialect of Chinese, more than a language itself. Chinese is pictorial so the word 'brightness' is the sun and the moon coming together. So it has pictures joining together to form words – that itself is a beautiful way to express. So calligraphy is an art form.

PK: It certainly is. What was your influence on Jack, do you think?

OC: Hmmm. I think he learned to ask questions a lot and he listened more. He learned how to white-water canoe which is why we were able to do a lot of the kayak and canoe trips in the wilderness.

PK: Would you like to tell the story of the eagle feather?

OC: Ah … He tells it a lot better than me. So you should take clips of him telling his eagle feather story. It's a beautiful story. You should hear it from the …

PK: … the horse's mouth?

OC: The horse's mouth! From people of the Aboriginal community about what Eagle stands for.

PK: What was his connection to the Aboriginal communities in Canada?

OC: He thought that the culture is really worth celebrating. He thought it was a complete injustice, the way the people lost in terms of their heritage and culture and what happened: the deep poverty and the cycle of poverty that was inflicted upon them. So he spent a lot of time visiting northern communities, visiting First Nations communities, understanding the despair that is settling in that caused all these young people to commit suicide. Which is why he spent a lot of time trying to push for a government that would treat the problem seriously and respect the First Nations culture and make sure that there is serious investment in education and all the aspects that need to be done. It takes political will. For him, this is almost the first duty of a government.

PK: Also to recognize their values … and the tradition which has almost been forgotten but is being relived and reborn.

OC: Of course, of course.

PK: His and your daily practice seems to be to consider policy decisions so that you get the abstract of what you want to do, the ideal, and then you put it into direct action.

OC: Mmm-hmm.

PK: What I admire most about both of you is that you stick by principles, no matter what, no matter whether they're popular or not. I'm remembering a time when you lived in a Toronto co-op that David Crombie set up as a mixed income setting. The press really misunderstood your living there. Would you like to tell that story, Olivia?

OC: Sure. Cooperative is really mixed income housing, where people, whether they have money or not, live together rather than in ghettoes and you wouldn't be able to tell what rent they paid. I don't think the public understood that. But some do. It's just that political opponents want to make a political point to say that it is all subsidized. Well, no, there are two types of housing, one subsidized, and one not. But that's neither here nor there: what we need as a nation is more affordable housing so that people don't spend all their salaries paying rent … or kids that keep on being evicted over and over again, having to change schools and as a result can't make any friends because they don't stay in the school long enough.

PK: They don't have the continuity.

OC: Mmm-hmm.

PK: How did Jack deal with that kind of misunderstanding of controversy, as in living in a mixed housing co-op, where noble intentions were misunderstood.

OC: One way of dealing with it is pushing even harder for affordable housing. The best way is to do what needs to be done and do it harder.

PK: It seems to me Jack lived privately as the same man of integrity all the way through. His public face was his private face. Would you add anything to that?

OC: What you see in public is what he is in private.

PK: He was a lot of fun and he accomplished so much in his life. I'm so grateful that you are continuing the work, Olivia.

OC: I want to invite you and others to post any comments you may have on a website called *www.dearjack.ca*. As you talked about, his last letter to Canadians talked about living life based on the values of Love, Hope and Optimism and together we can change the world. Since he wrote us a letter, perhaps we can write him a letter back to say what we have done to live by that spirit. Dear Jack, this is what I've done last year to make my neighbourhood a better place to be.

PK: Wonderful. And so necessary. Olivia, thank you so much for chatting with us today.

OC: Thank you for your time. Thank you for your interest. You take care ...

Life Choices and the Moral Compass

Wendy Valhoff

I am an American who came to Canada two and a half years ago largely because I became disenchanted with the political system in the U.S. The day that George Bush was elected as President for the second time, I applied for permanent residency. I had many reasons for coming here: Canada was a country that was not totally owned by corporations and dominated by the military industrial complex. It was not an empire and didn't want to be one. Canadians negotiated and reasoned rather than sending huge contingents of military all over the world. As a lesbian, my life choices would be respected here much more than in my native country. This was very important to me because at the time, not one national leader in the U.S. had stood up for equal gay, lesbian and transsexual rights. I just wanted to live my life with my partner of 29 years with equal civil rights and the respect afforded to heterosexuals. Canada had even legalized same sex marriage. Additionally, it was a country whose leaders understood the crisis of global warming. I felt freer every time I crossed the border.

Most of my Canadian friends were NDP members, and I recognized at once that the ideals of the NDP echoed my own. After landing, it took me a few months to become aware of Jack Layton. Bit by bit I started to hear about his policies and the stances that he took as NDP leader. As an American jaded by the political shenanigans in the U.S., I was initially cynical. I thought, "How could anyone get so far in the dirty business of politics and yet sound so truthful and so sincere?" I figured that he was just another clever political huckster. However, the more I listened to him, the better he sounded, and slowly, I started to believe that he really meant what he said. This gave me a great deal of hope and reinforced my decision to be a Canadian.

I was ecstatic when the NDP did so well in the last election, although I was extremely upset that the Conservatives ended up with a majority. I felt that with Jack at the forefront, the NDP had a chance of ousting the Conservatives in the next election, and just hoped that not too much damage would be done in the meantime. I noted that everyone I knew called the new minority leader Jack. It was like they knew him personally. Actually that wasn't too far from the mark. Many of my friends did know him personally, and if they didn't, they felt like they did. It seemed like he was incredibly accessible to everyone. Additionally, I saw that he stood for human rights, including mine as a lesbian who planned to, and did, get married in Canada.

Then last year while I was camping out in Vermont, a friend from Toronto came running up to me and cried tearfully, "Jack died, Jack died." I knew immediately that she was talking about Jack Layton, and I remember the sinking feeling that I had. Jack was the person who was going to take Canada back from Harper. He was the one who would be the next Prime Minister. He was the moral compass of the country.

In the days that followed, I realized even more acutely how much of a statesman Jack Layton really was. I was amazed at the sense of loss that everyone seemed to feel, including some of his political opponents. The grief was palpable. I realized that there wasn't one political figure in the United States that could even begin to afford so much respect. Jack was the real thing. He was a man who spoke the truth and backed it up with his actions. He stood for the highest human values, and was not afraid to buck the establishment. He was a man with real courage, someone who I could believe in, and now he was gone.

What eventually became clear to me was that I had left the U.S. and had immigrated to Canada because I thought that it was a land that reflected the values that Jack Layton had espoused. I never met him, but I too feel that I knew him. A charismatic leader such as Jack is a hard act to follow, but I have faith that his legacy will not be squandered and that the NDP will fulfill its promise. Nevertheless, as a new Canadian, I will mourn Jack's loss for many years to come.

Parallels

Nena Saus

In 1999, I came here from the Philippines with a working visa to work as a caregiver. At that time, immigration was not that strict. But now people who want to come to Canada find it difficult because of all the regulations that have been recently implemented. I would like to be able to bring over my daughter, a teacher, and my granddaughter, a registered nurse, but I cannot find employers who would sponsor them under the new rules. I know that Jack Layton would have helped to ease the restrictions so that more people could unite with family already here, and seek further opportunities for new lives in Canada.

I have not met nor talked to Jack Layton, just saw him on television. When I heard him speak, I could not help but compare him with our own beloved Ninoy Aquino in the Philippines. Both men were eloquent leaders of the Opposition. Both were articulate speakers with words flowing effortlessly from their lips; they never stammered nor paused to think of what next to say. They both were married to beautiful and powerful women, Olivia Chow and Corazon Aquino (herself part Chinese), who each carried on in politics when they were widowed and did very well for the masses. Both Jack's and Ninoy's fathers were prominent politicians and their sons are very active today in politics: the family tradition is ongoing: Ninoy's son is the President of the Philippines and Mike Layton is a Toronto councillor. Who knows, Jack's son might become Prime Minister!

Both Jack and Ninoy could have been great leaders of their own countries if fate did not intervene. Their lives were cut short: Jack's with an incurable disease. Ninoy was felled by bullets on a Manila tarmac upon coming home from exile to challenge Marcos, a long-time dictator, in an election. Jack died on August 22, 2011; Ninoy died August 21, 1983. So many people wanted to join the funerals for Jack and Ninoy because they were so well-loved. In both countries, the people were upset and crying and were roused to civic action. Our dreams of Ninoy becoming President or Jack becoming Prime Minister were doused when they died but our heroes are still in the people's minds. Their legacy lives on because of their sons and because of the people's trust and love for them.

Like Ninoy, Jack Layton represented hope, optimism and a good future for the country, especially for the poor. Both leaders worked hard for the rights of the poor. Jack could have helped many more Asians who wanted to come to Canada, seeking greener pastures … or maybe, like me, just wanting to see snow! Asians were close to his heart – indeed, he married one. I am very proud to be both Filipino and Canadian.

The Evolution of a Political Activist

Jennifer White

I have long been a supporter of the New Democratic Party. My family of origin suspects I was dropped on my head as a child, since they all lean to the political right. But if the story is true, it knocked some good sense into me. I have always had an unswerving sense of fair play and detested any hint of intimidation and bullying. For me, the NDP values are in line with that sense of equality and compassion.

For many years, I had been inching my way into the political scene by helping out in a marginal way on election campaigns, dropping literature in people's mail boxes. In the 2006 Election, I caught wind of Jack's visit to our riding, so I decided I would bring along a gift as my way of showing support.

I make my living as a full-time Canadian musician, specifically composing for and performing on the Celtic harp. In the instrument's early days, its players were known as harpers. It irked me that Jack's right-wing political rival had the last name Harper.

I autographed my CD, and my partner, percussionist Robert McMaster, designed a poster to go along with it. We put both in Jack's hands in the crush of that campaign stop and it brought a smile to his face. He said that while he was sure the music on the CD would be lovely, it was the accompanying poster that made his day. It read, "This Harper supports Jack Layton and the NDP."

I continued my marginal involvement with campaigns and the party in the interim. When I saw the momentum build to Jack and the NDP becoming the Official Opposition on May 2, 2011, after running a very positive campaign even while Jack was battling cancer, I figured it was time I stepped a little more into the hub of activities. I took out a membership. With Jack's death on the 22nd of August that year, and his letter about love, hope and optimism, I decided I would become more fully involved in the party. I signed on for office work with the fall of 2011 provincial campaign in London West.

My organizational skills got some notice and I was roped into the position of Secretary for the London West NDP Riding Association ... I've moved from marginal involvement onto the executive of both the local riding association and the provincial council in a very short time.

I certainly would not have predicted it, given my previous proclivity for skirting around the margins of most political activities. But I can sense Jack's spirit of optimism there, lending support, encouraging me on. I know, on some level, Jack's got my back. And around me has gathered a similarly optimistic group of fellow activists.

What sticks with me now, in my more central involvement with shaping and implementing Jack's vision and the evolving vision of the NDP membership, is Jack's direction to never turn down an opportunity to serve. And, of course, his good-natured, people-centred and fun-loving way of putting "party" back into politics.

Up and At 'Em, for Jack

Penn Kemp

When Jack asked me to write him a hip poem in March, 2011, this is what I came up with.

Who is always hip!

Hip enough to lean left,
very left of centre and
perfectly well balanced.

Hip enough to call down
injustice when he sees it.

Hip enough to calm down
doubt and call out for all

those whose voices are
silenced in the Harper din

minority. Hip enough to
know exactly when the next
election is called for.

Hip to the latest outrage
fraud too easily lent.

Hip enough to lead
opposition into power:

Our next Prime Minister
surely. In confidence.

When a hip poem is called for,
a hip poem responds,
comes out swinging.

Hip, Hip, Hooray!

March 6, 2011

From Nancy Layton's Blog on the 2011 Campaign Trail

Nancy Layton

At Jack's request, his sister Nancy travelled with him as Personal Assistant during both the 2008 and 2011 federal election campaigns. During the 2011 campaign, they worked out together for an hour a day. Having taught Physical Education for two decades, Nancy was well prepared to help with the physiotherapy that was essential after Jack's hip operation.

Saturday March 26.

It was a lovely sunny morning in Ottawa as I walked to the NDP headquarters with Jack's daughter Sarah (my goddaughter), her husband Hugh and their delightful daughter Beatrice. There were many young families as well as older generations at the launch, and once again I marveled at the respect that people have for Jack. There was lots of energy in the crowd and we all felt that "our guy" looks a lot better than Stephen standing by himself or Iggy with his little team marching out from the Parliament Buildings.

Wheels were up around 1:00 for Edmonton and it would appear that we will be well looked after on the plane. Lots of fresh fruit and veggies to snack on before a hot lunch en route. Many of the media are familiar from the last election although there are certainly new faces too. They were desperate to see Jack walk off the plane. They still wonder about his hip surgery, so it was decided to get it out of the way and he quite easily managed the stairs with the cameras snapping away. The rally in Edmonton was loud and enthusiastic with a good crowd. Back to the plane and now we are overnight in Vancouver. One change from last campaign is that I will tend to ride with Jack in the RCMP van rather than on the bus from the plane to hotels or events.

Sunday March 27.

I was all set to turn my eBook off and go to sleep but then I remembered that I hadn't written about our day. Waking up in Vancouver is always special with the coastal mountains covered in snow, apple blossoms and tulips blooming and the water shining in the early morning sun. Jack and I managed the morning routine for the first time and it seems to work if I get myself up and organized before making sure he is awake. A perk in this campaign is that I will likely have breakfast with him although I do enjoy getting to know the others on the tour, both staff and media, at meal times.

The morning rally was in Surrey and I gather Harper followed us to that area later in the day. Again there was an enthusiastic crowd and Jack also had his first scrum where the traveling media and locals get to ask questions. I sometimes feel sorry for the local press because the scrums are dominated by the national people who usually have more experience in this setting or just shout out their questions more loudly. There was an afternoon stroll at a small strip mall for the candidate trying to unseat Dona Cadman. I gather there is a real possibility.

Wheels up and off to Regina for overnight. Jack and I watched the Junos with a short photo op for the national CTV reporter. Tomorrow we will have a morning event here then bus to Moose Jaw for a visit before bussing back to the airport – next stop Hamilton. Jack seems to be feeling better by the day as he recovers from the hip surgery. We had time before supper for a good exercise/physio session and I know that made him feel good too. And so to bed ...

Blog 5.

This will be a short one as it is after midnight and I just set my alarm for 6:00 a.m. We awoke in Regina and had a morning rally. Again there was a good turnout with lots of applause and cheers. In fact, Jack had them finishing his sentences at one point, which was fun. Afterwards there was a fairly long scrum. Rosemary Barton from CBC tweeted that Jack stood for a "looping" scrum without his crutch. She was impressed as the media still wonder about his health. It was back to the hotel where Jack was able to do all his physio/exercise and have some lunch before we drove to Moose Jaw to visit the campaign office of a really impressive candidate, a young lawyer from the community. It was very windy and the roads were rather dicey in spots but our RCMP driver and the bus driver were obviously used to the conditions. Wheels up and it was off to Hamilton where we are spending the night. Jack feels that Harper is looking strong so it will be a battle to prevent a majority let alone remove him from power. Until tomorrow, oops I mean today ... Goodnight.

Blog 7, Toronto, Wednesday March 30.

It is a real treat to wake up knowing that one does not have to have all the bags packed and put on the bus before breakfast! Also nice to have Olivia here to spend time with Jack - good for his psyche and mine! Jack was delighted with the tenor of all three of today's events: a custom kitchen cabinet (and more) manufacturing plant employing about 100, a robotics company that I believe is involved in things like the Canadarm, and then the first significant Toronto rally. Just to make a good day even better, we had a session with his exercise therapist who was impressed with Jack's recovery from hip surgery and even gave the go ahead for him to start some aerobic work on a recumbent bicycle or elliptical machine. Jack was thrilled! . . .

We finished the day with a visit from Jack's granddaughter Beatrice along with her mummy and daddy. She does know how to light up a room! So tomorrow will still likely see lots of questions about the debates, candidates who flip and who knows what, since we will be in Québec. And so to bed with wheels up in Toronto at 8:00 a.m. for Montréal – it will be an early alarm!

Blog 8, Thursday March 31.

There is nothing quite like flying into Montréal on a sunny morning. Jack and I could see Hudson, our childhood home, in the distance on the shores of Lake of Two Mountains. The major policy statement was done at the old Angus yards that have been redeveloped into an industrial park with the buildings as ecologically friendly as possible. Jack had a number of local media interviews and had plenty of time for his first real "workout" since his hip surgery. He is almost ready to switch from the forearm crutch to a cane. Before we left for Sudbury, Jack did a taping on the very popular French Radio-Canada show, *Tout le monde en parle*. It will air Sunday night and usually has an audience of more than 1.5 million. ...

Blog 9.

April Fool's ... This might be shorter than usual since Jack has once again taken over my iPad. It has been an interesting day. The morning announcement presented the NDP policies on health care. It was done in a small hall in a student residence at Laurentian University. There was no public to speak of, just the media so the atmosphere was flat. In fact there were several questions during the scrum about the slow pace. The p.m. town hall meeting was a different story and boosted everyone's spirits. There was a good crowd and they interacted with Jack throughout. Off to Halifax. We have confirmed that the plane will be able to land and not having to detour because of the weather. Hopefully the tour will find sunny spots for us next week ...

Blog 16, Saskatoon, Friday April 8.

Once again I am blown away by the beauty of our country. The view when I woke up this morning was of Victoria's harbour with the morning sun reflecting off the still waters. The policy statement on ship-building and defense announcement was done at Fort Rodd Hill National Historic Site with Jack standing near the shore and a ship-building yard across the water.

The challenge continues to be getting noticed by the national media. As you likely have noticed, the focus has been on scandals involving candidates and the negative side of each party, its leader or its policy. Polls also seem to monopolize discussion. The planning team (people both in Ottawa and on the tour) focus on trying to get the NDP message out and certainly the focus has been on a leader you can trust and the need to fix Ottawa by electing a government that will work with the other MPs. ...

Jack and I do talk to our Mum every day, something all three of us look forward to, and she is following the campaign on her computer, which is fun.

The flight from Victoria to Kamloops took us over the coastal mountains covered in snow, again breathtaking. The town hall event was great – an energetic crowd, good questions and Jack having fun.

Blog 18, Toronto (o/n Ottawa), Sunday April 10.

It is mid-afternoon and Jack is to do a set of TV ads for use in the remaining weeks of the campaign. I am sitting in a room upstairs from the studio itself. A group of four are preparing/editing the script, discussing both the text and the delivery. When they have agreement, it is sent to the teleprompter. At the same time, several others are deciding what he will wear. I only found out yesterday that this was to happen and having been on the road for a week, my supply of clean shirts is limited but it seems as if there is a suitable one. Not like last campaign, when I had to be driven to Jack's by the RCMP and pick up any and all shirts there!

Yesterday's afternoon event in La Ronge was special. It is a community of about 5000, many of them members of the Cree Nation. The candidate seems like just the kind of man we should have in the House of Commons – a long involvement in aboriginal affairs, a community activist, a lay

Anglican minister and, at the end of the event, he demonstrated his musical talents as a guitarist with a great voice. I chatted with a number of those present, including a woman who had lived there for more than 60 years. She said that Jack was the first federal party leader since Diefenbaker to visit and, of course, he was from northern Saskatchewan!

Blog 21, Charlottetown (o/n St. John's), Friday April 15.

A sunny but rather chilly morning in Montréal as Habs fans are still talking about the game. Jack's picture was front page and above the fold in *Le devoir* wearing his hockey sweater and raising a stein of beer.

The tour visited the Jean Talon Market with our first stop a Premier Moisson bakery and all kinds of Easter chocolate. Don't tell Bea but Grandpa Jack might have a surprise for her (provided I make sure it doesn't break into pieces before we are next in Toronto). The whole gang then walked a couple of blocks to the closest Metro station. It was rather funny to have one of the camera guys saying that Jack was walking too fast!

Wheels up to Charlottetown, which is hosting the Eastern Canada Music Awards, a great celebration and an even greater party. Jack was asked to introduce a group called In Flight Safety. Then it was time to bundle up for an outdoor announcement. Did I mention it was even colder here than in Montréal? We drove out to Seven Mile Bay, which offers the most scenic view of Confederation Bridge according to our local RCMP. The announcement was about green energy with some specific projects that are needed in the Maritime Provinces. None of us have packed for winter! Fortunately Jack has long johns and a Gortex jacket so he seemed to be okay.

No room in the RCMP van for me as Peter Mansbridge joined us in Montréal. However, I am supposed to join Mansbridge, Jack and a couple of our senior staff for dinner as he gets background for the feature he will be doing. So, brothers Rob and Dave, do I tell all? Mum, just kidding! Off to St. John's after supper.

Blog 22, Halifax, Saturday April 16.

Many on the tour went out last night in St. John's and were "screeched." For the uninitiated this involves singing, repeating several inane phrases, downing a shot of screech and kissing a dead fish! A Newfie tradition like no other. This morning we strolled along Water St. and stopped in at a couple of shops. A family-owned bicycle store where Jack talked bikes with the son while his father looked on. A music store that specialized in fiddles, squeeze boxes and mandolins. Fortunately, Jack decided to stay small and bought a mouth organ which does fit into my knapsack. We finished up at a bakery/café, always a treat. With a little time to kill before the rally, Jack and I drove up to Signal Hill with our RCMP detail.

The rally was special. Jack Harris, the NDP incumbent, said that he thought it was the best turnout ever for a political rally in the province with over 600 cheering, dancing and having a good time. Coverage may focus on one dissident who kept interrupting Jack by yelling. Finally, he stopped and rather politely asked her to let him speak and he would speak with her afterwards. It worked. The crowd applauded and he did, in fact, take the time to meet with her for about 5 minutes. So unlike some other leader who will go unmentioned, the NDP do invite anyone and everyone to attend their events.

Before leaving the city, Jack had a further interview with Peter Mansbridge. Watch *The National* on Monday night. For some reason it was on a dock in the harbour amongst the fishing boats. It looked rather contrived to those of us watching and it was cold. It will be interesting to see what clips they use and what approach they take towards Jack and the NDP campaign. Wheels up to Halifax where we arrived in time to watch Les Canadiens win again!

Blog 23, 15 days to E-day! Halifax o/n Québec City, Sunday April 17.

A rather dreary day spent in Halifax but it didn't dampen the enthusiasm of the NDPers who came to say hello to Jack. Off to the Farmers' Market next. Cafés and markets are becoming regular photo ops and people greetings. Jack did a scrum at the end of his stroll through the market and then we went off for an interview with Craig Oliver, who hosts CTV's *Question Period*. Later, everyone drove down to Bridgewater, about 90 minutes away. Forty were expected to show up for a bit of a pep talk and meet and greet at the candidate's office. The RCMP said it was more like 140!

A postscript to yesterday's blog. Shaun Majumder of *This Hour Has 22 Minutes* had bumped into us at our hotel in St. John's and wanted to talk to Jack about a project he is doing in his NFLD hometown. He was invited onto the plane to chat with Jack before the bus with media and staff arrived and stayed on as they loaded. The crew had planned to "screech" the media and it was decided to have Shaun do it. Very funny and enjoyed by all!

Blog 24, Toronto, Monday April 18.

A look-back on yesterday as we spent the morning in Québec City before flying up to Val d'Or for a rally and meet and greet. All the talk both on our bus and in the national media is about the polls and the upswing in support for the NDP especially in Québec. It certainly has put a spring in everyone's step, including Jack's! He enjoyed finishing the afternoon scrum by telling the reporters that he was off to have a workout at a local gym called Momentum. …

Blog 25. London, Tuesday April 19.

The tour had to be up early this morning in order to be at CTV for a live appearance on *Canada AM* with Seamus and Beverly. The interview was low key with some serious questions but a chance for Jack to relax and be himself. It was very funny when they showed a clip of him from about 25 years ago as a young Toronto city councillor with longer, darker and more hair. As he finished it was time for the weather and Jack said that a lifelong wish had been to do a weather forecast. As we started to prepare for a media scrum, they invited Jack to come back on and he did the forecast - very funny and you could tell that he was having a blast.

A drive down to Welland where it is heart-breaking to see the number of plants that are closed down. Talking to some of the locals at the rally, there continue to be more closures as jobs get sent south to the US and Mexico as well as overseas. The rally was actually run like a town hall with Jack speaking for about 10 minutes and then answering questions. The first came from a younger woman who had made cookies with orange icing. Jack took a bite and then offered the rest of them to the crowd, suggesting that people break them in half so there would be more to share. Several of the questioners had really touching and sad stories as they asked Jack how he could help.

Blog 26, Toronto, Wednesday April 20.

This will be short as it is 1:30 a.m. on Thursday morning. We are settled into familiar digs at the Toronto Hyatt, four nights here! I have ironed several shirts and hung up all Jack's suits ready for Olivia to decide what he should wear tomorrow. It is nice to have her here at the hotel. She will do a few things with Jack while focusing on her own riding so I feel a little less pressure to get everything ready on time. And I know it makes a difference to Jack to have her with him.

A good day with a visit to a farm in Essex County where Jack announced the NDP platform specific to agriculture. The night before, the advance team noted that it would be rather muddy and purchased rubber boots for everyone. The boots were later donated to the local community center which was Jack's suggestion. I think the media had a bit of a chuckle as they wandered about in their "Wellies." Later we flew to Thunder Bay for a rally/town hall. The place was so full that they had to ask people to stay outside of the hall. One reporter tweeted that she had overheard someone complaining because there was no room in the parking lot!

A busy day for Jack tomorrow as he does a series of editorial boards. He says they are like comprehensive exams where over a dozen people fire questions at him. Unfortunately most of these are papers that do not support the NDP so they go after him.

Blog 27, Toronto, Thursday April 21.

It never pays to try something different. The tour was to have an early start so that Jack could go to Sun TV for an hour long interview. It was agreed that I didn't need to go as Olivia would be with him as well as the other regulars. But they got to the studio and realized that he had the wrong suit jacket! So off I went via cab to bring the proper jacket.

Nancy's husband, Joe Stairs, writes: I joined the tour mid afternoon. Nancy met me in the lobby of the Hyatt and brought me up to the penthouse suite which is Jack and Nancy's home for an unprecedented 4 nights in a row. The suite, with two bedrooms, is the size of our main floor at Toad Hall. I joined Nancy in the 3rd row seats of the RCMP SUV as we went to a very successful and energetic rally for the candidate in Brampton.

Illustrative of Jack's approach was a telephone interview done en route. When he was told the interview was with a blind communication group, he asked his chief of staff for the party's platform to be sent to a second BlackBerry that he could reference during the call. At one point he was asked about making voting accessible to the handicapped and he replied that they were very pro but that he did not have the specifics with him so he would get a staffer to call them back with details rather than get them wrong. Others would have blustered on.

Blog 28, Toronto, Friday April 22.

Joe continues: Nancy has temporarily deserted her position as bloggist, like she is allowed time off! The event today was a Catholic Good Friday parade in Little Italy. Jack has been a participant for many years but this year was special. I believe the count was four Jesuses, lots of Knights of Columbus, lots of other uniforms, floats and costumes for the stations of the cross and thousands of Italians and others (in Olivia's riding) cheering Olivia and Jack on as we walked about 2 km in about an hour and a quarter. The evening was spent in the hotel suite with Jack and Olivia, Sarah, Bea & Hugh, Mike & Brett and Nancy and I. Wine from room service, Chinese food courtesy of Olivia and entertainment by Bea. *Joe Stairs*

p.s. from Nancy: Today felt almost normal! It's the Joe effect.

Blog 30, Saint John, Sunday April 24.

I started to prepare for the final week. There is no question that the momentum is in the NDP camp so the challenge is now to keep focused on the message and to not react to the attacks from the other parties. The main event of the day was a celebration of Khalsa, a Sikh celebration of spring. Hundreds of people celebrated with a parade that ended up at Queen's Park with speeches from dignitaries. First up from the federal politicians was Jason Kenney representing the PM, followed by Ignatieff. The crowds were subdued and there was little reaction. Then Jack was unbelievable. First, he could be heard and engaged the crowd. They cheered during his speech and for several minutes after he was done. He was then swarmed by both media and regular folks as he tried to make his way back to the RCMP vehicles. It must have taken 20 minutes to cover a couple of hundred yards! I had watched Iggy leave with little more than his handlers. It was remarkable.

After a brief stop in Ottawa, we are now in Saint John and I expect will cross much of the country in the next week. An event in the morning and a second in the late afternoon is the plan with selected media events in between will mean that our days will be long but the end is in sight. Hang on to your hats, this is going to be quite the ride!

Blog 31, Montréal, Monday April 25.

Driving from Ottawa down to Montréal after two very successful gatherings today. The first was in Saint John where there was a good-sized crowd for a morning rally down on the boardwalk. Jack then did some radio and TV interviews while the national media who travel with us filed their stories. The cabin crew had seafood chowder and lobster rolls for our lunch – delicious! The day finished with a great rally in Gatineau where there are two really good candidates running for the NDP, both women and both with a decent chance of taking their respective ridings. The mood is so positive right now and the challenge is to not get carried away.

Joe says the pundits are starting to suggest the NDP are on the move and the bump in the polls is not just a blip! I gather the fact that the message is focused on the positive rather than negative attacks is being well-received. Time will tell, I guess.

Blog 32, Winnipeg and Yellowknife, Tuesday & Wednesday April 26 & 27.

Montréal - Toronto - Winnipeg - Edmonton. Now it gets hectic! The plan will be three-fold: stay in the public eye through interviews, talk shows and rallies; hit as many ridings as possible; and don't do anything stupid.

The polls are amazing and now somewhat reassuring as almost all show the NDP continuing to go up rather than having peaked. For those who don't want a Harper majority, the drop in their support according to some polls is good news. But polls are polls not votes so everyone involved knows there is still work to be done and no reason to be over-confident.

In Montréal, Jack did the rounds including CTV local and national. Same thing in Toronto before a town hall that included questions via twitter, phone and in person. The room was filled to overflowing and people had to be turned away. While the media filed, Jack and I watched the Habs score their first goal. We missed the Boston goal because he had switched to a news channel while I went to a scheduling meeting! I regained control of the remote just in time for the second goal, lucky for Jack. After the second period we asked the RCMP to get us to the airport fast as we thought we could watch the rest of the game in the lounge. It was closed! So we listened to the final few minutes on the radio. It turns out that some of the media were watching on the bus. Darn, we missed it. Now how are we going to make sure we don't miss a thing tonight... The Habs have won the 3 games that we were able to watch but there is a 5:30 MTN rally in Edmonton. I might just grab his iPad and watch live streaming while he gives his speech. After all I do have my priorities!

It was a late night arrival into Winnipeg and an early start this morning for a breakfast rally. Again a great crowd was delighted to see and hear Jack. Now we are driving from the airport into Edmonton for a BBQ rally. It will be another late night, as we will be flying to Yellowknife. After the morning there it will be on to Saskatoon. Friday Kamloops, whistle stops on Vancouver Island and overnight in Vancouver. Saturday a huge rally in

Vancouver then back to Montréal. Sunday, after a rally, we will take a bus back to Toronto with lots of stops along the way. Anyone feeling tired?

It is time for spring to be sprung for everyone. Jack sure has a spring in his step – he was whistling all morning! There. I didn't think I was going to be inspired.

Blog 33, Saskatoon, Thursday April 28.

The routine when we land is that Jack, Anne McGrath (his Chief of Staff in regular life and the Political Director on the plane during the campaign), and I deplane with the two RCMP officers and get into a six-seat SUV and drive to the hotel. I make sure our two knapsacks, the bag with our workout clothes and Jack's overnight bag come with us, often with the help of the RCMP who invariably grab them before I can myself. When we get to the hotel, Jack is able to get settled for the night while I wait for the bus to arrive carrying the staff and media and the luggage stowed in the belly of the plane.

Last night it was after midnight local time when we landed in Yellowknife. When I went down to meet the bus, I also caught a glimpse of the northern lights. We woke up to a beautiful but crisp sunny morning, -9°C and Great Slave Lake is still very frozen. The first event was a meet and greet at the campaign office of Dennis Bevington, the incumbent. He is in a tough battle primarily because of the gun registry vote. While Jack decided not to "whip" his caucus, thus allowing each MP to vote as he or she chose, a number of them have had to face the consequences and Dennis is one of those. It would be unfortunate should he not be reelected as he has championed a number of causes for the North and First Nations.

The second event in Yellowknife was at one of the most picturesque schools that I have ever been in. Jack engaged in a Q & A with a couple hundred students. While they were shy to begin with he was soon able to get them engaged in part because he turned the tables on them and asked them for solutions. As a former teacher, I was impressed with the students as they were attentive (no fidgeting) and posed some good questions. It was obvious that Jack enjoyed the encounter and I expect would have preferred to spend longer with them rather than to have to deal with the national media in the post-event scrum.

The reporters have got their daggers out now as they try to catch Jack and the NDP out on anything … At one point the scrum got so unruly that Jack got a little sharp with them, suggesting they were acting like the

Conservatives during Question Period, and telling them that he would answer all their questions provided they gave him the chance to do so. They did settle down a little but we also know they are being challenged by their news desks to get "a story." Hard to compete with the Royal Wedding and the playoffs.

A flight down to Saskatoon and then perhaps the biggest rally yet with perhaps as many as 2000 for a rally/BBQ. Jack is now mobbed wherever he goes and it usually takes about twenty minutes for him to wade through the crowds. They want to get their picture taken with him, have him autograph a sign, present him with a gift or letter (today these included a Saskatchewan Métis sash, an Orange Crush bottle, a bumper sticker and several letters and envelopes). And there are always those with difficult stories who think he can help. Unfortunately, many involve child custody cases. So another good day and we know that the election campaign will play second fiddle to the wedding tomorrow morning. Just as well, as we leave the hotel at 6:30 to fly to Kamloops.

Blog 34, Vancouver, Friday April 29.

… The day started with a very early flight from Saskatoon to Kamloops, so early we had breakfast on the plane. The morning rally was just as exuberant as those of recent days and everyone wants to shake his hand or get their picture taken with him. Sandra Clifford is the one tasked with leading him through the crowds with the help of the RCMP – only problem is that she is about 5 feet tall!

Jack and I did our workout while the media filed. It was just after that when Anne McGrath, Jack's Chief of Staff and the Tour's Political Director, broke the news to him that there might be a nasty story coming out. I could tell he was upset and disappointed that someone would smear him in this way but he seemed to take a deep breath and, of course, Olivia gives him strength.

Off to Comox on Vancouver Island where the story broke. Olivia put out a statement and it was decided that Jack would make a statement but take no questions before the event. The rally was fantastic and we slipped out the back way to keep the media away. It was a short flight to Vancouver to end a long and tumultuous day.

Vancouver, Saturday April 30. The final big rally is about to happen and we are looking out a 2nd floor window as people are lined up around the block to come into the theatre. Probably more than 1,000 at least.

The scrum after will tell the tale, but having spoken with a few of the reporters I am not sure how far they will go with the *Sun* story. They said it wasn't where they wanted to go. They also told me that the *Sun* reporter with us was almost in tears and apologized even though she had nothing to do with the story. Off we go for the final 36 hours of the campaign.

Blog 35, Toronto, Sunday April 30.

Talk about a surge! The rally in Vancouver had over 2,000 people, and today in Kingston, 500 showed up at a candidate's office to hear Jack say a few words – 75 had been expected. The tour had its last official flight on "Hipster Air. If it's broke, Jack will fix it." The media had written new lyrics to "Let It Be" – the chorus, of course, being "NDP." So we are almost done and it has been a wild ride. Now it is in the hands of Canadians. Thanks for keeping in touch during the past six weeks. Now just do me one last favour – vote! I am glad to have been able to help Jack get through the campaign in good health.

We are grateful to Nancy for keeping Jack well throughout both campaigns! And for such an insightful view into the dailies of a political campaign.

Election as Artwork: Before & After

Carolyn Hoople Creed

for Jack Layton

I. Topple
As with those who posted/ participated in
the domino game, you will cause watchers
to laugh, exclaim, marvel, all because
     NDP believers
    put hands on ballots,
      placed pens on paper,
      pushed, pushed
        sheets into slots:
pushed over stodge-clog boondoggle buck-lovers'
       dear-bought towers of power.

II. What Toppled
The towers of dominoes, performance art in the making,
created by college students, appeared to me to be
the brick walls that Layton faced in his last election,
symbolic of an attitude that not only other parties
but also his own (on figurative terms) might hold:

   Formidably dark, possibly
   solid, the walls turned out
   to exert the flimsy presence
   of smoke columns before
   a single energetic sneeze.

When it toppled, the domino artwork underwent
spectacular collapse, as did the challenge to Layton
in riding after riding after riding: I was quite right
to foresee opponents' political tumbles – if only
those were the only deaths to follow the analogy,
such a prodigy of power might have wowed the world.

Embracing the Nation, Jack Layton

Katerina Fretwell

Jumping Jacks and Leaping Lizards! For me, Councillor Jack was the Jack Russell terrier who would leap up indignantly and so vehemently that he seemed to be propelled into the air. Poet Katerina Fretwell shape-shifted this image into her own in the following piece.

Once a savvy toy poodle or pugnacious pit-bull, your initial rabid activism mirrored my bone-worrying political poetry. You cast off the hunter's stance; my poems shed their junkyard dog smell. No longer the yippy pooch nipping at wolverine Harper's heels or the pugilist pit-bull gnawing at his secret agendas, sacred guns, big biz prisons, corporate impunity, *robo-calls*, helicopter joyrides and F-35 billion dollar boondoggles. Cannier strategies.

Jazzing the ivories, you knew that a people without the Arts is a people without Soul, that the Arts express our nation's very being. Late arriving at a reading where I was featured, I had no time to waylay you on that sidewalk in my first sighting, lining up our ducks and decoys.

Obedience school for sensitives, your national rise inspired my gentler poetry: engage brain first, quills second – that blessed cessation when All Seeing Spirit romps in, that Pavlovian pause when trained dogs read the ley lands, Question Period, a *Renga*, not a fox hunt.

Brandishing your cane like a pedigreed vaudevillian, you implored us not to hate but to hope, not to leer but to love, not to divide but to diversify. Into my heart you thumped, humanity's best friend. Greatest NDP win in history, PMO within your power:

Tommy Douglas's health for all, Stephen Lewis's Africa-care bred bone-deep into you.

Compassionate border collie awaiting death, your last homily suffused us with pride – long absent during our graceless fall at home and abroad – to be Canadian.

Imagine a planet where policy trumps personality, where issues not insults greyhound the airwaves, where justice not juggernaut prevails, where the two Lefts: Mainstream and Anarchic, pooch and make up.

Reunited, we embrace downsized workers, silenced poets and playwrights, straggling suburbanites in a far wider gaze, eagle-eyed yet puppy-melting, in power and channelling your thoroughbred Spirit, undefeated by cancer, always with us.

Jack Layton, Stephen Harper and the Language of Public Representation

John Magyar

John Magyar has an interest in legal language, linguistics, and how language conveys meaning. When we were discussing the language of inclusion one summer day over coffee, John offered to look at and compare the victory speeches Jack Layton and Stephen Harper gave to the party faithful on the night of the May 2, 2011 election. For me, Jack's ability to connect with people could be summarized in Martin Buber's notion of an "I-Thou" relationship.

Public speaking is one of the more important skills required to be a successful politician and lurking within the many choices one has about what to say and what words to use to say it, there are dragons. Meanwhile, politicians are public representatives. They must constantly make decisions about how to talk about "us" – the people they are elected to represent, when speaking in public. The public, however, is not a homogeneous group, but rather a heterogeneous collection of individuals; and the politicians themselves are individuals. Public speaking, for a public representative, is inherently problematic.

A young Rob Ford provided a rather crude example about how badly one can go wrong in the language of public representation. As a city councillor, he made a speech in council, expressing what he, no doubt, believed to be a compliment about the work ethic he noticed in some people of Asian heritage (and I'm being diplomatic here. Mr. Ford claimed to be talking about people who immigrated from China.): "Those people work like dogs," he said, arousing much public outrage. Mr. Ford's grand mistake, in this instance, was to speak of Asians as "them," thus conjuring an "us and them" division, which implicitly declared Asians to be not "us." (I will disregard the stereotyping of "them" which is offensive but not relevant to the issue at hand). In a city as diverse as Toronto, this is something a public figure must not do, and the same holds true for a diverse nation like Canada. In political jurisdictions like these, a public representative's language must be inclusive.

With this in mind, it is interesting to compare the speeches delivered by Jack Layton and Stephen Harper at the conclusion of the May 2, 2011, federal election. Both speeches were given at nearly the same time, to their party supporters in the room and televised to the entire country, in the wake of outstanding electoral successes.

Structurally, the speeches were quite similar. They begin with a thank you and work through a number of common issues including praise for supporters, and how each party leader plans to deal with those who disagree with them when in office.

While structurally similar, there are some obvious differences. There is a difference with respect to the use of French, for example. Mr. Harper makes occasional brief statements in French, and speaks predominantly in English; whereas Mr. Layton recites all the substantive material in his speech in both languages. This is likely a reflection of each speaker's ability in French. Mr. Layton grew up fairly bi-lingual while Mr. Harper learned French later in life, and struggles with it to a certain degree.

With respect to the language of public representation, on the surface, both Layton and Harper appear to use a similar strategy to navigate the "I" versus "us" conundrum. Both alternate between talking in the first person singular, and the collective "we." Both use similar expressions like "my friends" when referring to the members of the audience. However, upon a deeper look, there are significant subtle differences to their linguistic choices that run through their speeches.

For example, after the initial "thank you very much," Mr. Harper begins by saying: "Belle soirée, what a great night." In contrast, Mr. Layton says "You are amazing" after the obligatory "thank you." A fair bit could be said about these different starting points. Certainly, Mr. Layton's statement is in keeping with his reputation as an inspirational figure. As well, by using the very direct, personal language of "me and you," the statement instantly engages the listener. Mr. Layton speaks to "you," which the listener instantly identifies as the self. This is the first word he utters, and it is the subject of the sentence: you. Although Mr. Harper is also addressing the listeners, they are presumed in his first statement. Ironically, he is expressing a similar sentiment. In effect, he is amazed by how great the night is. Yet, it comes across as less direct and less personal. It feels more like the language of "we" than the language of "you and I."

After his introductory comment, Mr. Harper employs the first-person language of "you and I" for the first two or three minutes of his speech to thank the various groups of people who contributed to the Conservative party's campaign. After that, he switches to the language of "we" and stays with that language for much of the remainder of his speech. "We," "us," "our government." This is how Stephen Harper speaks as public representative. He speaks for the Conservative party as a collective, and on behalf of Canadians, as our duly elected representative, as "we." This is an institutional "we." By using the first-person plural, Mr. Harper implicitly embraces the fiction that an individual truly represents a collective of individuals. This is certainly consistent with one of the Conservative party election mantras recited by Mr. Harper in his speech, which held that "unity of purpose" (as well as "hope" and "a strong Canada") were what inspired so many Canadians to vote conservative. This language emphasizes collective singularity. It conveys a comfort with the inherent authority of elected office, despite the heterogeneous nature of the "we."

In contrast, Mr. Layton resists the language of "we." He does occasionally rely upon the word; however, when speaking as a collective representative, Mr. Layton often chooses third person language instead. He speaks of "New Democrats" or "Canadians." For example, early in the speech, Mr. Layton said "in this campaign, New Democrats promised to get Ottawa working for you and your family." This was said in front of a room full of party loyalists, and it stands in very sharp contrast to the Harper "we." Within this choice is the implication that Mr. Layton is uncomfortable with the fiction that one person can represent many. He does not presume to speak directly on behalf of the party. His linguistic choice acknowledges that one person will always be only one person, despite being elected to represent a collection of people; and, that "diversity" rather than "unity of purpose" is what underpins an electoral victory. As with Mr. Harper's choice, Mr. Layton's choice is consistent with the NDP mantra that no Canadian should be left behind.

Ironically, Mr. Layton's third-person language is less direct and less personal than Mr. Harper's first-person plural language. Third person language comes across as rather distant and analytical. It lacks the immediacy and inclusiveness of "us." It also feels a little stilted and odd to refer to a group of people to which one belongs, as if it were a thing that is separate from one's self. It is a counterintuitive way of speaking. Yet there is an undertone of intellectual honesty to it – an inherent respect for the potential for one person to disregard the views of another in the collective process of democratic politics. It is a way of speaking that emphasizes unity through diversity rather than unity as a singularity.

Meanwhile, Mr. Layton does not stay with third person language for long stretches of his speech. Instead, he reverts to first-person language readily and often. It is the language he uses most often in his victory speech, and it is apparently the point-of-view with which he is most comfortable. Although he is up at the podium to figuratively represent "us," he is still himself. This is how he navigates the politician's linguistic dilemma of public representation – through honesty (at least in the context of this very narrow analysis).

There is need to state a caveat here. When analyzing political speeches one must keep in mind that these are carefully crafted works that might be written by someone else, and are most certainly vetted by many. The linguistic choices in a speech might not be those of the actual speaker. With this in mind, it is interesting that the choices are consistent with some of the principles that unite support for the respective Conservative and the NDP parties. There indeed might be larger social pressures at work underneath these choices. Regardless, this analysis should be understood as a comment on the public person and all that comes with it, rather than the private person. With this understanding in mind, there can be no doubt that both Mr. Harper and Mr. Layton are accomplished public speakers; however, Mr. Layton deserves praise for his linguistic honesty and linguistic respect for diversity. He was more than an inspirational speaker. He was a man who championed strength through diversity. This can be seen in his actions through the course of his life. It can also be found between the lines in his public speeches.

La fleur de lys

Alexandre T. Gingras

La Fête Nationale du Québec! June 24 ...

Take a look at the video on *http://www.youtube.com/watch?v=m7ENxGxOaKk&fea ture=youtube*, by Alexandre T. Gingras and edited for this book by him. Alexandre is Adjoint parlementaire / Parliamentary Assistant for Françoise Boivin, NDP Member of Parliament for Gatineau. Thanks to Alexandre, we can see the essential Québec NDP presence celebrated here on June 24, St-Jean-Baptiste day, and Jack so animated just two months before his death. How wonderful to see Jack dancing with the little girl who seemed to appear just for the occasion, and singing with the Québec caucus. After his speech, you can see Jack chatting with the youngster again, comparing their temporary tattoos. Lion, meet fleur de lys!

À la fin juin 2011, les députés néo-démocrates étaient retenus en Chambre afin de faire de l'obstruction parlementaire au projet de loi visant le retour au travail des employés de Postes Canada. Habituellement, la Chambre ajourne ses travaux pour l'été vers le 22 ou 23 juin, donnant ainsi la chance aux députés du Québec d'aller célébrer la Fête Nationale dans leurs circonscriptions. Toutefois, à cause de la stratégie d'obstruction, ceux-ci ont dû demeurer en Chambre jusqu'au 26 juin, si ma mémoire en bonne, question d'appuyer les travailleurs jusqu'au bout.

Toutefois, Jack, originaire du Québec, était bien conscient de l'importance de la Fête Nationale pour tous les Québécois. Après la vague orange du 2 mai 2011, il fallait absolument être là pour la province qui nous avait exprimé toute sa confiance.

Lors d'une courte période de repos dans l'antichambre aux Communes, Jack a demandé à Françoise Boivin, la députée néo-démocrate de Gatineau, si quelque chose était prévu dans sa circonscription pour la Fête Nationale. Françoise l'informa alors qu'une fête de quartier au Marché Notre-Dame devait avoir lieu vers midi, non loin du Parlement, et qu'elle devait aller y prononcer un discours patriotique si elle pouvait se libérer. Le Marché Notre-Dame se trouve quand un quartier moins favorisé de Gatineau, et sa direction chevronnée tente à chaque année de faire du marché public un pôle économique, social et culturel de plus en plus important. La célébration de la Fête Nationale est un véritable pilier de leur calendrier estival.

Je devais remplacer Françoise à l'évènement en question si elle était retenue en Chambre. Je me préparais donc à quitter mon domicile lorsqu'elle m'appela pour m'informer du changement de situation; elle serait présente et accompagnée par Jack Layton, Thomas Mulcair ainsi qu'une grande parti du caucus québécois. J'ai rapidement mobilisé ses amis sur Facebook ainsi que les médias. J'ai également informé les organisateurs de l'évènement, grandement surpris par l'ampleur de ce revirement. Lorsque je suis arrivé, les journalistes étaient déjà sur place. Jack et l'équipe du NPD sont arrivés peu de temps après et la magie fit sont œuvre. Le député Pierre Dionne Labelle avait apporté sa guitare et entonna des hymnes de Charlebois captivant les médias ainsi que les curieux se faisant de plus en plus nombreux. Par la suite, Françoise et Jack ont prononcé un discours patriotique, saluant l'importante contribution de la culture québécoise à la mosaïque canadienne, et appelant à être fier de notre différence et de la langue française en célébrant la Fête Nationale comme il se doit.

Tout au long de cette célébration, une petite fille s'est tenue près de Jack. Elle était âgée d'environ six ans, mais elle le reconnaissait. Elle est rapidement devenue la vedette de la journée. Elle a accueili le Chef de l'Opposition en dansant avec lui, puis ils sont passés à la table de maquillage; la petite fille s'est fait maquiller en lion, et Jack s'est fait dessiner une fleur de lys sur la main. Étant donné la chaleur intense de la journée, son tatouage improvisé perdit un peu de son lustre lors des discours, mais il retourna à la table de maquillage par après pour se qu'elle soit redessinée!

Fleur-de-Lys, Reframed

Alexandre T. Gingras

In June, 2011, the NDP was filibustering as long as it possibly could in the wake of the Canada Post strike against the government's back-to-work legislation. What usually happens is that the House of Commons traditionally rises around June 22-23: that usually gives the Québec MPs a chance to go back to their ridings to celebrate the Fête Nationale/St-Jean-Baptiste. However with the filibuster going on and the NDP not wanting to give up on the workers, the MPs stayed in the House to talk non-stop round the clock until June 26, if my memory is right.

But Jack, being born in Québec and knowing how important it was to celebrate the Québec culture in the wake of the orange wave, was very much wanting to celebrate the Fête Nationale as well. He was in the lobby behind the House of Commons taking a rest from the debates. Françoise Boivin, NDP Member of Parliament for Gatineau, was there too. So Jack asked her, "Françoise, is there something going on in your riding for the Fête Nationale? I really think we need to be there for Québec too!" Françoise said "Absolutely." There was a family fair-type event in the Notre-Dame public market in a struggling neighbourhood of the Gatineau riding at one of those events where the neighbors really come together and everything is coordinated and arranged by a top notch, dedicated and visionary social activist/social economy gang of community organizers.

It was originally scheduled that I was to replace Françoise on that day and give a speech on her behalf since she would be in the House of Commons at the time. But just as I was getting ready to go and about to get into my car, Françoise rang me, saying she was coming, along with Jack, Thomas Mulcair and a pretty big contingent of Québec MPs. I was to mobilize her Facebook friends, the media and so on. So I got there as fast as I could to inform the organizers: they were pretty shocked how the whole event had just jumped a few notches in intensity. The NDP MPs started to come in (they were kindly covered for in the House of Commons by non-Québec MPs). More and more of the public showed up (lots of people attracting lots of people, right ...). The media arrived and then Jack arrived. Cameras flashing. The Jack magic just worked itself out. Pierre Dionne Labelle brought his guitar; the caucus started singing Québec songs as the crowd grew bigger. Françoise and Jack's speeches just invigorated the audience and it made the day, if not the year of the market organizers. In fact, it was our first meeting together, celebrating our culture, a bonding moment between us and the Notre-Dame street community. Because of this day, we have closely collaborated ever since on a host of events and projects.

Throughout the entire celebration, a young girl stayed close to Jack. She must have been no older than six years old but she knew who he was. I have no idea who the little girl is, she was just there, but she truly was the star of the show! She greeted him by dancing with him, then they went to the makeup booth together. Jack got a fleur-de-lys drawn on his hand and the girl got lion makeup drawn on her face. It was a very hot day so Jack's fleur-de-lys dissolved a bit but after his speech he returned to the booth to get it redrawn!

Inspiring Hope and Optimism in Our Nation

Janet Vickers

In July of 2011, Jack Layton revealed he was battling a cancer separate from the prostate cancer that he had previously overcome. Inspired by Jack's integrity and courage, to carry on his fight for our country, even at the expense of his own health and life, I decided that Lipstick Press could take a diversion from exclusively writing on Lipstick Press publications and proposed a move into the political. Lipstick Press asked for poets' submissions of healing thoughts to send to Jack Layton. No, we were not venturing into spiritual healing, other than the kind of healing that comes with a flood of support and deep concern when someone's plans are interrupted so tragically.

Because Jack dedicated his life to public service, in an environment that barely yields any thanks from the electorate, the media or business, I asked for words to convey our thoughts and feelings to him and his family. What happened after that call was a steady stream throughout the summer months to September, from poets, some I hadn't heard of, with sincere heartfelt expressions of sympathy, and after his death – grief.

After that, the media was filled with expressions that revealed Canadians did indeed notice the politics and practice of a leader. Suddenly, we were reawakened to an appreciation for his leadership skills, and through that connection, our own capacity to see integrity in our political system. Suddenly, we knew we depended upon leaders who were willing to be authentic in a cynical media-scape. For a while, it seems we understood what was at stake in the governing of this land and we looked deeper than the clever sound bites and tricky slogans that had jaded so many of us.

> Your hope and optimism
> have found us
> like two pigeons
> on a cedar branch
> cooing in the morning's wake …

Hope and optimism are not light and airy
they are creatures of blood and bone
picking through grit and dirt
for anything they can use.

Mortal in pain
immortal in flight.

Dear Jack

Franci Louann

hearts break across Canada for your pain
we hold them together for your strength

you, who've done so much for so many
all the good fights let us win this with you

dare we say you've inspired us?
lest we compare the incomparable

not since Terry Fox has the C-word
hurt so many in this country

Dear Jack may you be a strong leader again
or just be Grandpa for your Beatrice

we stand united for your strength your triumph
hoping for one more win for Canada ...

The Last Line. To the Letter

Penn Kemp

I dream Jack Layton is sitting up in bed
joyously celebrating his win, beaming,
radiant: his indomitable optimism seeing
him through cancer and out the other side.

I know the game's over. He understands
what we won't till we too join him across
that last finishing line. Wherever you are,
Jack, we love you. Thank you for all you

won for us now that you are one with all.
His last line? "And we'll change the world."

August 19, 2011

Among Today's Dead and Sorely Missed

Penn Kemp

So there's Jack, standing at the gates with Jerry
Leiber, who co-wrote "Hound Dog," "Stand By Me,"
and "Jailhouse Rock." Sure hope Jack managed
to smuggle up his guitar. Wonder which song
he's singing first. A duet I wish we could hear.

August 22, 2011

The recently dead sometime become my familiars, whether in dream or at back of mind. I cannot consciously determine or guess who will turn up, who flits about my head, who stays. As I write, for example, Jack Layton stands behind me, about a foot high, just his face, beaming encouragement. He is like a headwind, propelling me forward, asking me to put into words what I would never have considered writing: a political narrative from a poet who is left-winged, for sure, but also very left-handed and not known for her logical power. For the last nine months, I have felt Jack's presence cheering (pushing!) this project forward, dismissing doubt. Even in dreams.

In reading the submissions to this book, I was intrigued by how often Jack appeared in other people's dreams during the last days of his life and long after his death. People felt he was offering the love, hope and optimism expressed in his last letter. Jack remains a symbolic emissary of hope and a guide to right action for many. "What would Jack do?" has become their watchword for living a more politically aware and active life.

In these moments
(for Jack and others just diagnosed)

Elsie K. Neufeld

Jack Layton. Is there a news-watching Canadian who didn't know who he was? Whose heart, upon hearing of his cancer's resurgence, didn't beat sadly – for Jack, for his family, for the NDP party, for the country!? When Jack was given his final, grim diagnosis, Janet Vickers of Lipstick Press created a poetry page to honour his life … After Jack's death, Janet invited us to submit a second poem … The first poem wrote itself as I sat in my apartment, pondering … and I dedicated it: "for Jack, and others just diagnosed" with cancer. The second poem came to me in a bout of insomnia the morning of Jack's death (August 22, 2011). I wrote it before I heard the news he had died. Though I never knew Jack, both poems felt somehow inspired by him.

"It is hard to have to leave so soon."

Ann Gelsheimer

On the morning of August 22, 2011, I was moved to tears when I read that Jack had passed away so soon after his tremendous political success. I felt what a great loss this was for his family and for our country, but I also felt personally touched and saddened. As I followed the media coverage of Jack's life and passing, and learned so much more about his advocacy efforts over the years, I was better able to appreciate the extent of our loss. And yet, at the same time, I strongly felt his spirit alive and so very present.

A few days after he died, I dreamt of Jack. We were at a huge outdoor party in his honour and he came over to chat with me as we ate food from the buffet. Jack was so warm and personable, and he surprised me by speaking to me as though I were a friend. Although he appeared very well and full of joy to be with everyone at the party, for a moment Jack became quietly emotional. I felt his sadness as he said, "It is hard to have to leave so soon."

This dream felt like an actual visit with Jack. It was so vivid at the time, and nearly a year later, I can still feel the poignancy of the encounter. Looking back over the past eleven months and the series of synchronistic events leading up to the writing of this reflection, I believe that this dream of Jack came to me so that it would be included in this book one day. I have the strong sense that this is Jack's way of getting the message out that he is "still kicking" in spirit: my role was to give it to you on behalf of Jack. So, Jack, your message is now passed, and it has been an honour to do this for you. Much love to you.

Hooked on Politics

Gay Allison

August 22, 2012

Dear Jack:

It's almost midnight. The moon is shining through my bedroom window. I am thinking of you and the "house that Jack built." Wondering what you are up to ... "up there." ... I'm sure you've run into my old friend Ayanna Black. She has probably challenged you already. Ayanna with her marvellous cackling laughter. I met you once with her when we were gallivanting on Queen West in Toronto late one night. Ayanna, the Black poet activist feminist from Jamaica. The moon was out that night too. And she was excited about you and Olivia ... and about your future, our future.

I told you then that I was a prairie poet from Saskatchewan. I grew up on a farm and was an avid CCFer. As a kid, my hero was Tommy Douglas. My parents took me to hear him speak and his oratory skills and passionate pleas were wired into my brain. Diefenbaker didn't cut the mustard with me but later my parents voted for him ...

After several years of Harper secrecy at the helm, with his focus on guns and jails and the military, I became very disillusioned with politics. And especially his lack of respect for democracy. I couldn't believe that we lost our UN seat to Portugal. I longed for leaders with vision. Sadly, the Liberal leaders who could have easily challenged Harper, i.e., Frank McKenna, Brian Tobin, Allan Rock, John Manley, and even David Peterson, all disappeared. I felt Canada had been deserted, either by choice or they were told not to run.

And then Jack, you came along, and entered my world. You were another visionary leader I could admire. I loved your wisdom, your search for truth, your intelligent common sense, and most of all, your love of ordinary Canadian people. You made me proud to be a Canadian again. I regained my faith in politics because of you. And when I watched you stumping along the campaign trail with your cane and your pain and your smile ... Your leg, Jack, reminded me of Tommy and his wonderful story about his leg. And I was hooked all over again.

When Tommy Douglas was a young boy in Scotland he fell and

injured his right knee. His osteomyelitis flared up again when his family moved to Winnipeg and the doctors told him his leg had to be amputated. However, a well-known surgeon offered to operate on his leg for free if his parents would allow medical students to watch the operation. When the surgeon saved his leg, Tommy was convinced that health care should be free for everyone.

Like Tommy Douglas, your vision and courage in adversity, Jack, will carry us into the future. I thank you, Jack be nimble, for regaining my faith in politics.

With gratitude,
Gay Allison

August 27, 2011. Toronto.

Shani Mootoo

This photo is truly iconic, with Olivia stepping into the future, followed by Jack's immediate family. Shani Mootoo writes: "Might the date, and place, serve as a title – suggesting, in other words, that on that day, in this city, that is what happened/mattered." Indeed.

PHOTO: SHANI MOOTOO

From where I was, on the rooftop of City Hall, I could see that the crowd had not gathered to see the spectacle of a politician's funeral, but had come rather to express their deep appreciation, their sense of this great loss, and, having stood quietly in place for hours as they waited – as we waited – to send a true citizen on his way. I saw from there, too, the power and the commanding stride of Jack's legacy as she, Olivia Chow – and they – his son Mike, and family – made their way through the concrete garden of messages chalked in different colours and different languages. It was as if I were looking at the past and the future, and what I saw – as represented by this photograph – allowed me to relax and hope.

Eulogy

Mike Layton

This Eulogy was given by Jack Layton's son Mike at the state funeral, Roy Thompson Hall, Toronto on August 22, 2011.

To our friends, to our neighbours, to all of you, we'd first like to say we are overwhelmed by the incredible support you have shown us. We are proud to have shared our father with you. Celebrating his life together today means so much to us, so on behalf of our entire extended family, thank you so very much.

Not many people are recognized practically everywhere by just their first name. Jack. His personality invited that kind of immediate connection. But while you all knew him as Jack, I want to tell you about my dad. It's true: he was never one to take the easy road. There was a time when I was 11 when we set out on a cycling camping tour of Prince Edward Island. Father and son awoke, ready to ride with the rising sun, our grueling route carefully prepared. What our map couldn't show us was that our main trail was basically impassable by bike. A trail literally of jagged shells. At best, we pedaled a few hundred metres before our first flat tire. Then another. Then another. And each time we'd hop off, patch the hole, pump the tire and push on. Dozens of flats, hundreds of tire bumps, increasingly colourful language. Sure, we could have given up, walked our bikes back and called someone for a ride. But, no. He wouldn't keep us from our goal. This is how my father lived his whole life. Undeterred by the height of the mountain, the storminess of the sea, or the rockiness of the road, he'd pour everything into achieving a goal. The only thing that mattered more to him was helping others achieve their goals. That's a pretty good quality in a father.

Growing up, our family used to rent a cabin near Huntsville, and dad was always planning fun activities for the kids staying in the cabins nearby. Plenty of campfire singalongs. One summer we noticed a sailboat at the dock. Dad suggested we go on a sail. I was excited but fearful. I'd never sailed before. I wasn't sure I could do it and I wasn't sure he could either. "No worries," he said, "I'll teach you. Everything will be fine." As it turns out, he knew how to sail, but the winds had stopped completely and we found ourselves stranded in the middle of the lake. Perfect stillness. You could almost hear the fish breathing. But was my dad fazed? No, he was not. Floating motionless, he talked me through every basic sailing skill he knew before we arduously rowed ourselves back to shore. "You could wait forever for perfect conditions," he said, "or you can make the best of what you've got." That's what he did every day of his life. He made the most of each moment. He was a man who changed this city and this country, and the loving dad I miss so much already.

Twenty years ago, he co-founded an organization dedicated to eliminating men's violence against women. What started as a meeting has grown into a movement against violence spanning 60 countries. Not long ago, my dad offered the new executive director some advice that I'll share with you now. He said, "Always have a dream that's longer than a lifetime. *If faut toujours avoir des rêves qui dépassent la durée de la vie.* Friends: be loving, be hopeful, be optimistic. Together we can build the world of our dreams." And as he always said, "Don't let anyone tell you it can't be done."

Eulogie

Karl Bélanger

Karl Bélanger, Jack's long-time Press Secretary, sent the text of the eulogy he delivered at Jack Layton's funeral, with these kind words: "since it was delivered only in French, I thought that many might appreciate reading it in English." The original speech follows.

C'est une aventure qui a débuté il y a plus de huit ans,
lorsque l'on m'a demandé de servir
pour le nouveau chef du Nouveau Parti démocratique du Canada.

Je ne connaissais pas beaucoup Jack Layton à l'époque,
mais j'étais une entité plutôt rare à ce moment – là ...
Imaginez, un Québécois au sein du NPD!
Disons que les temps ont changé ...

Au cours de ces années, on a traversé le pays ensemble à plusieurs reprises,
de gauche à droite, mais surtout de droite à gauche.

Mon travail était de faire connaître Jack Layton au reste du pays.
À convaincre les médias de parler de lui,
en bien dans la mesure du possible!

Par la force des choses, j'ai dû lui servir de chauffeur, de secrétaire,
de garde du corps, et même d'infirmier à deux ou trois reprises ...
Mais la force des choses a surtout fait de Jack Layton, mon ami.

Un ami que j'ai eu la chance de partager,
et on s'en est rendu compte pendant le dernier mois
et particulièrement pendant la dernière semaine ...
Un ami que j'ai eu la chance de partager avec des centaines,
des milliers, des millions de Canadiens.

Et je suis fier du petit rôle que j'ai pu jouer
 pour que tant de gens se sentent si près de Jack Layton.

Évidemment, la tâche s'est avérée de plus en plus facile avec le temps.
Car Jack Layton était un gars comme n'importe quel autre, dans le fond.

Un gars aussi à l'aise à négocier avec des Premiers ministres
qu'à réconforter des sans-abris.
Un gars qui savait manier aussi bien l'harmonica que le micro.
Aussi confortable à la Chambre de Commerce qu'à la taverne du coin.

Et pour tous ceux qu'il rencontrait, il devenait tout simplement … Jack.

Jack, un gars qui voulait être près des gens, qui aimait les gens.
Et les gens le lui rendaient bien.

Et plus les gens connaissaient Jack Layton,
plus les gens étaient inspirés par son message d'espoir, rempli d'optimisme.
Dans un monde où le cynisme fait trop souvent la loi,
plusieurs ont doutés des motivations profondes de Jack Layton.
Plusieurs en doute encore.

Mais pour lui, ce n'était pas important.
Parce que l'important, c'était de se rendre utile.
Et quelle meilleure façon de se rendre utile
que de se mettre au service de ces concitoyens.

Obtenir des résultats, changer les choses, améliorer le sort des gens.

Croire que c'est possible,
que non seulement c'est possible …
Que c'est nécessaire.

Oh, bien sûr, Jack Layton était ambitieux.
Pour son parti, bien entendu.
Mais il était ambitieux d'abord et avant tout pour sa communauté,
pour son pays.

Et si sa propre personne était le meilleur véhicule
pour se mettre au service de ces ambitions,
ça faisait parfaitement son affaire!

Mais ce n'était pas une ambition personnelle.
C'était une ambition collective, toujours un travail d'équipe.
D'ailleurs, son partenariat romantique et politique avec Olivia
en est la plus grande preuve.

Car il a toujours eu la volonté et la capacité de rassembler les gens
autour d'objectifs communs, pour changer les choses.
Alliés comme adversaires.
Travaillons ensemble, disait – il.

Pour faire du Canada un pays plus juste, plus équitable.
Pour que le Québec, où il est né, soit compris, respecté.
Pour que les communautés de partout au pays
s'unissent autour de ce qui nous rassemble
et trouvent des solutions en écartant les divisions.
Travaillons ensemble, disait – il.
Nous pouvons le faire. Nous devons le faire.
Pour nos enfants. Pour leurs enfants.

Merci, Jack.
Et à la prochaine.

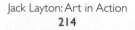

Eulogy

Karl Bélanger

This adventure started more than eight years ago,
when I was asked to work for the new leader
of the New Democratic Party of Canada.

Back then I did not know Jack Layton particularly well.
And I was somewhat of an oddity at the time ...
Just imagine, a Québecer working for the NDP!
Let's just say times have changed a lot ...

During these many years, we travelled the country many times together,
from left to right, but mostly from right to left.

My job was to make Jack Layton known to the rest of the country.
To convince the media to talk about him,
positively, whenever possible!

As things go, I also had to serve as driver, secretary, bodyguard,
and even as nurse on two or three occasions ...
But as things go, most importantly, Jack became my friend.

A friend that I was lucky to share –
as we realized over the last month,
and particularly over the last week –
a friend I shared with hundreds,
thousands, even millions of Canadians.

And I am so proud of the minor role I played
in making people feel so close to Jack Layton.

Of course, this task got easier with time.
Because, in truth, Jack was an ordinary guy just like everyone else.

He was someone who was as comfortable negotiating with Prime Ministers
as he was comforting homeless people. Someone who knew how to use a
harmonica as well as he knew how to use a microphone. As comfortable in
a meeting with the Chamber of Commerce as he was in the local tavern.

And for all those he met, he became known simply as … Jack.

Jack, a guy who wanted to be close to the people, who loved the people.
And the people loved him back.

And the more the people knew about Jack Layton,
the more they became inspired by his message of hope and optimism.
In a world where cynicism too often prevails,
many were those who raised doubts about Jack Layton's true motivations.
Some still doubt them to this day.

But for him, this did not matter.
What mattered was to make himself useful
And how could he have made himself more useful,
than by working for his fellow Canadians?

Obtaining concrete results, changing things, improving people's lives.

Believing that it is possible.
Not only possible …
but also necessary.

Of course, Jack Layton was ambitious.
For his party, of course.
But first and foremost he was ambitious for the future of his community,
of his country.

And if his own persona was the best way
to put these ambitions forward,
it was all the better for him!

But his was never a personal ambition.
It was a collective ambition, always a team's work.
And the best proof of this is
his romantic and political partnership with Olivia.

Because he always had the will and the ability to bring people together,
to work towards reaching common objectives, to change things.
Allies and opponents alike.

Let's work together, he would always say.

To make Canada a better and fairer country.
To ensure that Québec, where he was born,
is better understood and respected.
To ensure that communities from all across the country
join forces to reach common goals, putting divisions aside.

Let's work together, he would always say.
We can do it, we must do it.
For our children. For their children.

Thank you, Jack.

Farewell.

Notice that the colloquial last line, "Et à la prochaine" is translated more
formally into the English "Farewell." Somehow, then, that line becomes very
moving in French, directly addressing Jack as he must have done a thousand
times.

Homily

Rev. Dr. Brent Hawkes

Normally, it's Christmas Eve, and the Metropolitan Community Church Toronto occupies this space. Normally, I look up there in the balcony and Jack and Olivia are sitting there. Normally, I greet them outside in the hall with their Santa Claus hats on.

People have said to me, how do you prepare for this talk or speech. They said, it's probably the most crucial (speech) you've ever given. And I said, probably the most crucial. Probably the most nervous I've been was my first meeting with my future mother-in-law and father-in-law. I know that I speak for everyone participating today that we are all so honoured to be asked. We are all so honoured to participate today because we all want to do Jack justice.

Early in July, Jack and Olivia invited me to their home. To talk. The conversation began the way it always began with Jack. "Brent, how's John doing?" John is my husband. And then, Jack said that he wanted to talk to me about his funeral, and that he still intended to beat this cancer. He still wanted to come back but he needed to cover every option, to make sure all of the plans were in place no matter what the result was. We talked about making the plans and putting it in the filing cabinet and hopefully pulling it out years later. And so we began a number of conversations about this service and about life and death and dying. And so today I begin to talk to you about life and death.

Life is amazing. Every morning when you wake up, it's a new day, a new beginning. Every breath that you take is an opportunity to love and to be loved, an opportunity to go deeper spiritually. It's not about which spiritual path you choose, it's about choosing a spiritual path and going deeper, and respecting people on their various paths. It's about learning and growing and coming together. And, ultimately, it's about making the world a better place for those who will come after us. Yes, in life, there will be disappointments. Yes, in life, we will have the death of those close to us. And it's about how we face those situations, those disappointments and how we get back up and where we go on from there.

Life is a wonderful gift given to each one of us by God. You are intentionally placed here for a reason. Give thanks for the gift of life and every single moment you have and make the most of it. Jack and I talked about his life and he said that he was very, very grateful. Very blessed to have lived so long, very blessed to have met and worked with so many wonderful people. Inspired by many of you, particularly young people, he was in awe at the trust given to him of late, especially the trust from the people of Québec and what we can be together. He talked about his love for his family, and for you, Olivia. He talked to me about his love for you, his respect for you, for your wisdom, for your strength, for the rock you have been and for the partnership you have developed.

And while Jack was very grateful about his life, he was sad that he did not have more time. More time to continue and improve things, this movement towards a better Canada. Jack was a spiritual person. He didn't wear it on his sleeve, but in one of our conversations, he said to me, "Brent, I believe how I live my life every day is my act of worship."

I also speak to you today about death. I asked Jack how churchy I could be today, and he said, "Go for it." And while there are many questions we have about why, why now or why Jack? To some of those questions today we have no answer. But the reality is not why? but what now?

Many faith traditions have wrestled with the issue of death. It is my belief that death is not an ending but a transition. That sometimes we mistakenly believe that we are physical beings on this earth occasionally having a spiritual experience, maybe in a church once in a while. But the reality is just the opposite. Indeed, we are spiritual beings, and we enter this gift called life on earth through birth and we leave it to continue our spiritual journey through death. We don't know exactly what that journey will look like but we trust God.

Jack and I talked about his attitude toward death and he said he was not afraid; that he was not sure what it would be like but he sensed that somehow we would connect again with those who'd gone on before us. He talked about seeing his dad again, and he said I'll be standing beside my dad and looking up and hearing that booming voice singing "O Canada."

In one of those meetings, Jack shed a tear and he told me something and I asked him, if he wanted me to share it today. He said "I have had a great and blessed life but it has been far from perfection. I have made some mistakes." He said, "I am sorry that I don't have more time to make amends to some individuals. And if there was anything I said or did that hurt someone, I'm sorry."

I believe this reminds us to be quick to say I'm sorry, to make amends, to take the first step, to be quick to forgive each other.

Jack didn't have the time to spell out the details of this part of the sermon but he gave me some clear things that he wanted me to address.

In the details, I tried to capture the essence of his points. Jack didn't want this celebration of life to be primarily focused on him. He wanted to somehow talk about the issues and the themes and to be inclusive, gathering all of us together.

Jack believed that Canada was a great country and yet he was very clear there's a lot of work that is yet to be done. And that, yes, there are people coming from different places with different beliefs and different approaches. And yet, we can be one inclusive movement for a better Canada. And he wanted this service to inspire us and to challenge us. Each of us as individuals, and this was very important to Jack, not just as individuals but also working together in partnership. Bringing people together, young people together, diverse voices, different perspectives and opposing beliefs. Remembering that the best decisions are made together. And the best actions are taken together. It's not so much the organization you choose. Too often we get caught up in the organization. We know that Jack loved coalitions. We know that he loved his NDP family. We know that he loved serving the city and in Parliament. But Jack was clear that there were two things that were very much more important.

The first was the goal to make life better and not to leave anyone behind. What changes need to be done, what actions need to be taken, was the goal of making Canada a better country. That was important. The goal to inspire us and hold us together. Whether the goals were big goals, like ending homelessness or the rights of transgendered people or getting HIV/AIDS medication to poor countries, or whether they were little goals like helping your neighbour or picking up litter or turning off a light. Yes, making life better for others.

And the second thing that was crucially important is how we are with each other as we do the work. What are the values that will guide us? Caring for each other, forgiving each other, listening to each other, really hearing, taking the extra time to hear, to really hear the hopes and dreams, respecting each other, staying optimistic even when the disappointments come, optimistic even when the defeats come, and optimistic even when disease visits the first time or the second time. It is leaving every situation better because you were there and every person better because they met you. It's about how we care for each other, whether our hometown is Hudson, Québec or Bath, New Brunswick, whether across this country or across the aisles in Parliament.

Over the past few days something has been happening. Young people have said in Canada that they don't want this feel-good moment to be a fleeting moment. If the Olympics can make us prouder Canadians, maybe Jack's life can make us better Canadians.

I happen to be in the business of believing in miracles. We can do this. We can do this together. We can be a better people. We've seen how to try.

When all of the talking is done, when all of the tributes are done, when the chalk is washed away on the concrete at City Hall, when our crying finally stops, the legacy of Jack Layton will not be in how much power you have, it will be in how all of us exercise our personal power for a better world. It will be in our actions and how we take those actions together. Yes, bring your passion but also bring your compassion. Yes, bring your agendas of what you want to accomplish, but also bring a commitment about how we can accomplish that together. Yes, bring your seriousness about serious issues but also have fun – sing together and pick up a harmonica once in a while. It's about remembering to say, "Hi Brent. How's John doing?"

"Hi Prime Minister. How's Laureen doing?"

It's about saying, "Hi Olivia. How's Beatrice doing?"

It's about remembering each other and our love and our lives together. Over the next few years, we might not be able to say, "Hi Jack. How's Olivia doing?" But you can say, "Hi Jack. How are we doing?"

I met with Jack on the Friday and the Sunday before his passing. And Olivia left us together for a while. I said to Jack, "Jack, it seems like it's getting closer." And I said, "Jack, I want to say to you now:

Well done, good and faithful servant."

And may we rise to the occasion, because the torch is now passed. The job of making the world a better place is up to us.

Penn: At the service in Roy Thompson Hall, the Conservatives were appropriately seated to the far right, from the audience's point of view. The family sat in the centre, with Olivia and Nancy Layton in the front row along with Jack's children. Dalton McGuinty and former Toronto Mayor David Miller were seated in the left front row. Media folks like Jian Ghomeshi and Judy Rebick were seated to the left, about six rows back. Gavin and I were sitting with the family, also six rows back. As my sight line was straight to the Harpers, I was intrigued by their responses to the stage presentations. When Rev. Brent Hawkes addressed Stephen Harper directly by looking up from his script and asking how his wife was doing, in the line above, Mrs. Harper was startled, visibly shaken, shrinking down in her seat. Tears rolled down her cheek. Mr. Harper also looked startled, but he seemed to freeze, as if bewildered. Such a direct greeting broke the barrier between stage and audience and drew us all into an I-thou kind of immediacy, a very moving moment.

I recalled Jack telling us stories over an Ottawa breakfast we shared in April, 2011. He remarked then how much he liked Laureen, what a great sense of humour she had, how he enjoyed kidding around with her, usually on the phone. "Stephen Harper?" he said, "Not so much." After the funeral service was over, Mr. Harper passed very close by us in the procession out. He looked around from face to face. I would not have expected him to appear so vulnerable. I wondered if he was puzzled at all the attention given to Jack. Mrs. Harper followed directly behind him, downcast, huddled into herself, mourning.

When the Prime Minister offered Jack's family a state funeral, Jack became the first ordinary MP to be accorded such an honour, after poor D'Arcy McGee, who had been assassinated the year after Confederation.

When Parliament resumed in September 2011, the Prime Minister began the round of tributes to Jack Layton: "I cannot think of another leader, at least not in our time, whose campaign was described as gallant," Harper proclaimed. "However, Jack's campaign inspired and merited that description." He evidently thought of Jack as a friend, despite what he called "our strongest partisan instincts." *http://m.theglobeandmail.com/news/politics/parliament-resumes-with-tribute-to-former-ndp-leader-layton/article594827/?service=mobile.* I don't get the impression that Mr. Harper makes friends easily. But he talked affectionately of Jack.

Gestures
~ on the death of Jack Layton

Cecilia Kennedy

If civil rites attest the man he was one deserving
of high ceremony and the grandest lexicon of grief.
Well merited were all those obsequies of the state,
the honour guard, dress uniforms of white gloved pomp
under parliamentary arches and queues of solemn souls.
Worthy was he of processions through the streets
with drums, and the eagle feather blessing of a chief
come from Ahousaht, the Hallelujah sung, the sonorous
aches of eloquence and praise, coffin draped in a nation's flag.

and yet
the simple
small
and humble gestures
seemed truest to the man:
when his body passed
on the streets of Toronto
they rang their bicycle bells

My Memorial to Jack

Luba Goy

PHOTO: LUBA GOY

I had a little shrine in my side garden when Jack became very ill. I found a campaign sign I had not recycled. My memorial to Jack, the day I heard of his passing, grew ... I had a candle burning day and night for a week in the front and side gardens. One orange hibiscus bloomed the day Jack died.

Also had a little shrine in the front of my house. I had saved his campaign sign. I had to have this tree cut down ... I made it my throne.

The story of Marilyn Churley and the stone painted with orange dragonflies is a good one. I ran into Marilyn on the Danforth. She was looking for a small gift to give to Jack to help him feel better. I asked Marilyn, "How's Jack doing?" Marilyn didn't say a word, just looked into my eyes, and we hugged. We went into the shop and I noticed a basket of lovely stones, painted high gloss black with orange dragonflies. It was the orange dragonflies that caught my eye – I said they could be Jack & Olivia, so Marilyn bought one.

Two days later, Jack passed and I went back to Ten Thousand Villages and bought every stone left. I wrapped them in tissue and gave them out at Jack's funeral (about ten stones). I gave a stone to Lincoln Alexander … he was in a wheelchair, and he opened the tissue, thanked me and put it in his pocket. Then our "two mayors" Rob and Doug came over to talk to Lincoln, and ignored me. I introduced myself, and they seemed to know who I was. It was right before we went into the theatre at Roy Thompson Hall for the funeral.

I met this wonderful woman, Dee Barrett, after the funeral. She had a letter for Jack's granddaughter, Beatrice, about him coming to a tea at her seniors' residence. She had written Jack a letter inviting him and was shocked when he actually showed up at the tea! In fact, he came every year, after that! I gave her a stone. The stones are so high gloss, it's impossible to photograph them!

The Spirit of a Leader

Penn Kemp and J Peachy

The day after Jack's death, BC radio host J Peachy dedicated his show to The Spirit of a Leader. His interview with me about Jack aired on August 23, 2011. It is archived as Part 2, *http://soundtherapyradio.com/2011/08/23/the-spirit-of-a-leader-with-john-pippus-amanda-rheaume-and-penn-kemp/*. I've edited the transcription lightly here.

Dedication: to Jack Layton.

J Peachy: I just wanted to ask: how are you doing?

Penn Kemp: Oh, thanks, Jay. It's been such a communal time; everyone feels it far more than we would ever have imagined. I think everyone who saw him in his television appearance on July 25, 2011, guessed how close he was, and yet what an indomitable fighter he was.

JP: You've known him for quite a while? How are you related?

PK: I first met him in the early Eighties. I had lived for ten years on Toronto Island. As a young councillor, he was really helping the Toronto Islanders to defend their homes which Metro wanted to demolish for parkland. The Islanders won that fight, in part due to his help. That's where I first heard of him and met him. Then, fifteen years ago, his younger sister Nancy Layton married my husband's brother. We called ourselves outlaws because it's such an extended relationship, not quite orthodox … so outlaws we are.

JP: To those in the political community, like NDP MP Fin Donnelly, he felt like a family member. Can you give us an indication, outside of the political atmosphere, how Jack was personally, and especially that fighting spirit: how was that to be around?

PK: He felt like a family member to many. He was a great family man, very much interested in the goings-on, especially of young Beatrice, his granddaughter, and of all his friends and family. He was really so engaged in whatever was happening with them. After his prostate cancer last spring, I really noticed that fighting spirit, which you'd think would be difficult to be around. But he was so up all the time. He mellowed; his heart seemed to open. He became more and more luminous, which in a way is a dangerous sign. For me, it often means the person is ready to drop these mortal coils and leave us. Even though he was such a pragmatist. I know he knew he was dying, but he spent last Saturday composing that letter to Canadians. He always had the whole picture in mind.

JP: He wanted you to write something?

PK: Yes, when he had to have that hip operation. We had had breakfast with him in Ottawa [in April, 2012]. He told us then that the cancer had metastasized into his hip and he had to have that operation, that his hip was a latticework. So he asked me to write a hip poem. It was written on March 6. He really liked it. He passed it around to his friends and colleagues.

JP: He comes across as quite charismatic and polished on TV and interviews. Is that really part of his personality day-to-day?

PK: He was one of the very few people whom I have never met where there was no distinction between private and public persona. He was always up for a party, always up for dancing, for music, for singing. In fact, I just heard on our telephone a song that he and his sister Nancy sang in harmony to my husband Gavin Stairs on his birthday. I'd saved the message and just happened to hear it again. That was pretty poignant.

JP: How is the family doing? It's quite public.

PK: It is so public and that in a way buoys one. I would imagine Olivia especially is busy consoling others. They were such a team together. I know Nancy on the day of his death, yesterday, had to play golf. She's very much like Jack, the same sort of indomitable energy and positive attitude, action-oriented. She is a champion golfer in her age range. She had to play in a big professional game in Québec. We just cheered her on because we knew that that's what Jack would have wanted her to do. And she did; she did really well, between the laughter and the tears. It was very fitting for her to do that.

JP: It's almost that the busyness is part of the healing process. That's what he wanted.

PK: I think so, and that's what Jack wants for us all, to bond together and really move together collectively. It seems to me that the time for one-man charismatic leadership is passing over to a more collective group, especially with all these young untried but energetic MPs. It will be interesting to see what will happen to the NDP.

JP: Definitely. For someone who is a leader and very progressive, you have to be the pointy end of the stick sometimes to move things along and to make change. Sometimes that can be rough for people. Did you find that those kinds of strengths in his personality could have held him back? Was that a source of conflict for anybody? Did you observe that? How did he make his shortcomings not a limit to what he wanted to do?

PK: His way of handling diplomacy or controversy or opposition was to be the consummate listener. He was the best listener I've ever watched in action. He would treat every person on the level where they had something in common. His great mentor was Charles Taylor, who is the philosopher who actually campaigned against Trudeau as an NDP candidate in Québec, and lost, of course. He's a very well-respected scholar in dialectics. Jack studied with him at McGill and I think conceived of him as his greatest mentor. What he learned from Taylor was that to understand the opponent, you had to listen first, and then you knew both your ground and your opponent's ground. And then you could work together towards consensus or congruency of some sort.

JP: Did you find his strong personality hindered him in any way? Had he learned over time?

PK: It was very interesting to watch the development because I used to tease him that he had a kind of Jack Russell terrier personality, where he just would bristle and almost seemed self-righteous; he would jump up. But in the last year, his heart seemed to open and expand to become more and more inclusive, in that part of him that listened and welcomed controversy. He could somehow accept different points of view without denying his own. So people would really disagree with him politically, disagree with political decisions he had made, and yet still be friends with him and still love him. He was extraordinarily lovable in that way, because I think he was so present to the moment. But what changed in the last year was that he seemed to move down from his sharp, clear activist 'let's go get 'em' mentality into a really open heart, as he became more and more ill. He used military terms like fighting in battle, which I think are a little problematic with cancer patients. But I think he became more and more expansive and luminous.

JP: These are great stories. I really appreciate … Jack had quite a bit of energy; you can see that publicly. How do you think Jack kept his energy, the energizer bunny, going?

PK: The whole family has that kind of optimism and go-to-it pragmatism. Even more than a politician, Jack was an activist. He really believed in his causes and worked to get them done. So there wasn't any doubt or deviation from the path; it was very straightforward problem-solving. He really liked to solve problems. He would stick to very specific things that he could do. So there would be a great deal of satisfaction for getting bike paths in Toronto or bike lots set up, whatever specific things that he could accomplish. So there was a huge amount of satisfaction. As an extravert, he was energized by crowds of people and by individuals. There was lots of feedback in his life that gave him great joy. He really exuded love even when you disagreed with him – I sometimes disagreed with his policies, or wanted more arts emphasis … though the NDP does have the best arts policy. Nonetheless, he would listen to you and agree or disagree and state his position very clearly, so that you knew that whether or not he agreed with you, he still loved you. You could feel that.

JP: That's amazing. You have another reading for us?

PK: I'll preface this by saying that it's a dream poem that I had on August 20th ["The Last Line Is Yours," written several days before he died.] His last line? "And we'll change the world." I can just hear him saying that.

And then this poem I think is one he would really like. It was written yesterday. "Among today's dead and sorely missed." [The three poems I mention are included in this book.]

And the last piece is dedicated to Jack: "Now it feels significant to let Jack free, to dance or rest in peace, after such a monumental fight. Somehow I feel he's won the war, I feel him triumphant. As for the NDP, I have a vision of not one leader but a collective of MPs, riding the national swell of love. Now Canadians, in experiencing such devastating loss, can recognize his value and the values of the NDP. At last. This may be Jack's greatest gift to us. The time has come not for another charismatic leader to see us through but for the collective tribe to work in unity. For community."

JP: That's beautiful. Thank you very much!

An Answer to His Open Letter

Judy Rebick

Judy Rebick's original piece was published on *Rabble.ca* and simultaneously on her own site, *http://www.transformingpower.ca*, August 24, 2011. In her update, Judy, in her usual provocative and interesting way, draws out an aspect no-one else has mentioned. From the youth group in Hudson to youth uprisings over the last year, Jack would have been involved. He would have taken a stand for the protests. Whether he agreed or not in the particular, he would have supported and celebrated youth participation in social and political movements.

A couple of days after Jack died, I wrote a piece about why he was so special as a politician. It's pretty amazing that soon after Jack's death, almost as an answer to his open letter, there was a youth uprising in North America in the Occupy movement.

The part of the letter addressed to youth said, "Your energy, your vision, your passion for justice are exactly what this country needs today. You need to be at the heart of our economy, our political life, and our plans for the present and the future."

Even though Occupy is uninterested in electoral politics, I think Jack would have been happy to see it. He was always able to understand that while broad social movements don't usually support political parties, their existence changes social attitudes that can lead to electoral gain.

The current leadership of the NDP doesn't seem to understand this at all. I don't think Jack would have stood aside from the Maple Spring in Québec. I like to think he would have encouraged the young Québec members of his party to follow their hearts and join the protests there. I miss Jack personally as a positive presence in my life but mostly I miss his presence politically. Here is the piece I wrote at the time:

Le Bon Jack: August 24, 2011

Judy Rebick

Almost everyone I've talked to since what seemed like the sudden announcement of Jack Layton's death had the same experience that I did. It hit me harder than I expected. I've lost other comrades, many closer than Jack was to my politics and my practice but his death hit me harder. I've been thinking about why.

Maybe it was because we all believed with him that he could beat the cancer. And it seemed so cruel that just at the moment of his greatest triumph, it took his life. Such an archetypal tragedy. It might have left us in despair except for his amazing open letter to us.

"My friends, love is better than anger. Hope is better than fear. Optimism is better than despair. So let us be loving, hopeful and optimistic. And we'll change the world."

Yesterday, at the memorial in Toronto, a young man started rapping those words ending with "the change starts today."

The letter was so like Jack but it was the part addressed to cancer patients that took my breath away. His first thought was his responsibility as a public figure. He was dying of cancer but he didn't want that to discourage others who were struggling with the disease. How generous can a person be? In knowing his life was almost over, still he thought of others, not just loved ones but all the ones he didn't know but that he might influence because they knew him.

Jack was a rare politician whose driving force was not ego but his passion for social justice and his compassion for people. His famous love of the microphone, I believe, was about wanting to be heard not so much to be seen.

It was also Jack's spirit. He was always so positive, so enthusiastic, so loving. Even when I disagreed with him, which was pretty frequently over the last few years, he always accepted my disagreements with love. I don't know what else to call it. When I quit the party a couple of years ago over my disagreement with their support for Harper's law-and-order agenda, he accepted my decision with equanimity. He understood that this was a principle for me and never thought of it as betrayal. He still loved me as a comrade and a friend. In this Jack was extraordinary.

And then there is the comrade Jack. When I think of the battles I've fought in my life, Jack was always there. He was as much an activist as he was a politician. He stood up for what he believed in, not worrying so much whether it would win him votes or not. I think I first met him on the picket line in front of the Morgentaler Clinic where supporters would come to protect patients from the anti-choice gauntlet. He was a young city councillor then but he didn't hesitate to take a stand on an issue that meant a lot to him even though the clinic was still illegal.

And it was true on so many issues and for so many constituencies. You all know the list by now. He so thoroughly believed in a more equal society that he put his body where his mouth was time and time again.

I got to know him when he nominated me for provincial party president of the Ontario NDP in 1988. I was running as part of the group called Campaign for an Activist Party (CAP). The NDP leadership was determined to defeat us, so nominating me was a career-limiting move. He didn't hesitate.

When he ran for leader, a lot of people who supported the New Politics Initiative, which I helped to found, supported him, like Libby Davies and Svend Robinson. I stood aside because we wanted to remain independent from the party. I also wasn't sure that Jack necessarily supported our political vision for the party. Even if he did, I doubted it would be possible for the party to change without a bigger shake-up.

He didn't do what I wanted him to do with the party but he did something perhaps more important, something I think will create an even bigger shake-up, something I wouldn't have believed possible. He won Québec. His win in Québec was such a monumental shift in Canadian politics that it is still difficult to understand it. For me, it was Québecois saying to the people of English Canada, "We'll give you another chance. We can work together on issues like unemployment, healthcare, education, war and getting rid of Mr. Harper. On those things we have common interests." Jack understood that sovereignty is one issue on which we might disagree but that it is not the only important issue. By uniting on the other issues, whatever Québec decides about sovereignty, Canada will be a stronger, and fairer country. What a breakthrough for the Left, the most important in my lifetime, I believe.

I didn't thank Jack personally for that, but when he appointed Nycole Turmel as interim leader and the media descended on her like a pack of dogs, the people of Canada said no. It's a good thing if someone decides to give a federalist party a chance. The people of Canada refused to be polarized against the people of Québec as they have often been by the political elite. And that gives me hope.

So thank you, Jack. Thank you for showing us what working from a place of love means. Thanks for giving us a role model of a good politician who stands up for what he believes in and truly represents the people who elected him. Thank you for showing us that a difference of opinion is not about whether you are a good person or not. And thank you for showing so many people that politics is not a dirty word and maybe just maybe we can build a better world even without you.

two poems

Joy Kogawa

2.

Jack

Orange memories of times not gone
Orange scarves orange t-shirts, orange speckled
Dresses orange roses on the steps of the new
City Hall in Lethbridge this August 26
Friday twilight candles more visible
As orange moves to dark
Dear Jack how the light in which
You swim ignites this
Country from town to town singing
Early one morning just as
The sun was rising
I heard a country pleading
In voices sad and low

Oh don't you grieve me oh
Never leave – –

1.

Rushing through the drizzle

Late Toronto morning
August 24, 2011
Gasping my lungs out
To get to Nathan Phillips square
Before the rain washes away
The tributes in chalk

Almost there almost
There Jack, up Bay
Past Adelaide and Queen
As the downpour descends
And multicoloured chalk
Sluices down the ramp
The pink and yellow words

"Good night sweet prince ..."

And in the rain
One old man with no
Umbrella and no
Hair and his hand
Trembling

Photo: The Chalked Wall

Peter O'Brien

PHOTO: PETER O'BRIEN

Penn: The chalk, so ephemeral and yet such a statement of presence and process, represents so many different cultures. So many tributes to Jack and in such different places: from the impromptu shrines in private gardens and at his constituency office to grand ceremonies at City Hall and Thomson Hall. The people of Toronto displayed their love and respect for Jack Layton, wearing orange, marching in bands, standing in silent vigil, cheering. The tributes took various forms as temporary and permanent memorials.

Wind Horses

Chris Faiers

Given how Jack championed wind power, it seems appropriate that prayer flags are called Wind Horses in Tibetan. Here is Chris Faiers's Prayer Flag Haibun for the occasion:

Regarding the vigil for Jack, and hanging the prayer flags, I wanted to do something more uplifting (pun intended) than draw another chalk memorial on the concrete of Nathan Phillips. So I bobbled around the fixtures of the skating rink, frantically trying to tie down the flags in the downtown wind tunnel effect. An elderly couple stopped to encourage my efforts. They were possibly from India, and after I accomplished the hanging, they thanked me for displaying the prayer flags. They also felt the flags were a most appropriate spiritual honour for Jack.

> city winds
> carry our prayers
> over Lake Ontario

For Jack, Who Galvanized Me To Action

Honey Novick

It was important for me to go to Toronto's City Hall today, Friday, August 26, 2011 and pay my respects to Jack. That's the talk of the town, "Jack." I knew them, Jack and Olivia. I've been to their home, a couple of times. I know Olivia better than Jack. We sat holding hands at Tooker Gomberg's memorial. I sang the National Anthem for the Chinese Canadian Railway Workers Commemoration for three years. Our paths crossed again and again.

My wonderful friend, Pat, who is Chinese, called me from Guelph, Ontario, before I left home for City Hall. Phone call #1: "Please bow three times to the coffin, it's a Chinese tradition."

Response, mine: "How interesting a request is this. I'd already done that on Monday outside their home."

Phone call #2: "In the Chinese tradition, a loonie or other monies is placed in a red envelope as is candy wrapped in paper. It's o.k. not to take a loonie, but please take wrapped candy and pass it to someone and wish them a sweet life."

Response, mine: I only had three wrapped candies at home and a red silk pouch.

Upon arrival at the City Square, I asked directions of a woman on a bike. She became the first designated candy receiver. I opened the red silk pouch and offered her a candy telling her my friend, who is Chinese, requested I do this in Jack's honour. The lineup to view the coffin was long. Thousands of people waited to say something, "thank you, farewell …" I entered a line to sign the Book of Condolences. While waiting there, I turned around and Olivia was there. We saw each other and we hugged and cried in our own stoic way and placed our foreheads together. Then I said to her, "My friend is Chinese and she asked me to give people something." I pulled out the red silk pouch and gave Olivia a candy and one to Sarah Layton. Olivia looked at the candy and said, "They're orange!!!" She then explained the tradition to Sarah. Olivia told me to get back in line. I said, "We'll see each other again."

I signed the book and wrote my lyric: "I sing show me, show me, show me the love./I sing, show me, show me, show me the hope./I sing, show me, show me, show me the optimism and I'll show you the spirit of a smiling warrior. Nam Myoho Renge Kyo."

I think of Jack and Olivia as the embodiments of style and grace and action and art/culture. I see Jack playing his guitar/banjo, running the streets of downtown Toronto, sweat flying off him and I see him riding his bike. I see their love of pottery, my friend Elizabeth Block's beautiful pottery on their kitchen wall and hear Elizabeth singing at their wedding on Toronto Island. They were surrounded by culture: Chinese, French Canadian, anything that spoke to the heart. I remember him supporting the White Ribbon Campaign, "men against violence against women."… I remember missing Jack in Guelph. We waited in line for him to come. So many people, not enough burgers.

I see Jack gaining political momentum and using his passion for life to be open to ideas and suggestions and like riding an invisible bicycle uphill, inspiriting many to become aware of politics and to care for others. I believe his love of culture is what fuelled his political momentum; it reached the hearts of the people. Jack was a thinking person's politician, a cultured man whose legacy lives in culture, all cultures and is the inheritance we all were given.

Watching Jack Layton's Funeral with the Kids While Recovering from Wisdom Tooth Extraction

Adam Sol

Corpus, a body. Tonguing its wounds.
The idea that the tv is a distraction from
pain. The budget crisis. Percocet
prohibits reading the paper. The almost
comforting, because familiar, taste of
blood. Reports of robocalls. Vanilla
pudding. Strands of stitching in the
gums. I remember, a few months ago,
wondering if the shimmer on his skin
was the lights, the victory, or the screen.
Now I suppose it was the cancer. The
scar tissue. Not victory, exactly. The
chaotic pop music in the surgeon's office.
Asking for a different station just came
out Uhn. The reconfiguring of
priorities. The streamlining. The
yoghurt. The words "corporate" and
"cooperate" are not etymologically
related. The majority. The procession
of dignitaries. His body is in the coffin.
The clips are from the past. You may
taste garlic as the anaesthetic takes effect.
The public outpouring. The holes in my
head. People trusted him to do good
things for them. To try, anyway. The
impact. The impaction. The pinko
fringe. The wisdom. The future. The
full-on screed.

Can I have an apple? Who's that? Is he
the one who died? What's he talking
about? When is mom coming home?
Why is everyone all lined up to see the
coffin if it's closed and you can't even see
if he's really inside it? Who are the
people outside? Why aren't they dressed
up? What did mom mean when she said
you shouldn't overdo it with the pussycat?
We don't have a cat. Was she
joking? Was that a grownup joke? Does
your whole face hurt or just your mouth?
Cause your whole face looks weird.
What's "inspire"? Are there big holes in
your mouth where the teeth were? Will
your wisdom grow back bigger? How do
you know if there are going to be a lot of
people at a funeral or just a few? That
would be embarrassing if they reserved
that big place and nobody came. Is it for
the people who have more love or just
for people who are more famous?
What's the difference between famous
and love? How many people would
come to my funeral? Can I have an
apple? Is that his wife? Is that his son?
Who's that? She looks like she's funny
but she's not being funny now. I know
this song. It's from Shrek. Why won't
you tell me anything?

For Jack Layton: State Funeral and Celebration, August 27, 2011

Ellen S. Jaffe

Dream no little dreams (Indigenous prayer, spoken at the funeral)

The bagpipes play their strange sad lament –
TV lets us see everything without being there:
Olivia Chow's strained face, baby Beatrice,
the silent surging crowd.

This morning I cleaned my kitchen cupboards,
touched up the orange paint (Colorado Dawn) –
death does this, makes us clean, straighten, see, listen, and touch –
loved ones, flowers, household clutter.

Rise Up – Amazing Grace – Hallelujah –
O Canada, how can we lose this man, who gave a voice to the voiceless,
home to the homeless, a song of hope to people in need –
not a saint, but a very human being.

I regret I did not know you, met you
only once – an NDP meeting – shook your hand,
saw your smile. The political is personal,
the personal political – you knew this by heart.

Now you go from the ordinary world – bike paths,
jam sessions, elections – into the mystic …
Into The Mystic, where we can't yet follow.
All our love goes with you – love is all
we need to keep your dreams alive.

As someone who came to Canada from the U.S. in 1979, I especially appreciate
Jack Layton for embodying so many Canadian and human values – for being
a decent, loving, and caring person, and someone who championed human
rights because it is the right thing to do; he worked locally – in food programs,
the White Ribbon Campaign, in supporting the arts, supporting Aboriginal
and other minority rights, helping working people, trying to find solutions in
peaceful, inclusive ways – and still enjoying life, music, bicycling, and of course
his family. May his memory be a blessing.

Meeting the Challenge

Susannah Joyce

On August 27, 2011, I was writing the Conclusion to my latest book, *Meeting the Challenge*. It focuses on a subject I am passionate about: finding respectful, effective ways to help people who endure terrible things in the name of "treatment" for their dual diagnosis of mental health issues and developmental disabilities. The date was significant to me for two reasons: it was the State Funeral of Jack Layton, and it was also the birthday of the late Dr. Herb Lovett, a dear friend and colleague in the field of social services who was also a pioneer around the issues I was writing about.

There was a certain synchronicity in drawing on the combined inspiration and example of these two men, one of whom I was close to personally and the other who I felt close to because of shared values and vision. Both men had a passionate commitment to social justice and both were able to engage and galvanize others to rally for worthwhile causes. Much of their power to touch people came from their ability to share their own humanity with an open heart … to be vulnerable.

Some months ago, I had watched a TED Talk by social worker Dr. Brené Brown (*The Power of Vulnerability*, *www.ted.com/talks*). She speaks of the power of vulnerability among those who are whole-hearted and firm in their belief that what makes us vulnerable makes us beautiful and loveable: This is what I have found: to let ourselves be seen, deeply seen, vulnerably seen; to live with our whole hearts, even though there's no guarantee to practice gratitude and lean into joy in moments of terror … and last and most important, to believe we are enough. Then we stop screaming and start listening. Then we are kinder and gentler to the people around us and to ourselves.

Ultimately, this is what our work is about. To offer ourselves … our whole selves … to others and to see them and hear them and appreciate and be present with their gifts and their pain. Herb was a composer and a musician, and music was dear to Jack Layton's heart. Music invites us to listen and to move and it creates a common ground. So I felt that the final image in the Conclusion to my book, which was a work of whole-heartedness for me, should be the lyrics from a Canadian song performed at Jack Layton's service, with the invitation to step joyfully and lovingly, each into our own dance! "Rise Up!"

The lyrics to "Rise Up!" are on *http://www.lyrics.com/rise-up-lyrics-the-parachute-club.html.*

Two Photos

Jenn Jefferys

PHOTO: JENN JEFFERYS

As news broke of Jack's death, Canadians from all walks of life flocked instinctively to Parliament Hill to lay flowers, gifts, letters and tokens of thanks to Jack and Olivia for their life's work as progressive political activists.

PHOTO: JENN JEFFERYS

Candlelight vigil for Jack the evening of August 22, 2011 on Parliament Hill in Ottawa; candles placed in solidarity surround the centennial flame by heavy-hearted mourners.

On the Verge of a Renaissance

M.E. Csamer

I thought you were coming to bring us home.
Winds of change blew like a hurricane
the wind farm on Wolfe Island could hardly keep up.
Why does cancer get the last word? Will we let it?
I never met you, Jack, until your funeral; there you were
in every word, gesture; love so potent, prevailing,
I was shaken to my youth.

Voice without vote now, should we howl at the wind
as our dull masters pull their shade across the sun?
Why do we forget so easily the power of love?
Is it because we made a song of it?
Remember song is the sound of the world
coming to bring us home. It's when we forget,
we lose you, Jack, when we give in to those
who would make a business out of life.

Famous Last Words

Chris Vandenbreekel

Over the next few days, on the anniversary of his death, there are going to be hundreds, if not thousands, of articles and videos talking about the life of Jack Layton. People much smarter, more experienced, and who knew Jack a lot better than I will offer their thoughts, their analysis, and their memories. What I want to offer though, is the perspective of a young political science student, who saw the man as an inspiration. You see, even though I changed my major to Political Science, I never thought at the time that my end goal would be to become a politician. I saw them as self-serving, as people that had lost their way, people who had forgotten why they had decided to run for office in the first place. Jack Layton changed all that.

He was a man of vision, of integrity. He would grab onto an issue, and make sure that progress was made. He showed Canada that politics can be different, that the perception that many including me had of politicians as those self-serving liars, didn't have to be the reality. In May 2011, we decided to give that change a chance.

Jack brought the NDP into prominence. They had been the fourth place party for years, stuck behind the pesky Bloc Québecois and the powerhouse Liberals and Conservatives. Jack took the NDP and steadily improved their numbers. In his first three tries, he improved the NDP's numbers from a measly 18 seats, to a respectable thirty-seven seats. His voice was getting louder, and that year his message broke through in a huge way. He took the country by storm. He engaged voters like no politician my generation has ever seen before. He engaged young voters, actually encouraged us to get involved. It was the "orange crush" as everyone called it. My parents had a much more interesting take on it. As my dad put it: "This is exactly like Trudeaumania, only ... it's Jackomania. It's scary." That's when he had a Conservative sign on our lawn. By the time May 2nd rolled around, that sign was gone and my parents were determined to vote NDP. Jack had convinced them, as he had so many others, that change was a real possibility.

Some of you will notice that I have been calling him Jack this entire time. I didn't know the man, but neither did many of us. Yes, he was a famous politician, but you would never refer to the Prime Minister as Stephen, or Mr. Ignatieff as Mike. It just seems wrong. It doesn't with Jack.

He had that down-to-earth feel; he seemed like an everyday guy. A man I was speaking to earlier said that Jack was the kind of man you'd want to sit down and have a beer with. Nobody ever had his credentials, his Ph.D in Political Science, shoved in their face. It was never the reason people voted for him.

At the beginning, I said that Jack had changed my view of politicians, that he inspired me. No, sorry: that he *inspires* me. The man may be gone, but his influence is not. Jack's experiences, his life story, they inspire me to push forward. To be that change he envisioned for Canada. He makes me believe that I can make a difference, that we – the people of Canada – can make a difference. As he so beautifully put it in his letter to Canadians, "My friends, love is better than anger. Hope is better than fear. Optimism is better than despair. So let us be loving, hopeful and optimistic. And we'll change the world." Famous last words.

Polis Rising: A Glosa for Jack

Susan McCaslin

– from Jack Layton's final letter to the public

It's hard, dear Jack, to be optimistic without you.
I call you "dear" though we never met,
yet for decades I eyed your steady trajectory,
admired a public man speaking for ordinary Canadians,
passionate, while I wrote and rewrote the same
slippery poem that faded, returned, and would linger,
you arching past me with your bright demeanour,
so much my opposite, extrovert to my introvert;
yet we meet now at candle's quick where friends hunger,
knowing *love is better than anger.*

You made politics into poetry, the *polis*, a grand room
with room for disenfranchised voices,
brought us to our intimate, othered kin.
At the end, cancer magnified you,
your waving crutch, a semaphore for compassion.
When you rallied and sunk in your last year
you embodied something stronger than yourself,
your courage teaching what we've always known,
that hate is not love's opposite, but fear (that's clear),
and hope is better than fear.

In the museums there are corridors of defaced marble,
since to attack the arts is to grab a culture's jugular.
No arts, no blood, no bones, no health.
The arts, not mere concoctions,
not options, but another kind of food for the brood.
Shelter and daily bread; soul food and spirit care.
What are we, if not creatives creating?
Making, dreaming, spinning, elating?
You called us to an adventure in making, a dare,
saying, *optimism is better than despair.*

I used to think being optimistic was Pollyanna-ish.
But in you I found something other than the naïve,
a relentless restlessness that rests only in joy
and fullness, and fulfillment, a wild yes-saying
that takes up and includes all our divine darknesses.
To be other than this hopeful is atavistic,
since this is how evolution itself evolves.
When you left, you left a rarity –
legacy of surprise: ah, we are one (not atomistic),
so let us be loving, hopeful, and optimistic.

In Memory of Jack Layton by an Optimism of Canadian Poets

Sonnet L'Abbé

Sonnet, who contributes frequently to *Globe Books*, sent us an unusual poem, with the following note:

"Upon hearing of Jack Layton's death, people all over the country began tweeting, texting and posting status updates of love, grief and mourning. It was as though everyone wanted to write their own mini-elegy to Layton.

"This outpouring prompted 14 Canadian poets to come together, each providing their own small line of textual tribute, to create this poem, which is their collaborative elegy to the NDP leader. We hope it speaks to the spirit of Mr. Layton and to the ideal of working together across political and geographic divides.

"The poets are: Lori Bamber, Rachel Baumann, Karen Connelly, Adam Dickinson, Akin Jeje, Sonnet L'Abbé, Larissa Lai, Christine Leclerc, Tanis MacDonald, Sachiko Murakami, Billeh Nickerson, angela rawlings, Adam Sol and Rita Wong."

Here is their poem.

In Memory of Jack Layton

by an Optimism of Canadian poets

The night of Jack's passing, hundreds gather at the gallery – candles, songs, gratitude, grief. My own rapid aphasia but heart, heart. Rest, Jack Layton.

I tried to come up with something, but it just didn't work out. The man, brandishing his cane, suddenly/gone.

Ice in punchbowls on rooftops in Toronto. Love is better than winter speech breath bubbles. Love is better than women on vacation, better than anger. Hope is better than a headshot, or a Peace Tower.

They say his smile defined his politics. Out of optimism, out of an inward sunshine that took no rest. To refuse his opponent's foreclosure on the common good. In knowing that the growing front of culture war has no singular face.

Who will stand up for me now?

We will wave canes as wands as tuning forks as white ribbons as rafters as olive branches. We renew our commitment to his life's work. We will wear smiles as deep breaths as shared tongues as porch lights as changes of fortune.

Same perfect goals, imperfectly pursued: Cheers in Tripoli, tears in Toronto. Hope is better than silk scarves, than super-powers, than paint-chips the colour of the butterfly-hour.

A final footstep, patent leather-clad, steady and graceful. From the faded cobblestones of Place Jacques Cartier, from the leafy refuge of Hudson. He shall walk and walk and not feel the earth shift beneath his feet, he shall take easy air into his lungs, he shall be straight of back and great of heart, he shall not fall, nor stick, nor stumble; he shall move forward like a workman or a philosopher

don't go yet

the ones who need you
still struggle to drown out
the roar of greed

a star fades to darkness
only stardust remains

I met you once. We were at your house for an anti-violence thing. Lots
of people in the kitchen. Your mother-in-law in slippers on the stairs.
We sang loudly together, you and I, at that organ you had in the corner.
We sang "Hit the Road, Jack." What a cheeky note for an elegy! O, your
brilliant orange orchestrations! We sang "Hit the Road, Jack."

End of Summer

Terry Ann Carter

Trail
to Parliament Hill –
the ringing bicycle bells

State Funeral
his cane
by his coffin

on her father's shoulders –
a toddler
waves the maple leaf

all eyes
on the day moon –
his message of hope

the discordant final note
in the choral tribute

pond memorial
I plant a floating lily
for Jack

end of summer
the Great Blue Heron stretches
into its own shadow

Irving and Jack

Andreas Gripp

I dragged you to the celebration
of Irving Layton's
100th birthday,
you who know nothing of art
and politics,
me with my books
and orange buttons.

You noted my friends
were social democrats,
that the name *Layton*
cropped up again and again,
in different contexts,
as we schmoozed amid quaffs
of wine.

Too bad he came so close,
you said, adding *it's a shame
to miss a hundred
when you're alive at 99.*

He passed away in 2006,
I replied, with a rather terse
correction,
saying he'd made it to 93,
to which you said
*the election was just last year
and he only died in August,*
boasting that even *you* knew
that much about the players
on Parliament Hill.
*Though even with that white
moustache,
he didn't look a day over 60.*

I finally took you aside,
fearful your ignorance
would be overheard,
that we'd be snickered at
by the literati.

Irving Layton was one of Canada's
greatest poets,
Jack Layton was the leader
of the NDP.
They're two entirely
different people.

So did Jack write any poems?
you asked,
basing your question
again on assumption.
If his dad was such a great poet,
you'd think he would have scribbled some
himself.

Instead of explaining lineage,
those of the Lazarovitch clan,
or that "Jack"
was originally "John,"
I chose to simply nod,
exasperated,
say yes, Jack was indeed
a poet,
his words, eloquent
and elegant,
always speaking out
for the homeless man,
the struggling, single mother,
that we should cherish
our lakes and our trees,

holding his cane up high
in his final year,
quite poetic and prophet-esque,
like a raving Earle Birney,
or Moses
by the Sea of Reeds,

that father Irving
had taught him so well
and would be very,
very proud.

I LIKE LAYTON

Max Layton

I like Layton – it's a good name
Better than Lazarovitch, which
My dad abandoned when he
Began to self-create

For a while, as a child, I
Thought I was related
To Lord Athol Layton, the
Champion wrestler who always
Fought fair, even when tag-team
Midgets gouged his eyes
With sandpaper bandages

I remember, at a gathering of
Adults, being asked who my hero
Was, and everybody laughing when
I said Lord Athol Layton because
They thought I had a lisp

Later, asked if I were the son of THE
Layton, the magical name conjured
In a tone of hushed reverence, I knew
The questioner meant the millionaire
Who owned the big-billboard Layton store
On Ste. Catherine Street – a useful
Misconception when trying to rent
A cockroach-infested room in the
Slums of Montréal

And then, only a few years ago, a most
Surprising discovery: If spoken on the
Phone with a cough and one's hand over
One's mouth, Max and Jack sound the same!

Hello? Yes, this is (cough, muffle) Layton. Is
The PM available?

Oh, Mr. *Layton*! Well, sir, he's in a cabinet meeting
But I could transfer your call. Is this urgent?

Yes, very ...

Wondering if the Layton name had reached the ears of immigration officers,
I asked Max if he knew how his family received the name. Was it changed
from Lazarovitch at port of entry? It wasn't a common or well-known name.
Except in Montréal ...

Max replied with an even more interesting if enigmatic story:

About the name: My grandparents emigrated from Romania in
1913, bringing with them their seven children, including their one-year-
old youngest son Israel Pincu Lazarovitch (literally, "Son of Lazarus").
According to my father (which means this story may not be entirely true),
about a decade earlier, the eighth and eldest son, Abraham, had been sent
to New York where he lived alone and worked at whatever back-breaking,
menial jobs he could find in order to buy steerage places on a ship for the rest
of the family. The reason they came to Halifax (and then Montréal) instead
of New York was because Abraham knew he was dying of tuberculosis and
could only afford tickets to Halifax. He was dead before his parents and
siblings reached the New World shore.

Lazarovitch was the family name while my father was growing up.
However, some time in the thirties or early forties, his three older brothers
changed their last names to Latch. Dad did not like Latch and unilaterally
chose Layton. The University of Saskatchewan now has a number of his
books variously inscribed as "Israel Lazarre" and "Irving Lazarre" and one
where, gloriously, "Lazarre" has a pen stroke through it and "Layton" is
written above it instead ... Who knows, he may have seen the big-billboard
Layton sign on Ste. Catherine Street!

Dad knew and admired David Lewis and was himself a member
of YPSL, the Young People's Socialist League. Was Jack's father and/or
grandfather a member of YPSL as well? If there really is this connection,
then that, interestingly, might explain why "Layton" was such an appealing
Anglo name to him!

Penn: Jack's great-grandfather, Philip Layton, was a blind activist who led a
campaign for disability pensions in the 1930s. That might have impressed

Irving! From 1918 to 1932, Philip's son Gilbert was an executive in the family music store, Layton Brothers, which is still in business as Layton Audio. Gilbert ran as an Independent Progressive Conservative in the federal election of 1945. The Independent aspect might have intrigued Irving. So our speculations are possible. I think Irving would approve.

Everyman Jack – on His Would-Be 62nd Year

Leona Graham

Once upon a time
in a train station, Toronto Central,
I saw you in a crowd of folk
on your way to Ottawa.

Then, in NDP HQ Toronto-Danforth
with my sister Joan, your old political pal
who ran with you for the streets of Old York,
we met.

Jack Layton, as leader of the NDP (my life-long political persuasion)
represented a beacon of hope during my many years as a part-time UK
"expat." The closest we can come in the UK to the NDP is a very second-
best, the Liberal Democrats, since the Labour Party long ago abandoned
its commitment to its labour and socialist roots – a demise that reached an
apex with Tony Blair. Comparing Jack to the so-called top politicians here
(mainly from the upper classes), there's no contest. Jack wins, period. The
UK still awaits someone of Jack's stature. If only.

Looking into Jack's eyes in our one-time close-meet-up in Toronto-
Danforth NDP HQ, I saw a potent, canny man, determined to get what we
all really need: a just and fair society. I could see why my sister Joan Doiron
(an elected education trustee in Toronto for many years) had chosen to
work with both Jack and Olivia on behalf of the people of Toronto.

"Those Eyes"

Robert McMaster

I'm a long-time supporter of the NDP, but only became an official card carrying member in the last year. I was inspired by Jack's courage and the way the NDP seemed to run and organize for the common people of Canada and their rights. I loved to watch Jack speak, mostly through the media, but a few times up close and personal. And what really sold me on the man was his eyes. They twinkled. They danced with joy and friendship to those he was talking to, be it a one-on-one conversation or to a convention hall full to overflowing. You could see in those eyes the sparkle of his dreams of a better Canada for all.

When my partner, harpist Jennifer White, and I heard of Jack's new battle with cancer, we sent a message via his office offering more gentle music from "that NDP-Jack Layton-supporting harper," either on CD, or perhaps a live personal house concert whenever he felt up to it. It was only a few weeks later that we heard the tragic news of his passing.

I have heard, over the years, many positive things about leaving this Earth. "Death is like taking off a tight pair of shoes" is one of my favorites. But the one that strikes home for me about Jack is, "You'll leave this Earth when your job is done." I, like most people, think Jack left us way too soon. But maybe his job was done. Look at the good he has done, from his time on Toronto City Council to his glorious time with the NDP as its leader. Jack brought us all to the point of being the Official Opposition and I think he would have been the next, and long-term, Prime Minister of Canada. He brought us, the NDP, to the front lines of government. He inspired those who heard him speak, shook his hand, and followed his ways in politics to become engaged in making a better world.

Jack's eyes twinkled and sparkled when he talked. This is not something you can fake. Too many politicians have flat dead eyes, no soul. Jack's were different. Hasn't it been said that eyes are the windows to the soul? In Jack, I saw a happy soul. The joy of doing what is good, what is right: you could see all that in his eyes. He has passed on that twinkle to many.

Shortly after joining the London West NDP, I, like Jennifer, had the opportunity as voting delegate to attend the Ontario Convention. As the photographer for London West, I was able to get up close to both our provincial leader, Andrea Horwath, and our freshly elected national leader, Thomas Mulcair. As Andrea was making the introductory speech for Thomas, I watched him in the shadows through my lens. His eyes too were twinkling with tears. When he hit centre stage, they were dancing and sparkling, for real. You can't fake something like that. I feel Jack has passed on his knowledge, his love, his hope to his fellow NDP members of Federal and Provincial Parliaments, to the general membership of the people of the New Democratic Party, and to all the people of Canada. Jack's legacy is in good hands. Just watch our eyes.

Thanking Jack: Shifting the Political Sphere

Jenn Jefferys

Jenn Jefferys is a student of Departments of Journalism and Communications and Womyn's and Gender Studies at Carleton University and a critical/intersectional feminist. I love that this letter moves from the formal Dr. Layton to addressing him as Jack. No one else has referred to him as professor. It's interesting – and appropriate – that so many think of Jack as blue-collar, when his background was definitely upper middle class. But he often wore blue shirts, with the sleeves rolled up!

Dear Dr. Layton:

Every morning in my apartment, I wake up to your warm smile on my shelf; immortalized in a frame of the front page of the *Globe and Mail* from Tuesday, August 22, 2011. I recall that very day. When hundreds of heavy hearted Canadians (my twenty-three year-old self included) gathered in solidarity on Parliament Hill in our Nation's Capital to bid farewell to you, when you were Leader of the NDP Party and official opposition.

I know you hear us from heaven, and you yourself are reassured to know that you will live on in our hearts as many things; an outspoken fighter, feminist, environmentalist and humanitarian – not to mention a blue-collar family man, who wore a wide, charismatic smile below a world-famous "trust-ache" and seemed to have all the time in the world for a genuine, friendly conversation with anyone. You were just you: real. How a public figure *should* be.

Having forever shifted the political sphere from something dark, to something potentially beautiful, may you at long last rest in peace Jack, and thank you for changing this young, cynical feminist's perspective on the face of Canadian politics and instilling a sense of optimism I never thought possible. You changed my life with the following words:

"I believe in you. Your energy, your vision, your passion for justice are exactly what this country needs today. You need to be at the heart of our economy, our political life, and our plans for the present and the future."

I promise to persevere. This country will never be the same because of you and your life's work. So thank you Jack. I am grateful.

Jenn Jefferys

"Your words have made me an activist by nurture"

Melody Richardson

Muskoka, Ontario, August 2012

Dear Jack:

As a writer, I process everything through words. Writing this letter seems the best way to share my thoughts about you.

Jack, you are a metaphor for Canada – at least what Canada and Canadians should be: multilingual, empathetic, respectful, welcoming, possessing a highly developed social conscience and always anxious to seek common ground. I say *are*, Jack, because I only think of you in the present tense.

Actually, that makes sense. Canadian Prime Ministers have been obsessed with branding buildings and organizations and legislation as the legacy they leave us. Your legacy, Jack, is more fluid and organic and grows closer to the bone. Your legacy lives in all of us. It's the desire to serve; the need to share prosperity; the belief that individuals can cause change.

We met several years ago when you came to Muskoka. I'm certain you don't recall all the details of your visit – you've shared your time with so many across the nation. *I* remember. You talked about the state of the nation and your vision of our future. Then you asked for our opinions and you listened.

Man, did you listen! Not passively or absent-mindedly. As we spoke your eyes never wandered, your focus never wavered. Every atom of your being was engaged in our exchange. We knew in that moment what we had to say mattered.

I'll always consider you a literary artist, Jack. While all writers recognize the power of words, few make them powerful. You have. Your final words, your message of love, hope and optimism, continue to move us to *see* more, *do* more, *be* more. Like most writers, I'm a procrastinator by nature. Your words have made me an activist by nurture. Thanks, Jack.

Sure, there will be times when crap happens. I will own anger, know fear and wallow in despair. But when the worst threatens to take my breath away I'll stop to ask "What would Jack do?" I'll breathe deep, listen for your voice and move on.

The ability to inspire others defines leadership. Interestingly, inspire means "to breathe in." Perhaps that's your greatest gift to us, Jack. You continue to inspire, to make us breathe in. As proof, I'd like to share one of my poems. It's the first you've inspired me to write. I know it won't be the last. Anyway, here it is. Hope you like it.

In Memory of Jack Layton

We shall not weep
Not wrap sorrow round us
Not mourn what should have been.
We shall live as you lived
Turn *impossible* into *possible*
Emotion into *motion*
Reaction into *action*
Give your message meaning
As we share it with the world.

The Jack Layton Movie

Andrew Wreggitt

I'm not sure the country knew exactly why it cared so much when we lost Jack – why his death hit them so hard emotionally – even among his many political opponents. It was an unprecedented outpouring of grief for a politician who never managed to get his hands on the reins of power. Why did people care so much? When I took on the task of writing the CBC TV movie about Jack Layton, I knew that question would be at the centre of the drama.

Movies about real people and events are not meant to be answers or definitive statements. They are meant to open up questions – they ask you to feel something, to be free to think for a moment from a different point of view. My job as a screenwriter is to make choices – pick a few key sequences/ moments and let those glimpses of heightened reality add up to a final artistic statement. Some of those moments are by necessity fictional in content but truthful emotionally – scenes that need to stand in for years of complexity.

Making choices like that is a stern responsibility, especially when writing about someone as thoroughly known as Jack Layton – whose influence on the lives of so many Canadians was as profound as it was. But early in the process of "The Jack Layton Story," I was handed a gift by Olivia Chow – and by extension by Jack himself. Olivia said, "Tell a good story, don't worry if this didn't happen that day or whatever, just tell an entertaining story."

The license to play, to think outside the structures we are expected to labour under, is freeing. It's where new ideas are born. Researching Jack's political career, I was struck by how this spirit of play, of creative thinking, was often applied to very serious business with surprising results.

The Jack Layton movie tries to peek behind the curtains at a politician in the midst of his most important election campaign – a man who achieves the political victory of a lifetime and then is immediately faced with crushing tragedy. The portrait that emerged in the making of the film was of a man deeply committed to public service who lived his life openly – to experience new ways of thinking and challenges. His ideas didn't suit everyone, nor did his personal style, but no one could honestly say he didn't believe in what he said – that he didn't care.

And finally when Jack died so abruptly – on the brink of a new stage in his political career – maybe Canadians cared so much because he did.

Farewell

Ian Herring

ILLUSTRATION: IAN HERRING

Optimism and Action: Jack's Legacy to the Arts

Susan McCaslin

> In the following essay, Susan McCaslin provides a striking example of art in action, of what I am calling Applied Jack. Shortly after writing her piece, Susan developed the extraordinary Han Shan Poetry Project described below: hanging poems about trees in the forest she was trying to protect. With Jack as example, Susan bridges the gap between contemplative poetry and the activism that needs to emerge from that place of stillness and compassion.

When rereading Jack Layton's final, poignant open letter the other day, I noticed he uses the word "optimism" (or a variant thereof) five times, the word "hope" six, and the word "change" seven. When I first started to watch Jack on TV as the rising leader of the NDP, he seemed to me an embodiment of positive energy, someone fully alive. Since politicians can be accused of using language manipulatively, I'd like to reflect on how Jack's three powerful words form a kind of triumvirate for individual and social transformation. Thus the members of this trinity of political graces, so evident in Jack's life and thought, are deeply interrelated and constitute his lasting legacy to the arts.

The word "optimism" drew me in, though in the past I've been somewhat resistant to the word. Immediately I think of false optimism. I'm inherently suspicious of popular songs of the 1950s era like Frank Sinatra's "High Hopes," with those "high apple pie in the sky hopes." Yet Jack's optimism isn't Pollyanna-ish, nor is it a Monty Python skit with three guys singing a ditty from the cross: "Always Look on the Bright Side of Life." His kind of optimism doesn't blindly ignore the dismal facts. It's not about being in denial, never admitting doubt, or never surrendering to what we can't change. It's not about living in a bubble or refusing lamentation or tamping down anger in the face of injustice. Jack didn't offer a simple mind over matter recipe or simplistic notion that with positive thinking we can make bad things go away, or assume that always we create our own problems and illnesses.

So if Jack's form of optimism isn't merely a naïve form of positive thinking, then what is it? I would suggest his optimism is about acting in the midst of doubts, moving on, and claiming the power for transformation in each moment. Perhaps we need new language for it, something like radical optimism or deep optimism, or engaged optimism. Such an impetus commits itself to creating the positive conditions it longs for.

Whenever I come across a resonant, repeated word, I go scurrying to my dictionary to look up its derivation. An etymological search on the word "optimism" revealed some interesting things. Eighteenth-century writers like Leibnitz and Voltaire came to associate it with "the best" (Latin "opti" or "optimus"). Voltaire, however, satirized the notion that the actual world is the "best of all possible worlds," given the obvious discrepancies between the haves and have-nots. The Romantic poet Shelley and the American Transcendentalist Emerson tied "optimism" to a hopeful sense that "the good will ultimately prevail." I would say that Jack's use of it doesn't make assumptions about the future, but takes us to a deeper root of the word, the Latin "ops" or power, empowerment. For Jack's form of optimism isn't tied to results or beliefs about how things will turn out, but to the empowerment of individuals and groups within everyday life. Even when he came to accept that he was dying, his words were offered as a way of empowering others.

Returning to Jack's last letter, what is remarkable is how he splits the expected binaries that have become part of our language and dualistic thinking. Love versus hate becomes love versus *anger*. Hope versus despair becomes hope versus *fear*. Optimism versus pessimism becomes optimism versus *despair*. The changes seem simple but Jack has taken a big holistic leap. The old triumvirate of anger, fear, and despair is suddenly replaced by the trio love, hope, optimism. And when you think about it viscerally, psychologically and spiritually, anger is truly at the root of hate, fear at the root of despair, and despair is what keeps us from Jack's form of radical optimism. Jack offers an everlasting yes to being in the world.

Yet what exactly does Jack's form of optimism and the hope that accompanies it have to do with the arts? I believe his positive outlook represents a way of being that is inherently creative, one that can lead to change, transformation of the individual and of the *polis*, the community. A form of radical optimism lies at the very core of the creative process, even when an artist is writing about suffering, injustice, horror, and loss. In responding to what is with a sense of what might be, the artist acts as witness, participant, and transformer in her medium of words, movement, music, etc. as does Jack in his realm of politics.

Jack's support of the arts, then, comes from a sense that art and ethical politics are both forms of political action, *praxis*, twin forms of an ethical aesthetic. And, as every artist knows, to keep on keeping on with the creative process – the wild tumble of words, stories, images – despite writer's block and the vicissitudes of life, is to engage in art ("making" or *poesis*) as a positive force, an outpouring of energy and new life. Such engaged artistry pours from what the Romantic poet William Blake called "the prolific" as opposed to "the devouring." In true art, no matter how agonizing the process, there is at its base this life force, this primal *energia*.

I'm convinced that Jack was a spiritual person based on how he lived and acted in the world. By "spiritual," I mean that he worked at becoming an integral being in his inner life and constantly manifested this integrity in his outer life. As editor Penn Kemp has noted, there simply wasn't much of a gap between Jack's outer persona and his core self. There was a kind of transparency to his soul. That's a huge departure from the kind of duplicity we often see in politicians which makes us cynical.

Some might say Jack clothed his message in simple language to make it accessible to a wide range of people. Although Jack was associated with the United Church, I'm not concerned here with his particular beliefs or even his spiritual practices, but with how they manifested in the world. And what seems clear is that Jack's spirituality is inseparable from his sense of hope-based action. Rather than developing one art form (though he sang, danced, played guitar), he made his public life a work of art, an enactment of authentic being.

His legacy to artists and to the arts is the knowledge that art matters. It creates the conditions for and helps implement social change. The artist enacts a vision in a particular medium – words, paint, musical structures, the voice, the body. The integral politician (not always an oxymoron) is a kind of dancer in the public sphere. And as Jack knew, without the arts a society is soul-less, unkind, lacking in inclusiveness and compassion. The arts awaken empathy and help us know in our minds, hearts, and bodies how we are all interconnected. When the times require it, art offers resistance to oppression, inequality, injustice. It cries out for and has the capacity to inaugurate positive change, first in the individual and then in the political sphere.

To be an effective politician and to be a good artist one needs to be creative, tenacious, and transformative. Jack wasn't a prophet of gloom, but one who could "see before" or ahead to possibilities within the present. Such a person then places himself in the middle of things now so the future can be different. Art likewise is prophetic in this sense: it creates spaces for change.

At the end of her *Revelations of Divine Love*, the English mystic Julian of Norwich offers these powerful words: "And all shall be well, and all shall be well, and all manner of thing shall be well." Taken out of context, Julian's affirmation can be seen as naïvely optimistic, but it is not. Her statement emerges at the end of her autobiography out of a lifetime of suffering and resistance to the intransigence of religious institutions. It is an earned poetic truth that resonates far beyond her time. Jack's last speech isn't simply an attempt to encourage the troops in the face of his much too early demise, but a reflection of how he lived his life and how we might continue to live ours. Whether as artists or partakers of art, art sets us in the public arena, not outside; it connects rather than separates.

As a poet concerned with how language connects us, most of my life I've quietly written and published poetry, considering writing a mode of both contemplation and action. Yet last Thanksgiving, Jack's example compelled me to merge art and activism in what was for me an unprecedented way. I was introduced to a unique, mature forest that was slated for sale and development, despite it being prime habitat for some species at risk. Twenty-five acres would be sold in December if a local conservation group didn't come up with 3 million dollars. Many times I've wondered just what it would take to propel me into a more direct and communal form of activism. This was it. But what can artists do?

By December, our small group had organized a series of arts initiatives to bring attention to the issue. First, there was An Afternoon of Arts and Activism in the forest. Next, inspired by this event, a teacher from the local fine arts school brought three busloads of students on a field trip to the woods. Canadian poets have had lots to say about trees and forests, but not all can travel to Langley on short notice to lend their support. But what if we suspended their poems in the trees, thereby creating an anthology in the forest? I sent out a call for tree poems to all the writers' organizations to which I belonged and soon poems were flooding in. I received over 200 poems, which I encased in sheet protectors and mounted in the forest for the Han Shan Poetry Project. Local and provincial print media and two television stations covered two visits by renowned artist Robert Bateman.

As I write, the outcome is unknown. I've learned from Jack to live with optimism and hope in the midst of uncertainty, though it isn't easy. Jack has helped me resist discouragement and even despair. I never met Jack in person, but for me he is an embodiment of courage. I see him waving his cane, dancing in Québec, biking, living out his vision for a more equitable, kinder, more compassionate Canada. He has become a living parable for ordinary, extraordinary Canadians of all ages and circumstances. As much as we miss him, he is still with us. We too can dance, wildly swing our canes, attentive to those incremental shifts that move things along. Through a politics and an aesthetic of attention, we still have the freedom to create the world anew in our words, images, and lives.

J'Acktivist

Penn Kemp

Je suis activiste ... This sound poem was first performed along with an orchestra of participants on August 21, 2012 for Cabernet Cabaret, London Ontario: "Celebrating Jack Layton, the Environment and the Arts." This benefit concert for the London West NDP was a night to remember, and a night to remember Jack. On September 10, I performed the poem again, this time for Thomas Mulcair at a fundraiser sponsored by London-Fanshawe NDP. This time, the poem went on to celebrate Mulcair:

Won
Once
Once ha
Once half
Once having
Once having no
Once having no-one
Once having known
Once having known you
Once having known youth
Once having known youth sir
Once having known youth ccrtain
Once having known youth certain tea
Once having known you the certain T-off
Once having known you the certainty of see
Once having known you the certainty of seeing
Once having known you the certainty of seeing you
Once having known you the certainty of seeing you move
Once having known you the certainty of seeing you move some
Once having known you the certainty of seeing you move sometimes
Once having known you the certainty of seeing you move sometimes
through
Once having known you the certainty of seeing you move sometimes
through our
Once having known you the certainty of seeing you move sometimes
through our mine
Once having known you the certainty of seeing you move sometimes
through our mind sand

Once having known you the certainty of seeing you move sometimes
through our minds and all
Once having known you the certainty of seeing you move sometimes
through our minds and always
Once having known you the certainty of seeing you move sometimes
through our minds and always

through
through our
through our spear
through our spirit
through our spirits sooth
through our spirits smooth
through our spirits smoothes us
through our spirits moves us sir
through our spirits moves us sir ten
through our spirits moves us certainly
through our spirits moves us certainly too
through our spirits moves us certainly to ACT!
through our spirits moves us certainly to ACT, JACK!

Once having known you the certainty of seeing you move sometimes
through our minds and always
through our spirit moves us certainly to ACT, JACK!

The Winnipeg Toast to Jack Layton

Judy Wasylycia-Leis

Upon hearing the news of Jack Layton's passing, my first reaction was disbelief. Like so many others, I had seen his press conference the month before his death but believed he would conquer all as he had done before so many times in his life. I thought cancer would never defeat him – at least not at the pinnacle of his life before the significance of the orange wave had been fully grasped.

So many memories come flooding in at the mention of Jack's name:

– how he "dreamed no little dreams," resulting in historic breakthroughs like Bill C-48 and the transfer of $4.6 billion in the 2005 federal budget from corporate tax cuts to post-secondary education, aboriginal affairs, housing and the environment.

– how he always ended his speeches with the words, "building a Canada where no one is left behind" and "don't let them tell you it can't be done."

– how he never complained about anything – no matter how difficult the political crisis or painful the health challenge – and always asked about the well-being of his caucus colleagues and their families.

– how he challenged us to move out of our comfort zones whether it be in terms of trying new outreach strategies and use of social media or taking on new responsibilities as he did with me in moving me out of my role as health critic and into finance. (I initially believed this change in critic responsibility was punishment for not supporting him in the leadership campaign but quickly learned that it was about challenging us personally and that Jack didn't have a vindictive bone in his body.)

– how he practiced politics with a difference, never tolerating personal attacks or jokes that put down others; how he gave us the evil eye whenever we heckled in the House of Commons and never stopped talking about politics as a higher, noble calling.

– how he believed in inclusion, demanding the party do better when it came to nominating women as candidates and redressing the gender imbalance in Parliament; how he championed the rights of persons living with disabilities, made support for same sex marriage a matter of public policy and caucus discipline, fought for systemic solutions to address the historic injustice facing aboriginal peoples, and rejoiced in the ethnocultural diversity of his community and country.

– how he built a united Caucus and a strong Party that could withstand the test of time with a foundation based, not on personalities and individual contributions, but on values and collective efforts.

– how he was eternally optimistic, never doubting the possibility of an NDP federal government and always believing in the inherent goodness and potential for greatness of the human race. As he said, "Let us be loving, hopeful and optimistic and we can change the world." These words of Jack Layton and a lifetime of action devoted to building a better world will always be there for us. They are, in the words of an old poem, springs of water when we are thirsty, rays of light when we are in darkness, and reason for rejoicing always. Let us rejoice in the life and legacy of Jack Layton.

These notes were given at The Winnipeg Toast to Jack Layton on the anniversary of his passing, August 22, 2012.

Judy updated her piece with these remarks:

Jack Layton changed our party and this country forever and for the better. He transformed the NDP into a powerful force at the national level and he gave Canadians the gift of hopeful politics. For those of us who had the good fortune of serving in Caucus under Jack's leadership, the gifts he shared are precious beyond words but none more important than his unwavering commitment to the principles of social justice and equality and to the pursuit of those principles based on respectful politics and inclusive participation. Jack leaves for all of us the moral imperative that building a better world is our responsibility and that it begins with a belief in the inherent goodness in each one of us.

My favourite story about Jack is how he always asked about our son Nick who lives with a major disability and how supportive he was when family responsibilities took me away from Caucus and House business. One of Jack's legacies is his commitment to increasing the number of women in politics and creating a "family-friendly" Caucus.

Thanks for including me in this amazing project and major undertaking.

Judy Wasylycia-Leis

"A handsome heart"

Penn Kemp and Irene Mathyssen

This is an excerpt from my radio interview with Irene Mathyssen. It was produced by Ed von Aderkas for my show, *Gathering Voices*, now archived on *www.chrwradio.com/talk/gatheringvoices* (August 2012).

Penn Kemp: I am delighted to invite Irene Mathyssen, NDP MP for London-Fanshawe, into the studio. Welcome, Irene!

Irene Mathyssen: What a pleasure to be here and to be part of this remarkable project. I understand we're talking about Jack Layton. He was certainly the most incredible man. I am sure we will always miss him in so many ways. As a member of our caucus, he was always understanding, collegial and he listened very, very carefully.

PK: He had an ability to recall conversation from a year back or so and be right with you as if you were the only person in the world. That was an astonishing gift.

IM: It was! Thousands of people whom he came in contact with felt that they knew him. That always astounded me. They felt very much that he was a friend. He had that gift of making people feel that they mattered, because he believed they did. There was no one that he was willing to walk past or overlook, because they were *there*; they were part of his space and he wanted to embrace them. That's what we loved about him so very much. He looked at every individual as a unique person with something to offer, with tremendous gifts. He valued all of those gifts. Unfortunately, you don't see that in every leader.

PK: I think we have a good beginning in Thomas Mulcair.

IM: I think that Thomas is very cognizant of what it is the country needs and how we as New Democrats fit into that vision or can make that vision. There isn't a day goes by that he doesn't mention Jack. There's a collective wisdom that goes back many generations.

PK: There is a sense of working together rather than a master leading slaves.

IM: Yes, yes.

PK: There's a real sense of collegiality. In fact, in honour of Jack, I invented a word: 'inclusivity'. It is not in the dictionary but it certainly should be. I have never met a person who was more inclusive. There was no lack of integrity. He was the same person all the way through, whether he was talking to you, or to thousands of people. Although he was funnier if you knew him personally.

IM: Yes, a remarkable sense of humour and incredible warmth. The last time that I really had a chance to speak to him at length and enjoy his company was at Stornoway. He was determined that we would celebrate mightily. We would celebrate the breakthrough of New Democrats as Official Opposition. A tent was put up in the back yard at Stornoway. It's a really wonderful house, quite warm and comfortable, huge but there's an intimacy about it. We were ushered in and then out to the backyard into this marvellous tent. The staff was all there. There was wonderful music, our favourites, Rock 'N Roll. The neighbours had probably never heard such commotion. And the joke was, "My goodness, they've arrived, and there goes the neighbourhood!" It poured rain but the food, the company, everything was fantastic. A real sense that something quite extraordinary had happened and is happening and was going to continue.

PK: We are going to launch this book on May 2 in honour of the NDP becoming the Official Opposition.

IM: Yes. A remarkable day. I can remember watching the results coming in. As the numbers rolled in, I forgot to watch my own results.

PK: I happen to know that, over the years of being voted in, you have increased your numbers in every election. Before you ran, you taught drama.

IM: I taught drama, a little bit, here and there, and English.

PK: That should serve you in good stead!

IM: Well, I have to stick to Her Majesty's English; I can't descend into what I hear from across the way!

PK: I'm grateful for that. When I first had the idea for this book, it was called *Jack and the Arts*. It was primarily poets, writers and artists who responded.

In realizing the scope of what Jack offered, I've expanded that notion into three parts: Jack in the arts and cultures, including the Chinese, of course, through Olivia, and First Nations. He spent his dying days with an eagle feather in hand, significantly. And his ongoing influence on us through the year, and through the NDP. I think he's had an outstanding influence on raising the level of debate.

IM: Very much so. I should tell you about our first meeting at a caucus with Jack. We had it in one of the largest rooms in Centre Block, the Railway Room. It's quite historic, with pictures of pioneers building the railroad. A remarkable room, the only one that was large enough to accommodate 103 MPs and staff and those who were there for the first meeting of this brand new caucus. Bleachers were set up because there was going to be an official photograph. And, of course, Jack was going to deliver his first speech to the media with his caucus. So we arrived, milling about, greeting old friends and getting to know these wonderful new MPs.

PK: The young people from Québec.

IM: Yes! Brilliant young people, and so determined to be good MPs, to deliver service. They learned very fast and for all the right reasons. Nothing selfish, nothing self-serving: they knew this was an important message to carry. It was marvellous to go around and see new faces and to cultivate the beginning of new friendships. The Chief of Staff, Anne McGrath, was there, a most remarkable woman, brilliant and gifted.

PK: She took good care of Jack.

IM: Very good care of Jack. She was there for advice and support: they were great friends. Her gift to all of us was wonderful patience. Anne came into the Railway Room. You know how a mother looks dotingly at her new child, with awe and pride and love. That's what she was doing at the doorway.

PK: "My babies!"

IM: Yes, and they were all here, some as young as nineteen. Anne was very clearly pleased. We were all waiting in anticipation of seeing Jack because we hadn't seen him since the campaign trail. He came in glowing, an incredible aura. He was so happy and proud. I don't think for one instant that it was a pride as in "Look at what I have accomplished." It was a pride as in "Look at what we can do now together."

PK: Look at what we can do together.

IM: He greeted us with the usual hugs and greetings. Jack does not come into a room without hugs and greeting and welcoming. He'll remember the last time he spoke to you, and if there was something going on in your life, a distraction, kids, whatever … It was time for him to speak; the media was there. When he began to speak, a tiny tear rolled down his check. It was so emotional, but he was absolutely brilliant. He was on his game. It was this incredible moment: we can change things for the better. We can bring so much good to the people of this country. Those are moments that you can never forget. Jack was the master of that kind of moment.

PK: And moving!

IM: In terms of keeping Jack moving, he was the same with crowds of people. He always travelled light. He would probably only have two people with him, three at most, if Anne were with him. Karl Bélanger, his press secretary and maybe someone driving because Karl was the press guy. Jack insisted that the day be full. If he was going into a community, he was going to see as many people, do as many events as humanly possible. So it was always a matter of keeping Jack moving.

PK: What an extravert!

IM: But if there was someone in the crowd who needed to have a quick word or ask him for help, Jack intuitively found that person. It didn't matter if he was late. He had to hear, to offer advice and his card.

PK: *Art in Action* has a video shot at la fête nationale in Québec, online. You must see it.

IM: I'll look forward. Jack was in his element when he was back on home soil in Québec, in a way we hadn't seen in twenty or thirty years. It was inspiring, absolutely inspiring.

PK: Tell me about Jack's influence in other cultures as well.

IM: He had a remarkable gift for reaching out and understanding immediately someone who had come from another culture. He would create a sense of friendship, camaraderie, trust. Trust is probably the best word. He made every effort to come into every community. I have a significant Muslim population in my riding, quite a remarkable community, celebrating and encouraging one another to be the very best they could be. Jack understood that. When he first met them in London, they didn't trust politicians ...

PK: ... who had made promises and not delivered.

IM: Yes. So they wanted to get the measure of the man. It was clear to me that they knew where Jack stood – on the side of peace, respecting community. They absolutely trusted him.

PK: Especially respecting diversity.

IM: They are very much believers in the Jack Layton NDP. The Sikh community also has a big warm spot for Jack. In the Leader's office, there was this huge ornate sword, a ceremonial piece that was a gift from the Sikh community to Jack because he was special, a very valuable gift in his honour. I think it was a symbol of trust.

PK: Discriminating wisdom and awareness, cutting through.

IM: Very much, very much.

PK: He talked about that canoe trip up in the Northwest Territories, into the most beautiful country in the world. The eagle flying overhead and dropping a feather ... I'm so glad it was a feather!

IM: Yes, yes. It dropped onto the shore and they went to retrieve it.

PK: That's astonishing!

IM: Yes, and a significant symbol. He knew that it meant something important.

PK: When would that have been?

IM: That would have probably been in 2007.

PK: Just before the great Orange Wave. He had faith in our potential. He encouraged us to act and to rise above the negative.

IM: I don't think that any of us has the luxury to sit back and wait for someone else to do what we need to do. And he never stopped doing it. One time, Jack was going to take a week-long camping holiday, Jack's version of a holiday. He's going to be white-water rafting all day and in the evening he's going to finish his book. That was Jack.

PK: But it was balanced. He was very fit.

IM: Incredible energy. You couldn't be close to Jack without feeling that electricity. I can still see that smile.

PK: And you feel that you catch glimpses of him.

IM: Very much so. In what people are doing. There is an incredible sense of respect that would make him proud, proud of our desire to do what is right for the country. Thank you for this chance to talk about the good and the positive. Politics has a darker aspect. Jack was light.

PK: That's right. I focus on Jack as a mentor, an inspiration.

IM: You've reminded me of something I dislike. I will never say I hate my opponents because it is a diversion of positive energy. One last story about the last rally that Jack did in London during the 2011 election. It was a whirlwind as always with Jack. He climbed onto the stage and people were just mesmerized. My sister was there; she had never actually met him. After it was over, she said, "Irene, Jack is so wonderful. I knew he was smart and I knew he was incredible. But I didn't know he was so handsome!" So I invited her to come and meet him, "because he has a handsome heart as well."

PK: A handsome heart. What a lovely way to end. Thank you, again, Irene.

IM: We will be very pleased to carry the book on our NDP webstore.

From Tommy to Tom

Gavin Stairs

What will happen to the Orange Wave now? Poet John B. Lee writes: "I was recently in the post office when the postal clerk was being asked about the Tommy Douglas stamp. 'Who is Tommy Douglas?' asked the customer. 'I have no idea,' responded the clerk. We've been discussing that all morning here, and no one in the office knows who he was. Needless to say, however shocked I may have been, I leapt into the conversation and told them of his many impressive accomplishments. Obviously, I mentioned the western party he formed, the formation as well of the NDP, the establishment of universal medicine in Canada, his status as 'the most important Canadian' by the recent poll taken by CBC in the production of their popular series of biographies of essential Canadians, but when I mentioned that he was the grandfather of Kiefer Sutherland they were finally and truly impressed. How do you know all that? She asked. I said, 'I know everything.' Meaning it as a joke, but inside I was weeping. Only a year or so more, and the fact that he was Kiefer Sutherland's grandfather will be forgotten too. Who is Irving Layton? How quickly we forget."

Tommy Douglas was voted the greatest Canadian in a CBC poll a few years ago. If you were to ask why, I think the overwhelming answer would be Medicare ... Tommy lived through the hard times in the Prairies and helped to found the New Democratic Party there. He became the first NDP government leader there, and learned all the foundation lessons that have guided the party ever since. He saw the privation of the time in the kitchens and fields of Saskatchewan, so he knew that the great part of the suffering of the great mass of working people was caused by fear of loss of income or unsupportable debt owing to illness or injury, loss of employment and old age. He determined that these were risks that all people had in common, and that what was needed was universal insurance against such calamities. So he set about devising a plan to deal with the problem.

The beginning of the federal NDP is a history of the boom years after WWII. The NDP was led by a succession of great leaders, including T. C. Douglas. It was during this time, especially during the tenures of Tommy, his successor David Lewis and then Ed Broadbent, that the country developed into an industrial powerhouse that believed there was a social contract between capital and labour, between the corporate leaders and the workers at all levels on whose backs the wealth of the nation was being created. The membership and vote for the NDP grew over these years to a maximum under Ed Broadbent. The NDP had begun as a prairie populist movement supported by the small business men and women who both operated and worked the farms of Saskatchewan and the Great West of Canada. With the move to Ottawa, the party picked up unionists and industrial labourers in the East, as well as the fishers and seasonal workers of the forests and natural resources of the Maritimes and Newfoundland. Of course, this led to struggle and division in the party, but the NDP has developed a resilience based on strict adherence to internal democracy. This is still the basis of the NDP, even as the politics of the nation has shifted under their feet.

Toward the end of the Broadbent era, the old social contract began to disintegrate under a global shift away from the power of the ballot toward the power of corporate elites, empowered by a shift in the balance of wealth distribution from the broad middle class to the upper echelons of corporations and capitalists. And that disintegration has continued up to this day. Now there are new cries in the streets, for justice for the 99% of us who control less of the wealth of the country than the 1% who sit in the board rooms and executive suites of the banks and corporations.

It was during this disintegration that the two women, Audrey McLaughlin and Alexa McDonough, who have led the NDP were charged with holding back the tide. And to a large measure, they succeeded. But the NDP share did decline, until Jack Layton was elected leader. Under Jack, the electoral success went up steadily until the election of 2011. The Liberal Party more or less collapsed under the weight of too many scandals and too much cynicism, and the NDP surged forward in the so-called Orange Tide to capture the Official Opposition. Unfortunately, they failed to prevent the Conservatives under Stephen Harper from gaining a majority.

Jack fought the 2011 election while fighting off prostate cancer. The whole nation watched in awe as he went from weakness to strength, waging the electoral fight while walking with a cane, and becoming more and more confident and joyous throughout. By May 2nd, we had the delicious vision of a triumphal NDP in opposition, preparing for four years of Conservative onslaught until the 2015 election, in which the NDP under Jack would sweep into power.

Of course, that vision was shattered with the return of Jack's cancer, and his rapid decline and death in the summer of 2011. There has not been such an outpouring of grief in this country for many years as we witnessed at Jack's state funeral, and in the events surrounding his passing.

The extraordinary thing has been that the NDP has not collapsed under the weight of this tragedy. Rather the reverse. NDP members have declared that they are the legacy of Jack, and they will carry forward the Orange Tide, to victory in 2015.

Now we have a new leader: Tom Mulcair. Tom was Jack's Québec lieutenant during the last election, and he was the clear winner in the leadership convention. Whatever doubts there may have been have been dispelled during the current sittings of the Parliament and during Tom's tours of ridings across the land. The Orange Tide is reforming.

We went to meet and hear Tom Mulcair this evening. It was very encouraging, as he came across well, and spoke of carrying forward the legacy of Jack. He told us that there would be a lot of smiling on the way. I had seen that Tom was carrying this positive approach forward in his work on the Hill and elsewhere, and here he was confirming this as a personal policy. I am much encouraged. With sufficient men and women of good will, much can be accomplished.

Jack Pine

Nancy Layton

The tribute to Jack was lovely. It hardly seems possible that a year has gone by since his passing.

Jack's family and close friends travelled to Hudson last summer to bury some of his ashes in the small cemetery where his Steeves grandparents (Constance and Jack) and his father were laid to rest. So much of the man Jack became was influenced by this community where he grew up and it was very special to have some of the family's neighbours and closest Hudson friends join us and share their memories.

In early summer 2012 the family once again came together, this time on Toronto Island, to bury his ashes under a lovely Jack Pine tree planted in his memory by the residents. Jack had a special affinity for this community too as he lobbied on their behalf when the possibility arose that their houses might be razed for parkland. He and Olivia "house-sat" several summers with Jack's kids, Sarah and Mike, and they often talked of moving there when they finished political life. Jack and Olivia were married on the Island and on August 25th, Mike too was wed to Brett Tryon, and we felt Jack's presence with us on that special day.

On August 22, 2012, the family said their final good-byes to Jack as his remaining ashes were buried in the Necropolis, under beautiful old trees and surrounded by a garden lovingly planted by Olivia. On his headstone rests a remarkable bust that Olivia sculpted that somehow captured not just the joy one would see in his smile but also the energy and enthusiasm with which Jack lived every day of his life. The family sang, shared some final thoughts and tears to a son, a husband, a dad, a brother, a grandfather and an inspiration to so many Canadians.

Penn: That Jack Pine leans left, still thriving. It is marked by a plaque dedicated to Jack, east of the Algonquin Island Bridge on the north side along the Toronto Island road from the Ward Island Ferry.

Poem for Peace in Two Voices

Penn Kemp

PHOTO: JOE WILSON

Jack Layton is reading my "poem for peace" with me. He didn't take much convincing to perform the piece, gallantly leaping to his feet without a rehearsal. I took the lead in English and followed Jack as the second voice in French. You can read and hear many translations of the poem on *www.mytown.ca/poemforpeace*. The occasion was the NDP benefit dinner at the Fanshawe Pioneer Village, June 7 2007, in London, ON. I notice that the orange-ish door frame leading into the unknown is a motif repeated in Ian Herring's illustration. But hope prevails! The Mathyssen sign above Jack's head celebrates Irene, our beloved MP for London-Fanshawe.

Acknowledgements

This book is dedicated to Jack Layton, who, in the process of my writing and collecting work, became my mentor in more ways than I could have imagined. He taught me to make decisions quickly and to take direct action, to regret nothing and to risk asking for help, for anecdotes, for funding. His energy seemed to rest lightly on my shoulders. Like an intercessory between the worlds, he (as spirit or as memory) helped me negotiate political worlds unfamiliar to me. He taught me to take nothing personally. He helped me get over inhibitions of marketing because the book's purpose was greater than my fear. *Jack Layton: Art in Action* allowed me to take positive action in recording anecdotes as examples of what can be done in effective political action. "What would Jack do?" became my maxim, and that motif runs through the book. Jack is the wind behind the sails and (I hope) the sales of this book.

Deep thanks to Allan Briesmaster and John Calabro of Quattro Books, for their enthusiasm and support throughout this project. I'm entirely grateful for Allan's encouragement and editorial expertise. He is the kind of editor books are dedicated to. Thanks as well to Franci Louann for her sharp eye. The responsibility for any errors and for many of the titles is mine.

Special thanks to Nancy Layton for the use of her blog written during the last election campaign and to Doris Layton for her stories. To Irene Mathyssen, Shawn Lewis, and Gina Barber for their ongoing encouragement and contacts. To the NDP for continuing to follow the trail Jack's vision lit up. To all those who have been sustained by Jack's example. To Peter O'Brien, Kathleen Dindoff and Bob Siskind for advice on fundraising. To Palimpsest Press for the initial request to write about Jack.

For all those who contributed anecdotes about Jack by phone, in person and electronically, and to those who sent photographs or suggested stories and artwork. To Grahame Beakhurst, angela rawlings, James Stuart Reaney, and Ewan Whyte for their comments. To all who pre-ordered copies, made donations, and spread the word. To those who have organized launches for the book well before it was released, especially in BC.

To Radio Western, CHRW FM, for interviews with Olivia Chow, Mike Layton, Irene Mathyssen, and Shawn Lewis; and, for music dedicated to

Jack, to James Gordon and Laura Bird – all aired on my show, *Gathering Voices*, and archived on *www.chrwradio.com/talk/gatheringvoices*. Thanks to producer Ed von Aderkas. Special thanks to Irene Mathyssen, Mike Layton, Olivia Chow, and Shawn Lewis for the conversations we recorded.

To Edward Pickersgill for posting *http://www.mytown.ca/penn-jacklayton* and monthly updates at *www.mytown.ca/pennletters*. Thanks to my friends' enthusiasm, ongoing conversation and care, and Jake Chalmers' suggestions for contacts on Toronto Island. And most especially to my beloved Gavin Stairs, Jack's brother-in-law, for his constancy, sustenance and technical wizardry, and for his wisdom through long discussions throughout the gestation of this book.

Jack Layton: Art in Action was published with the help of a grant from the Douglas-Coldwell Foundation, a Canadian organization promoting education about and research into social democracy, activism and social justice. See *www.dcf.ca/*.

Previous Publications

An early version of Gina Barber's piece appeared on *http://www.thebeatmagazine.ca*. Reprinted with permission.

"My Olivia," © Laura Bird Wigborough Music 2011 SOCAN

Versions of the poems by Joe Blades, Ellen Jaffe, Franci Louann, Elsie Neufeld and me were posted in *Poems for Jack Layton*, *http://lipstickpoetry.blogspot.com/*, Summer 2011 (Lipstick Press). Reprinted with permission.

Terry Ann Carter's "pond memorial" was previously published in the *Haiku Canada Journal*. Her "end of summer" was published in *Frogpond: Literary Journal of the Haiku Society of America*.

Earlier versions of my poem "J'Acktivist" have been published under different titles in different books of my poetry, *Animus* and *Incrementals*.

Anne Lagacé Dowson's column in "Bloke Nation" is on *http://hour.ca/2011/08/04/jack-layton-the-personification-of-grace-and-courage/*.

"Jack's Dream:" words by Jack Layton, adapted by James Gordon. Music by James Gordon © Pipe Street Publishing, 2011.

Thanks to novelist Katherine Govier for suggesting that I contact Patricia Bradbury.

Cecilia Kennedy's poem was published in Waterloo University's *The New Quarterly*, Fall 2012.

"Poetry Makes Nothing Happen, Says Auden. True or False?" (title mine) is drawn in part from Susan McMaster's book, *The Gargoyle's Left Ear: Writing in Ottawa* (Black Moss, 2007), pp. 149-53.

Earlier versions of Glen Pearson's article appeared in *The London Free Press* and *Huffington Post*.

The link to Judy Rebick's original essay, which was published in August, 2011 is *http://rabble.ca/blogs/bloggers/judes/2011/08/le-bon-jack*.

My radio show, *Gathering Voices*, featured interviews about Jack. The shows are all archived on *www.chrwradio.com/talk/gatheringvoices*.

August 14, 2012. *Gathering Voices* features a conversation with London MP, Irene Mathyssen.

September 4, 2012. *Gathering Voices* features a conversation with Toronto MP, Olivia Chow.

September 25, 2012. *Gathering Voices* features a conversation with Jack's son, Toronto Councillor Mike Layton.

March, 2013. *Gathering Voices* features news about *Jack Layton: Art in Action*; a reading of "Jedi Jack" by Shawn Lewis, NDP Constituency Assistant, London-Fanshawe. James Gordon and Laura Bird sing songs dedicated to Jack, and Anne Anglin and I perform my sound poem for Jack, "J'Acktivist."

Contributors' Bios

Gay Allison is poet and feminist who was born on the prairies and now lives and works in Stratford, home of the Stratford Shakespeare Theatre.

Teresa Armstrong is a Provincial Member of Parliament for London-Fanshawe and the NDP Critic for Training, Colleges and Universities as well as Seniors. *www.teresaarmstrong.com*.

Susan Baker is the Executive Director of the Riverdale Share Community Association and produces Toronto's Riverdale Share Concert. She received Jubilee Medals for her contribution to her community.

Gina Barber, former teacher and politician, still monitors city hall through her blog, London Civic Watch.

Karl Bélanger is Secretaire Principal | Principal Secretary, Chef de l'Opposition officielle | Leader of the Official Opposition, Nouveau Parti démocratique | New Democratic Party.

Simon Bell, a Canadian photographer with a specialty in 3D photography, is the author of several travel and nature photography books: *www.simonbell.ca*.

Performing since 1990, Orangeville songstress **Laura Bird** shares her love of music and community on two acclaimed recordings and is currently working on a third; see *www.laurabird.com*.

Joe Blades is an artist, author, educator, publisher, radio producer-host in Fredericton, NB.

Patricia Bradbury is a writer and a professor at Mohawk College.

Ottawa poet **Ronnie R. Brown** is the author of six books of poetry and is the winner of the 2006 Acorn-Plantos People's Poetry Award for *States of Matter*, Black Moss.

Clark Bryan is the founder, Executive and Artistic Director of The Aeolian Performing Arts Centre. He is an accomplished concert pianist and President of The Ontario Registered Teachers Association.

Eugenia Catroppa is the founder and artistic director of The WHEEL: Art and Music for Pagan Toronto, committed to commissioning new, interdisciplinary art works that highlight pagan themes.

Terry Ann Carter is the president of Haiku Canada and the author of five poetry collections.

Dwight Chalmers is a retired special education teacher who worked on many of Jack's local campaigns.

Olivia Chow is the Official Opposition Transport Critic and NDP MP for Trinity-Spadina, Toronto. *http://www.oliviachow.ca*

M.E. Csamer's books include *Another Way of Falling*, *Paper Moon*, *Light Is What We Live In*, and *A Month Without Snow*. She is President of the League of Canadian Poets (2012).

Tina Conlon is a Philippine immigrant, community activist, and emerging artist. *http://macconlon.wordpress.com/*

Associate Professor in English at University College of the North, Manitoba, **Carolyn Hoople Creed** has published poetry across Canada, recently in the *Global Poetry Anthology* (Véhicule Press, 2012).

Kathleen Dindoff is a psychologist with extensive experience in organizational behaviour and career management and wellness. She is a professor of psychology at Fanshawe College in London.

Joan Doiron was a Toronto downtown school trustee from 1978 until 1994. She lives in West Island, Montréal, near where Jack grew up. *www/education/joan.doiron.htm~.*

Chris Faiers lives on the edge of the Canadian Shield, where he coordinates annual PurdyFests at his ZenRiver Gardens retreat. He was the inaugural recipient of the Milton Acorn People's Poet Medal in 1987.

Don Ferguson is a founding member of *Royal Canadian Air Farce*, which ran for twenty-four seasons on CBC Radio and sixteen on CBC Television, and continues to broadcast its annual New Year's Eve Special.

Peter Ferguson is a scientist who, inspired by Jack Layton, changed his career focus, including running for the federal NDP in the last two general elections. He and his family live in London, Ontario.

Kathy Figueroa's book, *Paudash Poems*, was published in July, 2012. Her work has appeared in numerous newspapers and magazines across Ontario, as well as on various international websites.

Robert Banks Foster, *CVII* editor under Dorothy Livesay, publishes across Canada, recently in *Event, Branch*, and *Other Voices*. He lives in Kaslo, BC.

Sylvia Fraser is the author of hundreds of magazine articles, six novels (historical and contemporary) and five non-fiction books. Two were travel quests – one to India; a second to the Amazon.

Katerina Fretwell's sixth poetry collection, *Angelic Scintillations*, was published by Inanna in 2011. Her poem "Kissing Cousins" was shortlisted for *Descant*'s 2012 Winston Collins Poetry Prize.

Gale Zoë Garnett is a writer, actor, arts activist, workshop leader, and initiator of The Canadafrica Kidlit Booklift (bringing Canadian children's books to the Nyaka Aids Orphans' School in Uganda).

Daniel Gautier lives in Hudson, QC by the Lake of Two Mountains. As a painter of the sea, his long Maritimes stays have become true rituals that give rhythm to all his work, reflecting the region's purity.

Ann Gelsheimer works as a Psychological Consultant for the Upper Grand District School Board. She loves her home in beautiful Hockley Valley, where she cares for her animal friends, domestic and wild.

Silence Genti is a Zimbabwean-born freelance writer, web developer, world music and world cultures aficionado, CHRW radio host and a Londoner with a passion for community.

Alexandre T. Gingras is the Adjoint parlementaire/Parliamentary Assistant for Françoise Boivin, NDP Member of Parliament for Gatineau.

Michele Girash is a former Ontario Regional Organizer for Canada's NDP, a campaign manager, community organizing consultant and a frustrated quilter.

James Gordon is a Guelph-based singer/songwriter, activist, playwright, community facilitator and provincial NDP candidate.

Luba Goy is a graduate of Montréal's National Theatre School. As a member of *Air Farce*, Luba received many awards including the Governor General's Performing Arts Award, fifteen Actras, and a Juno.

Leona Graham, Canada/UK. Sometime poet (*www.thegreatreturning.org*), all time community activist (Findhorn/Glastonbury/Ojai) and conservationist (WILD/CCF).

Heidi Greco, of Surrey, BC, lives and writes in a house that's nearly surrounded by trees. Her books include poetry from Anvil Press and a novella, *Shrinking Violets* (Quattro).

Andreas Gripp (London, ON) is the author of 14 books of poetry and 13 chapbooks. His latest releases are *The Apostasy of Daylight* and *Garden Sunrise*, both published in 2012 by Harmonia Press.

German Gutierrez is a journalist, writer, social activist and college professor.

Peter Haase: electrician / letterpress printer / musician / entertainer / ex-preacher-scriptural teacher / fisherman / writer / cook / gardener / house designer / environmentalist / political activist / mythology student.

Recipient of the Order of Canada, Rev. Dr. **Brent Hawkes** has been the Senior Pastor of Metropolitan Community Church of Toronto for 35 years.

Ian Herring is an illustrator based in downtown Toronto.

Bill Hiltz, 34, lives in London, Ontario and is active in several community endeavours, including politics and disability activism.

Joyce Balaz, an advocate for social justice, has dedicated a major part of her life to assisting Bill in his work to bring about changes that benefit society as a whole.

Peter Holt, a Toronto Islander for 44 years, a passionate New Democrat and Scandinavian Democratic-Socialist, this former Québecker's proudest moment was being Jack's first nominator for political office.

Ellen S. Jaffe, a poet and prose writer born in New York, lives in Hamilton ON, and is a Canadian citizen and NDP member. She teaches writing to children and adults and worked with Poets for Peace.

Jenn Jefferys digs progressive politics, art, music, social justice, and wit. Communications and Marketing Officer for the Canadian Heritage Information Network. Volunteers in Paul Dewar's Office.

Susannah Joyce, London, Ontario, is the Director of Realizations Training and Resources. She is equally committed to issues of social justice and the arts.

Rupinder Kaur has been a press secretary for the federal NDP in Ottawa for the past six years. The highlight for her has been working closely with Ed Broadbent, Alexa McDonough and Jack Layton.

Algis Kemezys is a seasoned image maker both in still photography and video. His photography and mostly-documentary videos have been exhibited worldwide.

Penn Kemp received the Queen Elizabeth II Diamond Jubilee medal for service to arts and culture. She is the 40th Life Member of the League of Canadian Poets and London's inaugural Poet Laureate.

Cecilia Kennedy is a writer and teacher in Brampton ON. Her work has appeared in *The Antigonish Review*, *The New Quarterly* and *The Robbie Burns Revival & Other Stories* (Broken Jaw Press).

Joy Kogawa divides her time between Toronto and Vancouver. A novelist best known for her essential work, *Obasan*, she is also an activist, working for Japanese redress as well as the Toronto Dollar.

Daniel Kolos is a Canadian poet, Egyptologist and erstwhile freelance broadcaster, living in rural southern Ontario.

Sonnet L'Abbé is a Lecturer in Creative Writing and Poetry at UBC. A frequent contributor to *Globe Books*, she sent in "An Optimism of Poets" shortly after Jack's death. The poets are:

Lori Bamber is a freelance writer and editor.

Rachel Baumann is writer-yogi living in Vancouver, B.C.

Adam Dickinson is currently giving himself to science in the name of poetry.

Akin Jeje is a Hong Kong based Canadian poet.

Sonnet L'Abbé vegetates in Kelowna, B.C.

Larissa Lai is the author of *Salt Fish Girl*.

Christine Leclerc is a Vancouver based author and activist.

Tanis MacDonald's latest book of poetry is *Rue the Day*.

Sachiko Murakami's latest book is *Rebuild*.

a rawlings is a mineral, plant, animal, person, place, or thing.

Adam Sol's most recent book is *Jeremiah, Ohio*.

Rita Wong is a Vancouver based poet.

Anne Lagacé Dowson is a freelance journalist and Director of the Tolerance Foundation. In 2008 she ran for the NDP in a by-election in Westmount-Ville-Marie.

Ann Lacey is a retired elementary teacher with a lifelong focus on social justice and children's rights. Her experience teaching conflict resolution to young children is documented in a book and film.

Doris Layton is a graduate of McGill, BA 1947, mother of four, grandmother of six, great-grandmother of six and counting. She is the mother, wife and grandmother of Layton politicians.

Eldest son of Irving Layton, **Max Layton** is himself a poet and singer-songwriter (*When The Rapture Comes*, Guernica Editions, 2012). *www.maxlayton.com.*

Mike Layton is the Toronto Councillor for Ward 19, Trinity-Spadina and son of Jack Layton. As Deputy Outreach Director for Environmental Defence, he championed a variety of successful initiatives.

Nancy Layton has been Head of Bishop's College School (Lennoxville) – the first female head of a Canadian boarding school – and Director of Development, Trafalgar School for Girls, Montréal.

Poet **John B. Lee** is Poet Laureate of Norfolk County, and of Brantford ON in perpetuity. He has well-over fifty books published to date and is the editor of seven anthologies.

Shawn Lewis is the constituency assistant to MP Irene Mathyssen. He joined the NDP in late 2002 to support Jack Layton's leadership campaign and has been active in many political arenas since.

Franci Louann, born in "our" Stratford, writes and reads and publishes in the Metro Vancouver area.

Nancy Loucks-McSloy is a community activist working within the London community of Argyle. She is a published freelance writer and was a recipient of one of the Queen's Diamond Jubilee Medals.

Donna Lypchuk is a Canadian columnist, critic and playwright who through the eighties and nineties hosted many charitable events onstage with Jack Layton for Clayquot Sound, Pink Ribbon campaign, etc.

Tanis MacDonald is the author of three books of poetry, the latest of which is *Rue the Day*, published by Turnstone Press. She lives in Waterloo, ON and teaches at Wilfrid Laurier University.

John Magyar is a legal scholar who specializes in statutory interpretation. Some of his research is published: "The Evolution of Hansard Use at the Supreme Court of Canada" (2012) 33 Stat L R 363-389.

Irene Mathyssen was elected MP for London-Fanshawe in 2006. She served as NDP Critic for Housing and Women's Issues, Deputy Critic for Veterans affairs, and is now Seniors and Pensions Critic.

Susan McCaslin's *Demeter Goes Skydiving* won the Robert Kroetsch Poetry Book Award. Since immigrating here in 1969, she has cherished the values embodied in Jack Layton. *www.susanmccaslin.ca*.

Christian McLeod, from Barry's Bay ON, is a visual artist based in Toronto who exhibits regularly there and in Halifax and most recently in Vancouver. *www.christianmcleod.com*.

Robert McMaster is a "SoundScape" and "FoundSound" percussionist who supplies the background textures and rhythms to his partner, Celtic harpist Jennifer White's magic original compositions.

Susan McMaster, Past President of the League of Canadian Poets, is an Ottawa poet, editor, and spoken word/performance poet, having published several wordmusic collections, recordings, and anthologies.

Michelle Mungall was elected to Nelson City Council in 2002, the youngest person elected in Nelson. Presently, she is the Member of the BC Legislative Assembly for Nelson-Creston, their first woman representative.

Shani Mootoo is an award-winning writer whose work has been translated into 15 languages. Her latest novel is *Valmiki's Daughter*, House of Anansi, 2008. A visual artist, she exhibits internationally.

Elsie K Neufeld is a Vancouver poet, personal historian, editor. Her chapbook is *Grief Blading Up* (Lipstick Press, 2009).

Honey Novick is a singer/songwriter/voice teacher/poet who lives in Toronto: *www.honeynovick.com*.

Peter O'Brien is the Director of Corporate and Foundation Giving for Massey Hall. He has published four books and has just finished a new book about studying Latin with his teenaged daughter.

Gianna Patriarca is the author of eight books of poetry. Her work is extensively anthologized and adapted for stage, radio and documentaries.

J Peachy is the Creative Director of Sound Therapy Radio, CJSF 90.1 FM, Shaw Cable 4, Vancouver, BC: *soundtherapyradio.com* and *jpeachygallery.com*.

Londoner **Glen Pearson** is a former Liberal MP and a professional firefighter who now serves as co-director of the London Food Bank and directs the NGO Canadian Aid for Southern Sudan.

Christopher Pinheiro is a Theatrician and Multi-Media Artist.

For more information about **Robert Priest**, singer, songwriter, poet and Broadview/Danforth resident, visit *www.poempainter.com*.

Judy Rebick is an author and activist living in Toronto. Her latest books are *Transforming Power* and an ebook, *Occupy This!* She is a founder of *www.rabble.ca*.

Melody Richardson is a writer and Recording Secretary/Publicity for the Parry Sound-Muskoka NDP Riding Association.

Lisa Richter is a Toronto-based poet and ESL teacher who can most often be found walking, dancing or cycling.

Larry Sakin is a writer and radio show host living in Arizona. *http://www.wordabuser.com.*

Darryl Salach is a poet residing in St. Catharines, Ontario. His work has been published in numerous literary journals and he is the editor of *The Toronto Quarterly.*

Nena Saus has been a Canadian citizen since 2006. She was a grade school teacher in Manila for 32 years.

Lorraine Segato is a diversely expressive creator best known as the singer-songwriter/co-leader of the Award-winning The Parachute Club. Her next CD and one-woman show is *GET OFF MY DRESS.*

Gavin Stairs, born in Montréal, April 1946. Idyllic childhood beside Lake Memphremagog and the Laurentides. Mostly autodidact. Lives with Penn Kemp in London, ON, publishing poetry books and cds for Pendas Productions.

Sandra Stephenson / Czandra is a Montréal-area college teacher of yoga who publishes and performs poetry and works with *www.poetsagainstwar.ca* and PEN Canada.

Adam Sol is the author of three books of poetry, including *Jeremiah*, *Ohio* and *Crowd of Sounds*. He teaches at Laurentian University's campus in Barrie ON, and lives in Toronto.

Jowi Taylor is a Toronto-based writer, former CBC broadcaster and creator of the Six String Nation project: *www.SixStringNation.com.*

Wendy Valhoff is a Nurse Midwife who practiced in Michigan, Kentucky and Nigeria. She and her long-term partner, Sarah, became Permanent Residents of Canada in 2010 and married in 2012.

Chris Vandenbreekel is a fourth Year Political Science student at King's University College in London, ON and an aspiring Political Journalist.

Janet Vickers is publisher of Lipstick Press. The blog [*http://lipstickpoetry.blogspot.ca/*] carried a series of poems on Jack Layton during his illness and after his death. *www.lipstickpress.com*

Joe Wilson is a retired English teacher, and current, enthusiastic NDP and labour activist. He has managed successful London-Fanshawe campaigns for MP Irene Mathyssen and MPP Teresa Armstrong.

Judy Wasylycia-Leis: Federal NDP Women's Organizer and Executive Assistant to Ed Broadbent prior to election as NDP MLA and Cabinet Minister. She was NDP MP for Winnipeg North for 13 years till 2010.

Jennifer White is a full-time professional musician, composer and storyteller. She is also a long-time political junkie who has recently become an engaged community and political activist.

Herb Wonfor was called to the ministry in Wyman United Church, Hudson, Québec 1961. His wife Margaret Wonfor and he now live in London, ON.

Andrew Wreggitt is a screenwriter, playwright and poet from Calgary. He wrote the script for *The Jack Layton Story* for CBC television and is a multiple Gemini Award winner for his screenplays.

About the Editor

London ON activist poet, performer and playwright, Penn Kemp is the 40th Life Member of the League of Canadian Poets. She received the Queen Elizabeth II Diamond Jubilee medal for her service to the arts and community from MP Mathyssen. As London's inaugural Poet Laureate (2010-12), Penn has presented poetry at many civic functions including the Mayors' Poetry City Challenge and the Creative City Summit. As Writer-in-Residence for Western University (2009-10), her project was the DVD, *Luminous Entrance: a Sound Opera for Climate Change Action*, Pendas Productions. She continues to host her *Lit-on-Air* program on Radio Western, *CHRWradio.com/talk/gatheringvoices*. Penn has published twenty-five books of poetry and drama, had six plays and ten CDs of Sound Opera produced as well as award-winning videopoems. Since Coach House Press published her first book (1972), she has pushed textual/aural boundaries, often in collaborative performance. Penn has been heralded by The Writers' Union as a one woman literary industry. Having performed in festivals world-wide, Penn now lives in London with her husband, Gavin Stairs. There she writes, grows herbs, edits poetry for Pendas Productions, and feeds a vast array of birds. Over the last year of working on this book, Jack Layton has been her ongoing inspiration for realizing art in action.